A Thousand Afternoons

Edited by
PETER HAINING

Cowles Book Company, Inc. • New York

To Philippa

Acknowledgments

The editor wishes to extend his sincere thanks to the following authors, their publishers, and agents for permission to include copyright material in this anthology: The estate of John Steinbeck and Time, Inc., for "I Even Saw Manolete" (1968); Sidney Franklin and Prentice-Hall, Inc., New York, for the extract from *Bullfighter from Brooklyn* (1952); Leslie Charteris and Doubleday & Co., Inc., for the adaptation from the Preface by Leslie Charteris to *Killer of Bulls* by Juan Belmonte (1937); Norman Mailer and the Scott Meredith Literary Agency for "The Crazy One" by Norman Mailer (1967); Barnaby Conrad and *Esquire* magazine for "The Greatest Bullfight Ever" (1948); James A. Michener and Random House, Inc., for the extract from *Iberia* (1968); Robert Graves and Collins-Knowlton-Wing, Inc., New York, for the extract from "The Decline of Bullfighting" (1959); the estate of Frank Harris for "Montes the Matador (1900); Viking Press, Inc., New York, for "None of That" by D. H. Lawrence (1928); Charles Scribner for "The Undefeated" by Ernest Hemingway (1928); Little, Brown & Company, Boston, for the extract from *Matador* by Marguerite Steen (1934); John Masters and Harper & Row, Inc., for the extract from *Fandango Rock* (1959); the estate of Robert Ruark and Manuscripts, Inc., for the extract from *The Honey Badger* (1965); V. S. Pritchett and Messrs. Chatto & Windus, London, for the extract from *The Spanish Temper* (1954); Vincent Hitchcock and Messrs. Frederick Muller, Ltd., London, for the extract from *Suit of Lights* (1956); Kenneth Tynan and Messrs. Longmans Green for the extract from *Bull Fever* (1966). Also to Leslie Charteris and John Masters for their help, guidance, and writings so generously given during the course of compiling this book.

Preface

The bullfight. To a large number of people it is one of the glories of Spain, a ritual of a proud, brave, and colorful people whose place in the sun has a harsh beauty unmatched anywhere else in the world. To others it is a throwback to the barbarity of less civilized times, a sop to rough, brutish peasants who thirst for the blood of man or beast. To those who really appreciate toreo it is neither; perhaps there is a little of both these elements, but certainly nothing about it that allows one to categorize, explain, or define it in mere words. No corrida de toros—the assembly for bullfighting—is ever the same, no *faena*—the ultimate encounter of man with bull—ever follows quite the same pattern. Nothing that takes place in the plaza de toros on a sunlit afternoon is ever repeated and—for those true aficionados this is the crux of the matter—never will be.

Bullfighting has been the subject of controversy for over two hundred years—probably longer. But here we are only really concerned with the modern art of toreo as developed by

Francisco Romero in the early years of the eighteenth century. Naturally enough, as a spectacle primarily of drama and death it inspires passionate reactions: those of admiration and loathing. There is probably no other single spectator-witnessed spectacle— at least I have not experienced one— which can draw from those Anglo-Saxons present such fervent parise (accepting, of course, that the corrida is good) or such outright condemnation. Certainly it is impossible to watch without becoming committed for or against, impossible to study without becoming aware of the skill, the splendor, and the courage of both man and beast.

This fascination has been shared not only by tourists but also by some of the greatest writers from England and America who, over the years, have been irresistibly drawn to this unique death—or life, as some will have it, for the matador is also staking his life— in the afternoon. Mention a famous author of the past two hundred years and, if he visited Spain at any time, it is more than probable that he endeavored to register on paper his thoughts about this most difficult of all events adequately and expertly to describe. His work may well show great understanding and admiration for bullfighting—but, equally, there have been instances where sensitive writers have been horrified and sickened by it.

A Thousand Afternoons is a collection of just such varied writings. It is not intended to be merely an anthology of the best material on bullfighting; rather of those documents and stories that demonstrate as clearly as possible the obsession of the writers in question with the ritual. They may well have written better on the corrida, but not often with more fervor. The items have been assembled, too, from the widest possible range of available sources, to illustrate as many of the facets of this incredibly complex ritual as possible. In my five years' researching, I have tried to give both the voices for and against toreo their due regard, but if in the final selection those in favor tend to outweigh those who condemn, you must rather blame my own aficion and not any obvious weakness in the case of the latter. Let me add, too, that this anthology is not intended to be exhaustive, but rather one that offers a diverse selection of material, fact and fiction, by some of the most celebrated writers from both sides of the Atlantic. Finally, let no expert look for total accuracy herein; aficionados though many of the authors are, the very intricacies of the bullfight breed errors in the writings of all but the most experienced.

It may come as a surprise to those not closely involved with toreo to learn that the single most important influence on the literature of the ritual was not a Spaniard, but an American, Ernest Hemingway. Hemingway, absorbed with death and man seeking his moment of truth, spent much of his life in Spain and was naturally drawn to the plaza de toros. His book *Death in the Afternoon* is not only a classic of modern literature, but also a brilliant study of the matador's art. That someone who had never stood in a sunlit arena face to face with one of the towering black fighting bulls should have created a work of such authenticity is remarkable.

Finally, a word to those who, like me, have a strong feeling for Spain (in my case it is Andalucia). I hope they will find much to interest them in this selection. I trust, too, that the book as a whole will satisfy those many people who gave so generously of their time and knowledge in its compiling—in particular Mr. Benjamin Rook, the secretary of the Club Taurino of London, who has my profound gratitude for his guidance and my appreciation of his patience in teaching me so much more about toreo than mere books could do.

In conclusion let me say that if just one aficionado who reads these pages has, albeit briefly, memories revived of an afternoon in a thousand when man and beast were truly brave, noble, and courageous, then I shall feel my work has been worthwhile.

Peter Haining

Andalucia, Spain
1969

Contents

Who would go to see this posturing
bully, the matador, if he were dressed
in workman's clothes and cap? It is
slaughter-house work and in any decent
country the public is denied the
sadistic satisfaction of abattoirs.

George Bernard Shaw

The bullfighter is a champion, a
paragon.

Ernest Hemingway

Introduction
By Barnaby Conrad

"I'm aficionated," a Little Old Lady in tennis shoes once remarked to me as we headed for the plaza de toros of Tijuana. "*Real* aficionated!"

Well, there would appear to be more and more aficionated folk in America these days. And since only a small percentage of them can get to Spain or Latin America to indulge their *afición*, what are they to do in the long arid spells between corridas?

They do what trout fishermen and baseball addicts and skiers and the like must do between seasons—they read about their favorite passion. This volume, then, will be greeted with extra loud *olés* by the dyed-in-the-wool aficionado.

Perhaps he will have read some of the selections in other books or periodicals, but they have never all been assembled in one handy and attractive package before. Each reader will have his own favorite selection; I certainly have my own likes and dislikes and prejudices among the contents.

For instance I didn't believe that story of Sidney Franklin's

when he first told it to me in Los Corales café in Sevilla in 1944,
and I still don't. I like Norman Mailer's account of El Loco very
much. And then, there's Mr. Ruark's exacerbating contribution of
such a momentous taurine event as a girl's getting her britches
horned off at a tienta.

(Incidentally, wasn't it Mailer who wrote of Ruark so devasta-
tingly: "He has the kind of personality that Hemingway would
have had if Hemingway had been a bad writer"?)

The editor has selected well and truly. For example, I had never
read D. H. Lawrence's tour de force, "None of That." It is over-
written—but, by God, it is written—*written!* ("He looked at me
with his yellow eyes, and that pleasant look which was really hate
undreaming.")

Then, too, the Steinbeck piece is new to me. It was not a surprise, however, that he was interested in the bulls. I have a wonderful letter from him back in 1952 in which he tells of going to
a week of bullfights in Sevilla and sitting next "to a nice little man
in a business suit who very kindly explained things when I asked
him. It wasn't till afterwards that I found out his name was Juan
Belmonte."

(In that same letter Steinbeck wrote: "I like bullfighting—to
me it is a lonely, formal, anguished microcosm of what happens
to every man, sometimes even in an office, strangled by the glue on
the envelopes. In the bullring he survives for a while sometimes.")

I like many of the selections so well that I will not pick a
favorite. But what a pleasure it is to reread "The Undefeated"!
It is so very good, so absolutely right, so clean, so true. Perhaps it
does sound like a parody of Hemingway at times, but that is not
his fault; it is simply that he has been so universally—and un-
successfully—imitated.

I enjoy the Michener narrative; he has a great feeling for Spain,
as do Pritchett and Tynan. And the ever-excellent Charteris dis-
sertation, and the durable and amazingly fresh "Montes the
Matador."

I must emphatically denounce an extraordinary statement contained in Robert Graves's article. With appalling sangfroid or

innocence or ignorance, Graves tosses this off: "Manolete, to be frank, was a bad matador, in the sense that he seldom killed at the first attempt."

Wow. This statement rivals Hemingway's atomic gaffe in *Life* to the effect that Manolete was a great matador but "with cheap tricks," a remark that did great damage to Hemingway's previously high taurine reputation on the Iberian Peninsula. The hue and cry and bleats of pain that went up in Spain and Mexico were astounding; Hemingway was denounced on all sides as a charlatan and unknowing *villamelón*, for he had stated one thing that simply could not be said of Manolete, no matter what else one felt about that matador. It would be tantamount to saying: "Marciano would have been a good fighter if he hadn't been knocked out so often, Louis could box but he couldn't punch, Sugar Ray could hit but he couldn't box," etc.

There were many critics of Manolete. People criticized him for being cold, for his small repertoire, and so forth, but no one before or since Hemingway—(who confessed subsequently he had never even seen Manolete but merely relied upon the word of his wife)—ever accused him of "cheap tricks."

And I don't believe that anyone before or since Robert Graves has ever said he was a bad killer. Maybe Graves, whom I respect enormously in every nontaurine matter, saw Manolete miss with the sword on a bad day. Wouldn't that be somewhat like saying: "Ah, yes—saw that chap Nureyev once—tripped, fell flat. Poor devil, fine dancer, too bad he stumbles and falls all the time"?

I saw Manolete perform some ninety times in Spain and Latin America, and with the possible exception of Rafael Ortega, no one ever killed with such style and efficacy.

But anyone who writes books like *I, Claudius* should be forgiven anything, and I am running on too much about it. But that is the sickness, the occupational disease of the aficionado, and this book will provide the nucleus and glorious opportunity for much spirited discussion when we aficionados get together. It will recall afternoons of great emotion, of thrills of the kind that only the fiesta brava can offer.

Recently a prominent British scientist announced that when aroused by emotions of excitement or fear, a man's beard grows more rapidly; aficionados knew this a long time ago when Belmonte wrote in his autobiography that "on the days of a corrida the beard grows more." And Manolete mentioned the phenomenon the very day he was killed.

"Haven't you shaved yet, Manolo?"—"Yes, I've shaved, and if it doesn't look like it it's fear that's making the whiskers grow."

Such are the various talents and vivid writing contained in this volume that I feel that there are selections herein that are sure to cause the reader's beard to grow at a great rate.

¡*Orejas, rabo, y la pata para Peter Haining!*

—San Francisco, 1970

I

Fact

Bullfighting: An Explanation

Leslie Charteris

LESLIE CHARTERIS (*b.* 1907), *creator of one of the most famous characters in modern detective fiction, "the Saint," is British by birth but became a naturalized American subject in 1957. Deeply interested in bullfighting, his contribution to the literature of the art has been his work as editor and translator of Juan Belmonte's autobiography*—Killer of Bulls.

The origin of the bullfight as a standardized spectacle is the subject of a good many speculative theories; but as it exists today, it consists in the ceremonious killing of a number of bulls, generally six, according to a formalized and traditional sequence of manoeuvres designed to display the skill and valour of the *torero* and the power and bravery of the bull, while at the same time taking advantage of the bull's fighting instincts to bring it into the condition and position in which it can be perfectly killed according to the rules of the art.

Anyone who plays the bulls is a *torero*. The man who kills the bull is a *matador*. The word matador means "killer." Usually from two to four matadors will take part in a *corrida*, and each of them will fight and kill two or three bulls. Each matador is the head man of a *cuadrilla* which probably consists of two *picadors*, men on horseback armed with lances, and two *banderilleros*, which means simply the men who place the *banderillas*, or wooden darts, about two feet long, wrapped in paper of

various colours and tipped with steel barbs. Sometimes the matador will do this himself, if he is any good at it, and sometimes
even if he isn't; but the men are still called banderilleros or
peones. Only the cuadrilla of the matador whose bull is being
fought will be inside the arena at that time; the other cuadrillas
wait on the safe side of the *barrera*, which is a circular wooden
fence running round the arena and forming a kind of trench between the arena and the spectators in the stands. In this trench
also walk about the carpenters, the *monosabios* or bullring attendants, the *mozos de espadas* who look after the matadors'
swords, the various officials, managers, photographers, reporters,
and policemen waiting to capture any of the spectators who may
jump into the ring and try to take on the bull themselves. The
safety of this trench is more or less relative, for bulls have been
known to jump over the barrera into it and do much havoc. The
other matadors will not be inside it; they will be in the arena,
ready to come to the assistance of the working matador in case
of accidents, and also to play their proper part in the *quites*.

The bull is only distantly related to the animal which is reared
for beef in other countries. It is a practically wild animal whose
chief instinct is to fight, and it is one of the fiercest and bravest
animals in the world. The bull you will see today has been bred
from some famous strain renowned for many years for its fighting
qualities, and for many years a deliberate process of scientific
selection will have been employed to ensure that the product will
combine the finest qualities of strength and courage and ferocity
in the breed, just as other cattle have been bred for years to give
the maximum quality of milk, or race horses are bred for speed
and stamina. This bull, to meet the regulations which govern
bullfighting, will weigh not less than 543 kilos on the hoof, about
1,197 pounds, or nearly half a ton; probably it will be bigger
than this. The most distinguishing thing about it, apart from its
obvious size and power, will be the tremendous hump of muscle
running from the back of the horns to the centre of the back.
This is the bull's fighting muscle; it is what holds his head up and
lifts his head, with anything on it, so that he can lift and throw up

a horse and rider together on his horns. Now the regulations pre-
scribe that the matador must kill the bull with a sword by thrusting the sword into the bull's back between the shoulder blades
and into the bull's chest, while facing the bull and thrusting in
over his horns; so one of the objects of the fight is to tire the
bull's neck and tire this great muscle so that the bull will lower
his head, because until the bull will lower his head and keep it
down it is impossible to make this thrust. The other object is to
steady the bull so that it will be possible to get into position to
make the thrust. And these things must be done valiantly, artisti-
cally, gracefully, and according to a fixed and timed procedure, so
that the tempo of the fight rises through a crescendo like great
music to the supreme emotion of the last moments.

When the bull is let out to the *toril,* or pen, it is a wild and
savage animal. It has been shut up in the dark for some hours,
and now it is prodded out into the blazing sunlight of the arena,
at first thinking that it is charging out into the freedom of the
pasture in which it grew up, and then finding that it is only in
another enclosure, even if this is a larger one. The bull is raging,
fighting mad; and you only have to see it as it comes thundering
out into the arena to have half your humanitarian instincts
numbed. You will stop thinking about the poor helpless bull and
feel about it as you would feel about a tiger, the same admiration
and awed respect tinged with fear. You will feel that you would
as soon be in a cage with an angry tiger as down there in the
arena with the bull; and this is the animal that the matador has
to dominate until he can stand in front of it and dive in over its
horns after his sword.

Now the matador is not in the arena when the bull comes in;
he is standing in the shelter of one of the *burladeros,* which are
small secondary fences built out a man's thickness from the
barrera and parallel with it, where a man can take refuge if he
is hard pressed. They also mask the openings in the barrera itself
through which the toreros can enter and leave the ring. The only
men in the ring now are the banderilleros with their capes, which
are just like ordinary long heavy capes made of raw silk, yellow

on one side and cerise-coloured on the other—bulls are no more sensitive to red than to any other bright colour. The banderilleros "run" the bull, while the matador watches: that is, they run away from the bull, trailing their capes behind them and letting the bull charge and gore at their capes, without letting it get close to them, and if it comes dangerously close they will duck behind one of the burladeros. You may think they are all afraid of the bull and none of them dares to stand up to it and pass it properly as the matador is going to do. You would be wrong; they are simply playing their appointed part in the fight, and they are not allowed to make passes with their capes, which they only use to protect themselves in the same crude way that a man might use a coat to protect himself if he were being pursued by an angry bull in a field, if he had the knowledge and presence of mind to do it. They are doing two useful things: they are taking the first fierce, wild, uncontrolled impetus off the bull's charge, which is important, because the matador cannot sculpture the tight-disciplined figures which his art demands out of a wildly charging bull, and they are also giving the watching matador his chance to observe and study the fighting characteristics of the bull, whether it charges in a straight line or in a curve, and how it moves its head, and whether it has a tendency to hook with the right horn or with the left. It is on what the matador learns from this first study, only a few seconds of it, that he is going to gamble his life, when he will be working so close to the bull that the bull's horns will brush against his legs and the bull's shoulder will brush by his body, if he is any good, when he makes the formal passes which are required of him. And as soon as the matador feels that he has learned enough, he steps out from behind the burladero into the path of the bull and gives it a few passes with the cape.

There are many different passes with the cape, and there may always be new ones if the bullfighters are born who will invent them, as Rudolfo Gaona and Chicuelo have given their names to the *gaonera* and *chicuelino*, but all of these passes are formalized and standardized like the steps in a ballet, only that this is a ballet with agonizing death for a partner, and the foundation of all work with the cape is the *veronica*, which is one of the supreme tests of the torero's skill and courage, and which was one of the brilliant peaks of Belmonte's work. The *veronica* is the cape equivalent of the *pase natural* with the *muleta*, which we shall come to presently, and you could probably say that it is the most natural pass of all. The torero holds up the cape by the shoulders, with his left shoulder towards the bull, and standing in the straight line of the bull's body, with the cape spread across the bull's probable line of charge; and as the bull charges him he lets the bull take the cloak and keeps its attention on the cloak, so that it follows the cloak instead of driving its horns into him, and charges past him, while he keeps his feet and legs firmly planted and only turns himself from the waist, sculpturing such a figure . . . and then if he has done this perfectly you will hear a concerted staccato roar of "Olé!" from the *aficionados*, whom you might call the fans of bullfighting, and the matador will have turned a little so that as the bull turns and doubles on itself to charge again he will be ready to give it another *veronica*. He will give it a number of passes, the number depending on how courageous and skilful he is and how brave the bull is and how well he can control it to keep it charging him instead of galloping away in search of another target; and when he is finished he will terminate with a *recorte*, a pass ending in a deft flick of the cloth, like a *media veronica*, which begins like a *veronica* except that the matador fixes his hands at his hips as he turns and turns in the opposite direction so that the cape winds itself round him like a spread crinoline. The sudden distracting flash of colour serves to fix the bull where it stands, so that it stands still and is momentarily baffled, and the matador should be able to turn his back on it and walk slowly away with the cape over his arm, to the tune of a round of applause if his work has been good, while the bull simply watches him without charging; although if he is mistaken and he has not fixed the bull he may get a horn in his rectum and that may be the end of him. But if this is not the end of him, the trumpets will be sounded for the second quarter of the fight, which is the *suerte de varas,* the feat of the lances, the work of the picadors.

Now while the picadors are riding in on their shabby horses, you must think a little more about the bull, for all the work in a bullfight is directed against the bull with an intelligent object. The bull is also intelligent, so intelligent that if the tempo of the fight is not perfectly controlled and if the fight goes on even ten minutes longer than it should go on, the bull may become so wise that it will be unplayable and unkillable according to the rules. The assets of the bull are its power and strength and speed and courage, its fearless fighting instinct to charge any other creature on sight; its asset to the bullfight is its natural tendency to charge in a straight continuous line once it has picked its object; and its handicap to itself is its tendency to have its attention distracted by any movement in its field of vision, which is the handicap on which all the matador's work is based, by directing the bull's attention away from himself toward the cape or *muleta.* This bull which we are seeing fought has no knowledge of man, and it has never been misled by a cape or *muleta;* if it had ever been played before it would be unplayable now, for it would have learned too much; this is its first experience of the wiles of a new enemy, and all through the fight it is searching for ways to overcome them. All its life, in its fights with other bulls on the ranges, it has been used to normal objects behaving in a normal manner. It has been used to charging a target and finding the target there when its horns arrive, and it has never dreamed that it might be possible for a target to dissolve into unresisting silk when the charge hits it. Now it has charged several times and met no resistance, and the last *recorte* of the matador has completed the work of upsetting it. The bull is baffled, and it is thinking: "Am I wasting my time charging shadows? Am I just being made a fool of?" It is also thinking: "What can I do to give my charges more effect?" And while you may now be beginning to think pityingly about the poor bull, you should really be thinking about the poor matador, because his bull is becoming wiser and more dangerous, and it is going to charge more dangerously, more deliberately, even while you are thinking that it has lost heart. It is like a tennis player who has been hitting and smashing wildly in a first attempt to slog his opponent off the court, and who finds every shot neatly returned, and who has to settle down to play more methodically and try to discover his opponent's weaknesses. The bull is no nearer than that to admitting defeat; and as it tires a little it is conserving its strength only to use it better, to make every charge and thrust to the best effect.

So the picadors ride in, and the bull's attention is drawn to the man on horseback, who looks more like the creatures the bull has been used to; and the bull is encouraged and charges again, at the man and the horse. These horses are protected by a kind of mattresslike armour strapped over one side and under the belly, which the law has required since 1928. It is supposed to save the horses, and sometimes it does, but not always. The picador's right leg is also protected with steel armour, and this is supposed to save him, but it will not help him much if he is thrown off. As the bull charges, the picador will place the point of his lance in the bull's hump of muscle, if he is skilful and quick enough; and he is theoretically supposed to prevent the bull from reaching the horse. The trouble is that there are not many picadors today like José Trigo, who could hold off a six-year-old bull with the blunt end of the lance, or Corchado, who never wore armour and would use the same mount through an entire corrida and never get a scratch either in the horse's hide or his own silk stockings. Besides, there are many matadors who believe that a bull must *enganchar*, must get its horn into living resisting flesh, to make it good for the fight, and also if the bull gets the horse and lifts it, it helps to tire the bull's neck and make it carry its head lower, which we have already listed as one of the objects of the fight, and also there is a superstition that a goring from a horn which has been sunk in a horse's body will never turn septic and will heal quicker than a wound from a clean horn. Also it is not so easy to sink a lance in exactly the right place in the hump of a charging bull, and besides if the bull does not upset a few horses the public may think it is not very brave; so the chances are that the bull will get the horse, with or without taking the *pic*. A picador acting on the instructions of a cowardly and unscrupulous matador can ruin a bull for the rest of the fight: for instance, he can place the pic too far back and injure the bull's spine, or when he has the pic in and feels the resistance of the bull he may twist it about and try to make a large wound so that the bull will be weakened by bleeding. But even if he does his work well and turns the bull away, the bull may free himself and return to the charge too quickly and get the horse in the flank which is unprotected; or he may place the pic right and find the force of the bull too great for his strength. The guard above the point of the lance will still allow the blade to drive in about six inches; but I have seen bulls with the pic in them driving steadily in against it, with their feet thrusting and their whole bodies leaning forward, still trying to get at the man and horse in spite of the punishment. That is the kind of bravery a fighting bull has. So the bull may always get the horse, even if it is only the battering-ram force of the charge blunted by the mattress that topples the horse over; and once the horse is down the bull may go on charging before it can be taken away, and get its horn under the mattress to rip the horse's guts out. It may just as well do the same thing to the picador, but no humanitarian would worry very much about him. In any case, it is now the duty of the matador to make the *quite*.

In the *quite*, the matador must first take the bull's attention away with his cape, and then continue to play it with the same kind of passes as were used in the preliminary cape work, finishing with a recorte which serves to fix the bull in position for the next horse. In these *quites* the matador should do his best work with the cape, for the bull is in the best condition to be played. It has found new heart from charging and achieving something, and it should charge now with more zeal and shrewd ferocity than ever before; but it will still be less wild, and more dangerous, because it has not forgotten its first lesson in the untrustworthiness of the lure, and because it is tiring a little more and has to make every movement count.

In the *quites* you should begin to feel the pull of that quality

in the fight which the Spaniards call *emoción*. "Emotion" doesn't
have quite the same meaning in English, but you can't find any
other translation for it. You have seen the bull in its first wild
fierceness, you have seen proof of its strength and fierceness and
bravery in the way it went in against the pic and threw over the
picador and his horse like a sack of potatoes; and now there is
one man, the matador, armed only with the cape and his skill
and knowledge of bullfighting, meeting the bull alone, playing it,
keeping it charging the cape and not himself, controlling the bull,
steadying its rush, keeping it close to him, dominating it, holding
it with the cloth as if with a magnet, weaving that earth-shaking
mass of savage flesh around his body as if it were something
smooth and plastic, and doing all this, if he is doing it well, as
smoothly and gently and gracefully as a dancer, sculpturing the
poised and airy attitudes of his slender body against the dark
destroying mass of the bull, seemingly without effort, seemingly
without risk—until you remember what the bull did to the horses
and you realize again what a bull can do and what it would do
even more easily to the matador if he made one miscalculation.

It is a regulation—not always observed—that each bull must
take a minimum of four pics. The first *quite* is made by the matador whose bull it is, and the subsequent ones by the other matadors appearing in the corrida in order of seniority, and their individual rivalry should show in each of them trying to make a
better and more valiant *quite* than the others. Then, at the next
trumpet signal, the surviving horses are ridden out and the fight
goes into its third quarter, which is the placing of the banderillas.

Unless the matador is placing the banderillas himself, he rests
during this quarter in preparation for his *faena* with the *muleta*,
while one of the other matadors stays in the ring to be ready to
come to the rescue of any unlucky banderillero. To my mind it
is the least interesting part of the fight, probably because it is
usually done without any inspiration, which is because the matador would not want one of his banderilleros to steal the limelight
with any showy work. The banderillas are placed by a man standing with one in each hand, held by the blunt end with the point

downwards, and his arms held above his head and opened a little; he cites the bull, and as the bull charges him he runs towards it at an angle, halts at the right place, brings his feet together for an instant, leans forward over the horns, and nails the banderillas in the hump, where they stick by reason of the barbs, after which he runs on to safety, while the bull checks and tosses its head up, distracted by the sudden pain, and gives him the chance to get away. Three or four pairs of banderillas will be placed by the banderilleros working alternately, and if they are perfectly placed in a perfect bull there will be three on each side of the centre, avoiding the wounds made by the pics, and marking round the exact spot which the matador will later have to aim for with his sword when he makes the kill; but they may be deliberately placed on one side by a skilful banderillero to correct a tendency that the bull has to hook to that side, which the matadors have not been able to cure with their cape work. There are several other fancy ways of placing the banderillas which are more ornamental to watch, but these are nearly always performed by the matador, if he fancies himself in this phase of the work; and the room for emotion is there, with the posing of the man with his feet together at the moment when he places the darts, the statuesque moment when the darts are going in and the bull's horns are passing under his belly as his body sways aside. But you will very rarely see it, and it must always be inferior to the emotion of the moment of death, when the matador is one with the bull, not separated from it as the banderillero must be. The banderillas of course, like everything else in the bullfight, have their use: besides correcting any of the bull's tendencies to hook, they go on with the work of tiring the bull, particularly tiring its neck as it shakes its head to try and shake out the darts, and they encourage the bull to concentrate on a smaller target, the banderillero unshielded by a cape, in preparation for the *faena* or work with the *muleta*, which comes next.

The *muleta* is an oval piece of red cloth with a stick about eighteen inches long laid and fastened lengthwise in the centre. The cloth is doubled over the stick so that it hangs down like a curtain. The matador may hold the *muleta* in either hand, but the sword is always held in the right hand; so that if he holds the *muleta* in his right hand the sword helps to spread the cloth and make it larger, whereas if he holds the *muleta* in his left hand he has a much smaller lure with which to keep the bull's attention away from his own body. For this reason work done with the *muleta* in the left hand is esteemed more highly.

With the *muleta* the matador goes out alone. He stands under the presidential box and holds out his hat in salute, and either dedicates the bull to the president or, with the president's permission, to some friend among the spectators; or he may go into the centre of the ring and wave his hat around the circle of the stands to dedicate the bull to the whole audience. Then he throws his hat away, to whoever has received the dedication, to hold for him while he is doing his *faena*, and goes towards the bull.

Now you are going to see the quintessense of bullfighting, the final crescendo of emotion rising to the supreme moment of the kill. It is on his work with the *muleta* that a matador's reputation ultimately stands or falls: it was with the *muleta* that Belmonte touched his greatest heights. The passes again are as varied as the lances with the cape. . . . They are founded on the *pase natural*, the natural pass, which is the simplest and most dangerous and most beautiful to watch. In the *pase natural*, the matador stands with the *muleta* in one hand, his arm hanging down at full stretch and spread a little from his side, so that the cloth barely covers his legs; he cites the bull, and as it charges he leads it past him, so that its horns brush his thighs if he dares to bring it so close, and its shoulders will rub his waist, while he sculptures the same kind of graceful figures as he did with the cape, keeping his feet and legs firm and gracefully placed, turning from the waist only, controlling the bull, dominating it, working with all the knowledge he possesses of its instincts to weave it about him like a flowing veil; and then he should be ready and the bull turned and controlled so that it will charge again. Then he will give it another *natural* or a *pase de pecho*, all the time playing with the bull, moving it as he wants it to move, commanding it, forcing it by his art to join him like a conscious partner in that strange and sinisterly beautiful dance of death. And then he will change his position and go into another series of passes, continuous, linked together by form and rhythm, which should be as complete and conclusive as a melody in music; and then perhaps he will have the bull fixed and baffled and at a standstill, and if he is valiant and trusts his judgment he will pause for an *adorno*. He will put his hand out slowly and take hold of the bull's horn, or take hold of its ear, or kneel down with his back to the bull and face the stands; and by this time they will be cheering and applauding him if he has been good, and he will get up again and go on with his *faena*. All this is the final stage in the work of tiring the bull, and lowering its head, and steadying it so that when the time comes the matador will be able to make his kill properly; and if he is going to attempt to kill valiantly and conscientiously, and if the bull has not been ruined before this by a pic in the spine or some cruel work with the cape that has strained its back by turn- ing it too quickly, it will depend very much on his work with the *muleta* whether the matador will see the bull swaying and foun- dering after he has gone in with the sword, or whether the horn will catch him in the thigh as he goes in and send him up to the sky and down again to his death. But this is not what you need to be thinking about now, because the work must be done in such and such a way and it must be beautiful to watch, and if it isn't beautiful to watch it is a bad *faena* even if the matador does kill the bull properly at the end of it. What he should be doing is performing his task with so much grace and beauty that you are not conscious of the practical end of it. It must not be monot- onous, but full of variations; it must take you through all the emotions that the genius of the matador is great enough to wring from you. It must have light and shade, it must be sometimes grave and sober and sometimes airy and lighthearted, sometimes tragic and sometimes gay. You must feel that the matador is giving you his best, because this is the best thing he knows in life and he is doing it in the best way he knows; and you must feel that he is serious even when he is being gay, because the end of all this is death, and he must not make you feel that he is being flippant about death even when he is lightening it, because death is not flippant to him. You must feel that he has pride and responsibility, because if the death of the bull is not justified by the beauty which eventually necessitates it, then the bullfight is as cruel and pointless as the humanitarians would like you to believe.

But if you have seen the perfect *faena*, and all the emotion of the fight has reached its peak and held it just so long as is necessary for perfection, the time has come for the kill.

The bull is standing still, with its forefeet together and its head lowered. The matador stands facing the bull, at the right distance, with his feet together and his whole body poised straight on the balls of his feet, with the *muleta* held in his left hand and hanging down over his feet and the lower part of his legs. He has fixed the bull's eye on the *muleta*, and he is "profiling," as they call it: the sword is held in his right hand, stretched out towards the bull, and he is sighting along the sword at the place where the sword has to go. Now he may either kill *recibiendo*, receiving—that is, letting the bull charge him and receiving the bull on his sword; or with a *volapie*—that is, diving in with the sword while the bull stands still; or *al encuentro*, which is a combination of the two, with both the bull and the man moving towards each other; but whichever of these he is doing he will have to move his left hand across his body with the *muleta* at the crucial moment to draw the bull's head to his right while he himself sways to the left and slips out over the bull's right horn. If this has been a perfect *estocada* the bull will stand there with the sword in it and only the hilt showing, with its four feet squarely planted as if to brace itself, and in a moment or two it will crumple down and be dead. If it was a bad *estocada* the bull may not be mortally wounded, and it may shake the sword out if the sword ever stayed in. Maybe the matador never went in, if he was frightened: that is to say that he may have started to come out before he was in, and the thrust was only a *pinchazo*, a pinprick. Then you may see the peones flapping their capes to make the bull turn round and round in a circle, to make it dizzy and help it to bleed internally and make it go down so that it can be finished off easily. The law requires the matador to go in once over the horns, but only once, so that if he has no stomach for another attempt he will try to get rid of the bull with a *descabello*. This is quite humane if he can make the bull lower its head so that he can find the right place at the back of its skull with the point of his sword and sever the cervical vertebrae with a quick downward thrust; but if the bull is still full of life it will rear its head when it feels the point, and the matador will make a lot of bungling attempts before he gets rid of the beast, and the stands will be howling and whistling, and it will all be a very messy and disgusting business, spoiling all the effect of the *faena*, if there ever was an effect with a matador like that, and you will be quite right to throw the bottles you have thoughtfully brought with you, if you think you can get away with it without being spotted by a policeman. But if you see a perfect *estocada* at the end of a perfect *faena*, it is the final resolving chord, the supreme breathless moment. You will see man and bull, who have been gyrating together like partners in a dance, suddenly welded together, the man merged with the bull, bound to the bull by the sword, with the steel vanished altogether and only the man's hand grasping the hilt of the sword on the crest of the bull's back, the matador with the bull's horns under him and his body bowed over the bull; and it will be something that you will never forget.

So now that is your bullfight, and if it still means nothing to you you should go and see some for yourself—the mere description of it, after all, can convey very little more than the verbal description of a symphony. You will have to see at least a dozen bullfights before you can begin to recognize and understand their finer points, even with the help of all the books in the world, because your eye will not be quick and trained enough to grasp them; just the same as, if you were taking up music for the first time, you would have to go to a lot of concerts before you could hear much more than tunes. And then you may have to see twenty bad or mediocre bullfights before you see a complete and perfect one, because matadors are as temperamental as any other kind of artist, and they all have many off days, and because almost as much depends on the bull as on the matador, and the bulls are not always good, and finally because there are always many unscrupulous and overballyhooed matadors, and a man who is getting five thousand dollars for each corrida is inclined to do a lot of simple arithmetic about what it will cost him to get a goring that will lose him half a dozen fights, and it is impossible for a matador to do any good work unless he gets close enough to the bull to run a genuine risk of being gored. But if you ever do see a sublime *faena* you will know you have seen it, and if it still means nothing to you you had better give it up and go back to fox hunting and pigeon shooting and other inelegant but humanitarian activities.

A Man Called Hemingway

Sidney Franklin

SIDNEY FRANKLIN *(b. 1905) was the first American to become a matador. His autobiography,* Bullfighter from Brooklyn, *gives a fascinating account of his career, from boyhood in New York to bullfighting in Spain. Franklin was described by Hemingway, who was his friend and contemporary, as a "better, more scientific, more intelligent and more finished matador than all but about six of the full matadors in Spain today."*

Shortly after my debut in Madrid, a duke who was the King's uncle became one of my most outspoken admirers. He formed a caravan of about twenty cars which travelled with me all over the country. Each car belonged to some titled person. These people were in the habit of doing most of their business at the fairs, much in the manner of those of our big business men who prefer to discuss their projects on the golf course.

The duke always got my advance schedule from Argomaniz and we could take to the road for tours of a month or so before returning to Madrid. His party would reserve a floor or two in the swankiest hotel in each city or town we would visit. We carried our own chef. And before long I had to arrange for a chef to prepare food exclusively for me. I couldn't take the rich banquets as a steady fare. My stomach definitely affected my performances.

Internationally famous artists who appeared at the fairs

where I was booked entertained us privately in our suites after the theatre. They were violinists, pianists, 'cellists, singers of many nationalities, and artists in many fields. Pavlova gave some performances for us I'll never forget. And so did Caruso, Mary Garden, Farrar, Kreisler, Schipa, Pablo Casals, Andrés Segovia, and a great many others. They all gave brilliant performances. Practically all of the world-famous artists who toured Spain at that time entertained us privately at some time or another.

The day after returning from our first short trip round the country, I was sitting at a pavement table of the Café Gran Via, just across from the telephone building. There were about twelve in our group. It was just before noon and it was one of those days for which Madrid is famous. The air was crystal clear. The sky was a brilliant blue without a wisp of a cloud in it. The usual mob were making things difficult for the traffic and police. We were having a pre-lunch Tio Pepe when I noticed a great big fellow talking quietly with our waiter. The waiter pointed me out to him and then came over and asked if I'd permit him to present "a *paisano* of mine" who wanted to speak with me.

"Bring him over," I said, reaching into my pocket for some change. By his appearance, this fellow looked as though he needed a handout. Since my first success in Sevilla I had been swamped with all sorts of requests and demands for money by Americans. Some had what I believed to be legitimate hard-luck stories. Some were wise guys who lived by their wits. And there were quite a few crackpots. This man hadn't shaved and he needed a haircut. He wore a shabby suit which looked as though it had forgotten what a tailor's iron felt like. Battered bedroom slippers were on his feet. He approached very meekly and in a very small voice asked if I were Sidney Franklin, the matador. I rattled my pocket change in anticipation. But he didn't want money. Rather, he said, he'd like to know when he could speak with me.

"What about?" I asked.

He asked if I had received a letter from a Guy Hickock who was the Paris correspondent of the Brooklyn *Daily Eagle*. At first I didn't recall any such letter. But when he mentioned that it said something about my going to Pamplona to meet a certain Ernest Hemingway, I remembered it. "That's right," I said. "I remember this Hickock made some silly suggestion of that kind. Whoever this Hickock is, he doesn't seem to understand that for me to go to a place like Pamplona when I'm not appearing there would mean cancelling engagements. And for what? I don't know Hickock. And I don't know who this fellow he mentions is either. The way my contracts run right now, I can't go anywhere unless I'm booked there."

"That's what I tried to explain to Hickock when he told me he was going to write to you," he said. "I know a little about these things. But you can see that Hickock doesn't understand anything about bullfighters or bullfighting. So please don't hold that against me."

"Why should I? What has all this to do with you?" I asked.

"I'm the fellow he mentioned," he said. "I'm Ernest Hemingway, the one he asked you to go to Pamplona to meet."

At this point Count de la Peña, who was sitting on my right, offered his chair to the fellow. After a quick glance at me to see if it would be all right, he asked my permission and sat down. "What'll you have?" I said.

He thought a while, then said he'd order what he wanted if I'd permit him to pay for this round. But that was out of the question. "That's quite all right," I said. "Just order what you want. I don't pay for it, and, for that matter, I don't know who does. But somehow everything gets taken care of at the right time. So go right ahead and order."

"I can't do that," he said. "It wouldn't be right."

"That's a strange thing to say," I said. "Why wouldn't it be right?"

"What I'd like to order is about the most expensive drink there is," he said. "And this is one of the very few places in Madrid where it can be had. No, on second thoughts, I guess I'll have a beer."

I clapped for the waiter. This seemed to be an entirely new

line. I decided to play along with him, just to see what his game was, so I insisted he order what he first had in mind.

He ordered Pernod and explained that it was really absinthe. Absinthe? I hazily recalled having heard something about it. It seemed to be shrouded in a certain mystery. Something like cocaine, heroin, or opium. They all evoked visions of the mysterious. Something to stay away from. I definitely wanted to see what this absinthe was like.

The way he handled his stemmed glass, the ice tray with the tiny hole in it which sits on top of the glass, and the way he dripped the water, all made me wonder just who this fellow really was. His language and manners definitely didn't go with his appearance. I had a strange feeling that he either had had means at some time and was now down on his luck, or was somebody so well known that he didn't want to be recognized. Maybe this could explain his appearance.

So I asked who he was and what he did.

He stated simply that he was Ernest Hemingway and an author.

"What kind of an author?" I asked. "Books, newspapers, magazines? Do you make a living at it?"

"I manage to get along," he said.

"Are you any good at it?" I asked. I never had heard of Hemingway or read anything that wasn't directly concerned with bullfighting, except the *Saturday Evening Post*. I had no idea that he had already written A *Farewell to Arms* and *The Sun Also Rises* and was world-famous. When he offered to get me some of his books, I told him I wasn't interested. I had read so many pieces of tripe in English by people who said they were authors of repute that I had better use for my time. And far from being annoyed he seemed to take my statement without the slightest feeling of any kind. So, at his own suggestion, we just ignored the fact that he was an author. More to our mutual interest, we began to discuss bullfighting.

As we chatted, I realized that this fellow had a choice selection of English terms for bullfighting which up until then I had been at a loss to translate. And he used them very casually, as though it were old stuff with him. Besides, he was the first person who spoke to me in American English who appeared to have a deep understanding of the business. Since I knew that some day I would want to write on the subject, this was a perfect opportunity to learn. I drew our conversation into channels which would show me just how much he knew about bullfighting. And, little by little, he amazed me. He was familiar with events and instances which only a deep and sincere student of the subject could know about. We kept up this discussion until someone remarked it was time for lunch.

Hemingway asked me if I'd permit him to invite me to lunch. He said he'd been looking forward to this moment ever since he first saw references to me in the professional journals. He'd been thinking for some time that he'd go to Mexico to see me perform. But now that I had come to Spain, he was glad he didn't have to go so far.

Truthfully, I didn't believe he had the means for anything like that. I listened with half an ear to whatever he said about himself.

When the subject of lunch was brought up, he immediately invited me to lunch. I explained I was in the habit of eating at home. I had one of the most wonderful cooks in the country, and Spain is noted for her good cooks. So I invited him to come home with me for lunch if he didn't mind Spanish cooking. Mercedes always prepared enough for six or eight guests who dropped in at almost every meal. I was sure he'd enjoy it.

He accepted so enthusiastically that I smiled to myself smugly. This must be his gag, I thought.

When we reached the house, Ernest stopped at the door. He said he wouldn't feel right accepting my invitation unless I let him bring some wine. For the moment I thought the idea silly because my pantry was loaded with quantities of packaged food-stuffs and wines given me by manufacturers who were fans. He seemed to know of a very good wine house nearby and said it wouldn't take but a few minutes. So I told him to go ahead.

He finally came back with half a dozen different wines. Without the slightest suggestion of being pretentious, he explained that each wine was noted for some particular quality and was at its best when used with certain types of food. He said I'd soon see that a particular wine would bring out the finer flavours in certain dishes. He did it in such a manner that I could tell he knew what he was talking about. I didn't know the first thing about wines. Here was an opportunity to learn something I had wanted to know about for a long time. I had begun to entertain on a scale I'd never known before. As a host I'd be expected to understand all the things a good host should know for the benefit of his guests.

We began lunch with smoked clams and mussels, *percebes* (a sea barnacle with a meaty stem), *cigalas* (a delicious long-armed large shrimp found only in Spanish waters), several kinds of Spanish olives, small cubes of a very special Spanish Serrano ham, anchovies, Spanish sausage, pickled artichoke hearts, and marinated herring bits. Ernest went into the pantry and prepared the Cinzano for that.

When we had had our fill of appetizers, Mercedes brought in the first course, a light vegetable soup. Ernest opened a light white wine.

We talked and talked about bullfighting.

And here was Mercedes with a vegetable course, *acelgas*, as only she knew how to prepare them. Ernest now opened another white wine. We ate slowly and talked and talked and talked.

Then Mercedes came in with a platter of *lenguado*, baked in butter with a lemon sauce. Here we call it fillet of sole. I've never tasted any sole like the *lenguado* of Spain. And Ernest opened still another white wine for the *lenguado*.

I asked if he'd like to try some *calamares en su tinta*, baby squid done in a sauce made with their ink, which Mercedes had prepared for my approval. He said he'd love to try it to taste the real thing done by a cook who knew how. It was delicious, with a very rare flavour which can't be described. I made a note to get her to repeat this several days later. And of course Ernest opened a very light red wine he said was especially good with *calamares*.

Then we had partridge in orange sauce. After that we had

some wafer-thin slices of Serrano ham with a very light amontil-
lado. And then dessert. While I was preparing the express coffee
machine to make coffee under steam pressure, Ernest suddenly
asked if I'd mind if he followed me round the country to watch
me fight. By then I really liked the guy and didn't care what he
looked like. But when he mentioned following me round the
country, I looked to see if he really meant what he was saying.

"That's an expensive proposition," I said. "Do you realize the
kind of money a thing like that would take?"

"I'll manage it, I guess," he said with some hesitancy. "But I
don't want to do it if you don't approve."

"What has that to do with it?" I said. "Whether I approve or
not, anyone who can afford it can go where he pleases. I can't
stop anyone from coming to see me fight. You seem to know a
lot about bullfighting and I don't know how long you've been in
Spain. But do you know how expensive such a proposition would
be?"

"I guess I can take care of the expenses," he said without the
slightest sign of boasting.

"Let's not kid ourselves," I said. "In the first place, the travel
part would cost you an arm and a leg. Then, when you got to a
town where I was to appear, and since it would be right in the
middle of the fair dates, unless you had reserved some accommodations from six months to a year in advance, you'd never be
able to find a place to sleep standing up, much less in a bed!"

He was on the point of saying something, but hesitated. So I
continued. "Let's say, for argument's sake, that you managed by
hook or crook to get to these towns. It wouldn't be possible, but
let's say you also were able to find some hole in the wall where you
could stay so you wouldn't have to spend each twenty-four hours
on the street. You may not know this, but since my first appearance in Sevilla, the moment my name appears on a card you can't
find a ticket. If I didn't have it stipulated in my contracts, even
I couldn't get tickets to my own fights. Now how do you suppose
you'd get in to see these fights after all the expense and trouble of

getting to the places where they are held? Can you answer that?"

"That's not worrying me," he insisted. "All that bothers me is that I don't want you to feel annoyed at me for doing it. I guess I'll be able to manage everything. And even if I miss some of your fights, at least I'll have tried. On the level, what do you say?"

I particularly liked this fellow because he took a deep and sincere interest in my favourite subject, and I didn't want to offend him by constantly harping on expenses. So I told him I'd be in town for a day or so and would let him know where and when I was to appear. We were so engrossed in our discussion that I hadn't noticed Luis, who was now trying to attract my attention. He reminded me that I was supposed to meet Argomaniz at the Frontón Madrid. Then, for the first time, I suddenly realized what time it was. It was eight o'clock in the evening. We had been eating for five and a half hours! So I asked Ernest if he was free and if he'd like to accompany us to the *frontón*. He excused himself, claiming he'd already taken up more of my time than was right. Besides, if he intended to follow me round the country, he had a number of things which demanded his attention. But he promised to meet me at the *frontón* next evening when I'd be there again with my manager.

The following night, as soon as I had introduced him to my friends, we went to another box where we could be alone. I gave him my advance schedule for the next month and a half. He showed me a *kilómetrico* with seven thousand miles in it but I brushed it aside.

"You won't need that," I said. "I've spoken with some of my friends who make up our travelling caravan. If you'd care to pack in with us, I guess we can find room for one more person in our some twenty-odd cars. If you don't mind sharing a room with Luis, my *mozo*, I can manage it so they can put an extra cot in it for you. How does that strike you?"

For a moment I thought he would burst into tears. His eyes watered. I don't know what may have caused it, but I saw his eyes wet. After some time he spoke very slowly.

"It's too much! I can't let you put yourself out like that for me! I couldn't accept anything like that unless you let me pay for my share of the expenses!"

"Look!" I said. "Let's not kid ourselves. The travelling, even with your *kilómetrico*, would be very expensive. And you'd never be able to get accommodations. I don't pay for any of this and I don't know who does! I've tried to find out many times. But whenever I send Luis for an accounting, he always comes back and says he doesn't know who paid the bills. I like you and I really want to help you. You're the first guy I've ever spoken to in English who really knows something about all this. That's worth plenty to me. And there's another thing. The tickets I get are all spoken for. If you won't mind and would like to watch the fights from behind the fence, if you're not afraid to see them that close, I think I can arrange it. That's the only way you'd ever be able to see the fights. Now, what do you say?"

He finally accepted my invitation and left to make his arrangements.

The first few nights out of town we talked until about three in the morning. When he noticed me dozing off, he would go to his room quietly so as not to wake me. And although I didn't notice it at the time, later I marvelled at how well he got along with all our hosts. I found out much later that he had known most of them intimately for a number of years. He never let on, and I was so absorbed in other things that I never guessed. When we visited the great estates and hunted and fished, he outdid himself in teaching me the finer points of handling a gun and rod. He was an expert with both. Now and then he'd tell me stories of things he had done and places he had been. He never put himself in a good light. He was very unassuming. And the more I got to know him the more I liked him. He was definitely an outdoor man. There didn't seem to be a thing he didn't know about nature and sports. And once in a while our conversation would drift to a point where I'd stop him and ask who the hell he was! All he'd say was that he was an author, and a lousy one at that, and once in a while he did some newspaper reporting.

He offered to get me some of his books to read so that I could tell him what I thought of his stuff. But I told him that no matter how well he might write, he couldn't possibly add up in his writing to what I already thought of him as a person. So again we deliberately forgot about his writing and didn't mention it any more.

After the first week or so on the road, we reached a point where it began to bother me that he had to go to another room when I'd fall asleep during our discussion. So I had his cot or bed placed in my room to make things more convenient for him. And when we couldn't get the extra cot or bed, if I had a double bed in my room we just shared it.

He questioned me about past great matadors. Why was it, he wanted to know, that nowadays we didn't see such things as made Guerrita great? And Joselito? And Franscuelo? And Fuentes? He made me describe in detail exactly how each manœuvre was done. And wouldn't it be a good stunt to try some of the specialties of former days once in a while? I promised to try a couple on the following day. In the next fight I did one or two of the passes which hadn't been seen in Spanish rings for more than fifty years. The effect on the critics and old fans was electric. It started a whole new series of endless discussions.

The press fell all over me. Who was I, anyway? And where did I really come from? Who taught me all these manœuvres since it wasn't possible I had seen them and only a few people alive actually had? They wanted to know all about my background. I must have Spanish blood in me. I couldn't be possible otherwise. And as though to show they knew more about me than I did, I began to get photostatic copies of what were purported to be birth certificates and baptismal papers which seemingly proved beyond any doubt that I was born in Sevilla, and then in Madrid, and then in Valencia or Bilbao or a dozen other places which had produced some famous fighters of the past.

All this proved that Ernest was right in his approach. So we worked out a series of signals between us. He would give me an indication of how things were going from the spectator's angle and what I should do next. Only he and I knew what was going on. This direction from him was the cause of my meteoric rise. My appearances were causing demonstrations which began to take on the dimensions of riots. Meanwhile, we spent more and more time in the country when we were inland, and yachting and fishing when we were near the coast.

I began to live in a goldfish bowl. I couldn't take a bath in privacy. I couldn't even go to the bathroom alone. They thought there was nothing strange about wanting to observe me at all times. By the time we had finished that second tour, my price had risen to fifteen thousand pesetas per fight. You can understand what this meant when I say that the top full professional matadors of the day were getting the long-established rate of twelve thousand pesetas. I was even naming the breeds I appeared with as well as the matadors on the cards.

When we got back to Madrid, Louise Whitney was waiting in my home for me. She said she had been ordered by the Ambassador to wait until she saw me and to make me promise to bring Ernest Hemingway to the embassy for tea.

"All Spain knows you've been travelling with Ernest Hemingway," she said. "And you can name anything you want if you'll only bring him to the embassy!"

"What do you mean, I've been travelling with Hemingway?" I said. "Don't be silly! He's been travelling with me as my companion on the whole trip!"

"What difference does it make who's been travelling with whom?" she said, annoyed. "The important fact is that the Ambassador wants you to bring him for tea!"

"The Ambassador wants him for tea?" I said incredulously. "Why, the poor fellow doesn't even have the clothes for such a thing!"

"The idea of such a thing!" Louise said impatiently. "I'm surprised at you, Sidney!"

"Let's quit horsing around, Louise," I said exasperated. "I ought to know what I'm talking about! After all, we spent the last month and a half together."

"Well, it's apparent you don't even know who the man is!"

"Who is he?" I twitted. "All I know is that his name is Ernest Hemingway. I don't know what he does. He told me once or twice that he wrote, or something like that."

"Good lord!" she said, throwing up her hands in genuine surprise. "You mean to stand there and tell me you don't know who Ernest Hemingway is? Can you really mean that?"

"Of course!" I said. "Who is he? Tell me! I'm waiting!"

"Why, he's only the greatest author of our time!" she said. "There are millions of people who would give their right arms just to see what he looks like in the flesh! Can it really be possible that the two of you have been together for more than a month and you don't know who he is?" she said.

As soon as Louise left, I hurried to the Hotel Victoria on Calle Victoria where Ernest said he would be staying. I sat down and told him what had happened and demanded that he tell me who he really was. He tried to tell me, but I couldn't grasp most of it. He just said he wrote and some people thought he wrote all right. Then he asked me if it would do me any good to have him accompany me to the embassy. I balked at that. I didn't want him to go solely because it might serve me in any way. The only way I'd agree to go with him would be because he really wanted to go for his own purposes. Otherwise we'd forget it and I'd tell them I couldn't find him. In the end, this was what he preferred.

We spent four months together that year and the whole eight months of the following season before I got up enough courage to read *A Farewell to Arms* and *The Sun Also Rises*. After those two books, he couldn't write fast enough to keep me satisfied.

El Inglés

Vincent Hitchcock

VINCENT HITCHCOCK (b. 1925) was the first English matador. Despite a career marred by a number of bad accidents—he did, also, score several notable triumphs—Hitchcock displayed considerable skill and bravery and became known as "El Inglés." His autobiography, Suit of Lights, describes his uphill struggle to gain acceptance—and be taken seriously—in this most Spanish of all Spanish events. Here is Hitchcock about to face his moment of truth and make his début at the La Linea bullring near Gibraltar.

It was 11 A.M. when Pedro, my swordhandler, came to wake me. He laid out the pale blue and silver costume over a chair in the corner of the bedroom and after seeing that everything was to his satisfaction, turned to me.

"Are you going to Mass, *jefe?*"* he enquired.

Until this moment I hadn't thought about it but it seemed to be the right thing to do and, after all, I had plenty to pray for.

"Yes, I'll go to the 11:30 Mass. Have you been yet, Pedro?" I enquired of him.

"I haven't had time to yet, *jefe.* I'll come with you," he replied.

I suspected that he had already been, but thought that I might like to have someone to accompany me. He was right. I had never been to Mass before and it would be easier having someone to follow.

We walked down the Calle Real towards the little white

* Chief.

church that stood in the square at the end of the street. The pavements were lined with people sitting at café tables taking an early *aperitivo*. As we passed I could hear my name being mentioned and once or twice, out of the corner of my eye, I caught sight of people pointing in my direction and caught the words— *El Inglés que va a torear esta tarde*—the Englishman who is going to fight this afternoon. There was evidently a lot of interest in the coming fight.

When we arrived at the church Mass was already being said and we had to stand at the back. There was still a steady flow of people entering and soon the church was uncomfortably overcrowded. Looking around me I could not help but notice that to most of the congregation religion seemed more of a habit than a devotion.

The service came to an end and I walked back with Pedro down the Calle Real towards the café Anglo-Hispano where we were to await my manager and Adolfo Beaty. Finding ourselves an empty table on the pavement outside the café, we sat down and Pedro called the waiter.

"You better have a fruit juice, *jefe*," he said.

"No alcohol?" I asked.

"It's better not to have any. It affects the nervous system even in small quantities," said my swordhandler, "though most toreros have a coffee with a tot of cognac in it just before they leave for the ring."

The waiter approached and Pedro ordered two glasses of lemon juice. The facts that Pedro drank lemon juice with me and not wine as he would have preferred, and that he had gone to Mass a second time just to keep me company, were examples of attributes which I came very much to admire in him.

It was with a great deal of impatience that I awaited the arrival of my manager and Adolfo, for they had gone to the bull-ring for the *sorteo*, the sorting out of the bulls.

The *sorteo* usually takes place around noon on the day of the bullfight. The six bulls to be killed in the afternoon have been brought in from the country and enclosed in the corrals of the bullring. At the appointed hour the matador's representatives, usually his manager and senior banderillero—known as his confidential banderillero—go down to the corrals and with the representatives of the other two matadores pair the bulls as near as possible into three equal pairs. Perhaps a big bull will be paired with a small animal, or one with large horns with one with a small pair. After a lot of discussion and argument, the six bulls are paired and the numbers of each pair are written on separate cigarette papers which are then screwed up into tiny balls and dropped into a hat. That hat is shaken and the banderilleros draw the papers out according to the seniority of the matadores they represent. The bulls are then separated and penned in semidarkness in order to quieten and rest them. In no way are they starved or provoked before being set loose.

Pedro and I had been sitting at the table about a quarter of an hour when he pointed up the road saying, "Here they come." Following his eyes I saw my manager and Adolfo approaching together with Fernando Naranjo, my confidential banderillero that afternoon.

I started to get up. "Come on, Pedro," I said to my swordhandler. "Let's go and find out what bulls we've drawn."

"You had better wait here for them to arrive, *jefe*. They will tell us soon enough. You mustn't appear impatient," he said. "Matadores are supposed to be above worrying about what bulls they draw."

I took his advice and sat down again to wait for the trio to arrive. On seeing us sitting outside the café, they hurried towards us.

"This is certainly your lucky day, Vicente," began Miguel, "you have drawn the best pair by far."

"A couple of beauties. Horns like this," said Adolfo, crooking his two index fingers inwards to indicate the shape of the horns.

"We'll cut the ears all right this afternoon, *jefe*," Fernando joined in.

Adolfo must have read the look of disbelief in my face for he continued, "Believe me, Vincente, you have nothing to worry about."

Miguel, my manager, as if reading my mind, backed Adolfo up. "I know that we should have said this in any case," he said, "but I swear by all that is holy, Vicente, you have drawn two dream bulls for your debut."

Adolfo left us to go to the box office to see how the sale of tickets was progressing. Miguel and Fernando sat down at the table and after ordering wine for themselves, continued describing the two bulls that I was to fight later that day. We had sat there for an hour or more when my swordhandler suggested that I should go to bed and rest until the hour arrived for me to start dressing.

"I had better go and have my lunch now," I said to my swordhandler.

"Toreros do not eat on the day of the fight, *jefe*," Pedro replied.

"But why not?" I asked curiously.

"It—er—it is in case of a goring in the stomach," said my swordhandler nervously, stretching out his hand and touching wood as he did so. My surprise at seeing Pedro's nervousness made me forget the implication of his words. I walked back to my room.

Back in the solitude, doubts and fears again began to crowd my mind and the full realisation of what the afternoon might bring dawned upon me. I pictured all the gorings that I had seen and tried to imagine how it would feel to have a horn ripping through my flesh. I wondered how I would react to an injury. It had always amazed me whenever I had seen bullfighters being gored, how unworried they appeared to me. I thought of a boy I had known, Luis Miguel Sanz, who had been killed by a bull; gored through the heart, some months previously.

That would be the best way to die, I decided; it would be quick and probably painless. But what if I should lose a limb or even an eye? It had happened often enough. I began to feel sick and getting up from my bed, I went outside to the lavatory. Somehow my bladder had become weak. That was the third time that I had relieved myself in the last half an hour.

A radio blaring out from a nearby house played a *pasa doble torero*, music of the bullring, and this had a stimulating effect on me. Like the feeling of intense patriotism and national pride one feels on hearing a Guard's band play a stirring march. The music stopped and a shrill feminine voice began announcing the afternoon's corrida.

"This afternoon in La Linea a grand bullfight. Six brave bulls from the ranch of Don Juan Belmonte for the following bull-fighters: Miguel Campos of La Linea, Pepe Chapi of Sevilla and Vincent Charles (she pronounced it Vicente Charlays) of London, the first Englishman to become a bullfighter. Do not miss this great . . . etc. . . . etc. . . ."

It seemed strange and unreal to hear the fight anounced like that over the radio. It sounded like somebody announcing a freak show. Come to think of it, that's what it is, I thought, a bloody freak show. People won't be coming to see what I do, but what I don't do. I got up and went to the lavatory again.

Returning to the bed, I lay down and lit another cigarette. How many had I smoked since Pedro had left me? The ashtray was full of stubs, some of them two inches in length. My hands were sweating so much that they soaked the cigarettes and made them fall apart along the seams.

The radio was blaring out the announcement again when the door of my room opened and Pedro came in.

"They're a bit late," he said, indicating the radio.

"The tickets are all sold. It's going to be a full house today, *jefe*."

At that moment there was a knock on the door. Pedro opened it to admit the barber who had arrived to shave me.

Whilst I was being shaved, my swordhandler arranged an altar on the dressing-table. He placed photographs of various holy *Virgens* and a figurette of *La Macarena* who from her church in

Sevilla stretches a guarding hand to all bullfighters. Pedro placed three candles before the altar and lighted them.

When the barber had finished shaving me, the complicated process of dressing began. First of all Pedro made me put on my *montera*, the black hat worn by bullfighters. He then selected a tuft of hair at the back of my head, just below the lower edge of the hat; to this he would later fix the traditional pigtail. Twisting the strands, he slipped them into a split screw, the ends of which he tightened together with a nut. The reason for attaching the clip before combing my hair was to prevent it slipping once my hair had been brilliantined.

Next I put on my vest and the white linen underpants which reached to just below my knees and two pairs of stockings, a white cotton pair first to prevent the following pink silk pair from wrinkling. These I held taut under my pants whilst Pedro tightened the tapes below my knees to hold the stockings in place.

Now came the difficult part of wriggling into the skin-tight *taleguilla*, the figure-moulding breeches. I sat on the edge of the bed, stiff-legged, while Pedro pulled the *taleguilla* over my feet and up my legs. I then stood up, and with Pedro holding the back and the barber the front of my breeches they lifted me off the floor and shook me down into them. Pedro then took a towel, twisted it, and told me to sit astride it. Then he and the barber each held an end whilst I wiggled until my breeches fitted like a tight glove. At last they were on, and I slipped my feet into the black pumps whilst Pedro tightened the laces on the breeches just below my knees. The lacing up of the breeches is most important; they must be laced to just the right pressure. Too much and the circulation is restricted, too little and no support is given to the bullfighter's legs and he feels insecure. All these details have a psychological effect on the man in the ring, just as much as has his physical fitness. Naturally a bullfighter can never hope to compete with a bull in strength nor, as it is his obligation to stand still unless he is placing the banderillas, is it necessary for him to be agile. However, the fact that he feels strong and agile gives him

the will to dominate the bull. It's just a question of wills. When
Pedro had finished lacing my trousers he tied the ribbons on my
pumps into neat bows.

The worst was now over. All I had to do was to put on shirt,
sash, waistcoat and jacket. First the shirt of fine white linen with
lace and frills down the front, with which I wore a red tie about
an inch wide throughout its length. After buttoning the *taleguilla*,
first the inside fly which is placed to one side and which acts as a
sort of built-in support, then the outside fly, Pedro helped me
into the red sash which he passed once around my waist, tying
it in front and intertwining the ends round the lower part of my
braces; then into my waistcoat, and I was nearly ready. I had been
so busy that I had forgotten my fears. I lit a cigarette but noticed
that my hand shook slightly. It was now nearly time to leave and
I awaited with impatience the arrival of the car that was to take
me to the bullring. Pedro slipped out of the door and returned
shortly with a cup of black coffee and a tot of brandy. I poured
the brandy into the coffee and drank it down hurriedly and then
while Pedro was helping me into the stiff and heavily embroidered
bolero jacket that completed the costume, there was a knock on
the door to announce that the car was waiting.

Picking up my dress cape and hat, I said a silent prayer before
the altar, then, carrying my cape over my arm and my hat in my
hand, I went out to the car, Pedro following with the leather
box containing the fighting capes and *muletas* and the leather
sword case.

I sat in the back seat of the car between my manager and Pedro.
A small crowd had gathered on the pavement to watch us leave,
and, as we moved off, an olive-skinned gipsy girl, carrying a baby,
leaned forward, touched me on the shoulder and assured me that
everything would go well.

We turned into the road that led to the bullring. The pavements were thronged with people as indeed was most of the
roadway. A steady stream of humanity slowly flowing towards a
common goal.

We passed one of the huge posters announcing the fight and I couldn't stop myself looking at it to see my name again. It still seemed unreal. Surely that could not be me, billed to kill two bulls on this Sunday afternoon of 5 June 1949? Surely it was a mad dream and any moment I would wake up and life would be simple once again.

The car moved slowly because of the press of bodies we had to pass through. People kept waving and shouting to me, wishing me good luck, and I thought how false they probably were; that in reality they were all going to see what sort of a fiasco I would produce. Suddenly I realised we had reached the bullring and were outside the gate where the bullfighters enter. My cuadrilla, who had gone ahead, were just alighting from their vehicle and waiting for me to lead the way. We shook hands and greeted each other, then I led the way into the *patio de caballos*, the courtyard where the bullfighters await the signal to make the parade across the ring. The door through which we came into the bullring was set midway between the *patio de caballos* and the yard where the bulls were butchered, and I caught a glimpse of two men from the slaughterhouse sharpening their skinning and cleaving knives in preparation for the coming afternoon's work.

Someone called my name. It was Pepe Perez-Ponce, the photographer. He wanted to take some photographs before the fight started. I walked stiff-legged to where he was standing with Miguel Campos and Pepe Chapi, passing as I did so the mule team which was already in harness to drag the carcasses from the ring. The mules looked splendid, their bell-covered harness gleaming, and brand-new red and yellow pennants fluttering from their collars. I greeted Miguel Campos and Pepe Chapi and we wished each other luck for the afternoon's performance.

Three photographers tried to lead me to different positions for photographs and everybody, it seemed, wanted to be in the picture. I have no idea how many photographs were taken but a good length of film must have been used.

Pedro, who had disappeared into the *callejon*, the narrow corridor that runs round the bullring between spectators and the arena and in which the bullfighters and bullring attendants stand when not in action, reappeared and told me it was time for me to put on my dress cape.

Unfolding it, I swung it on my left shoulder and pulling the rear corner under my right arm, grasped both points firmly in my left hand whilst Pedro gathered up the lower edge and tucked it up under my left forearm, tight against my body, leaving my right arm swinging free at my side. I had to carry my hat in this hand during the parade, out of deference to the public of La Linea, this being my presentation in their bullring.

I took up my position between Miguel Campos and Pepe Chapi and our cuadrillas formed up in columns behind us, the bullring attendants and the mule teams bringing up the rear. It was a tense moment.

At last the trumpet sounded and the gates in front of us were flung open, revealing a blaze of yellows and surrounded by a seething sea of faces. The vivid blue and cloudless sky formed a canopy high above our heads.

The photographers dashed out in front and took last-minute pictures before the parade began. Then it was Miguel Campos saying, "*Que Dios reparta la suerte. Vamos*"—May God share out the luck. Let's go. We all muttered "*Suerte*"—luck. The band struck up with a *pasa doble* and we swung out across the ring.

It seemed even more dream-like now. I felt as if my feet weren't touching the ground. I made a conscious effort to emulate the bullfighters I had watched, marching slightly pigeon-toed and swinging easily from the hips. I began to feel the part.

Arriving below the presidential box we bowed to the president, who in this case was the local chief of police, and then made our way to where our respective swordhandlers were waiting ready to give us the heavy fighting capes. We slipped off our dress capes and handed them to our swordhandlers, who in turn handed them up to friends in the front seats who would spread them out over the barrier dividing the seats from the *callejon*.

Opening our fighting capes we tried them in a couple of passes to see how they handled and what wind there was, if any. Then we slipped in behind the plank shelter and through the opening in the main barrier which it covered, and thence into the *callejon*. The bullring attendants, called *areneros*, were smoothing over the sand that had been disturbed during the parade. One man shovelled up a heap of dung dropped by one of the mules.

Miguel Campos was due to take the first bull and with his banderillero de confianza by his side he moved into the space behind the plank shelter and the barrier.

He did well with his animal and made a clean kill and afterwards was obliged to make a circuit of the ring to acknowledge the applause.

Pepe Chapi did likewise.

It was now my turn. Fernando motioned to me to slip into the ring with him while Pepi Chapi was still acknowledging the cheers of the crowd. When the cheering subsided and Pepe Chapi had left, Fernando and I slipped in behind the plank shelter. My other two banderilleros had taken up their positions in the two plank shelters which were set one on each side of the ring; one to my right and the other to my left. The *areneros* smoothed the sand of the arena.

A heavy and tense silence fell on the crowd as I waited for my bull to be set loose. Fernando whispered last-minute words of advice.

"Now don't forget, *jefe*, wait until I've run the bull at least once on each horn. I'll tell you when to come out," he instructed.

"All right," I replied.

"Just keep calm and you'll be all right. Imagine that you are at a *tienta* and forget about the public."

"O.K.," I murmured. I was beginning to feel scared again and wanted to relieve myself, but knew that this was impossible now.

The president gave the signal and the trumpet shrilled. I watched as the man who was in charge of the bull-pens advanced towards the gate where the bulls came in. ("The gate of the big fear," the bullfighters call it. I now know why.) He reached the gate, unlatched it and swung it wide open. I tried to penetrate its inky blackness but could see nothing.

A shout went up from the crowd, but it was not to greet the

entry of the bull. A little black cat had walked into the ring from
the bull-pens and everybody, myself included, burst out laughing.
The tension was broken and my confidence was restored.

In came my bull and a cheer broke from the crowd. It was a
perfect specimen of a fighting bull: short, stocky and perfectly
proportioned, with symmetrically curving horns. It halted a few
paces from the gate to the pens and stood still. I could see the
hump of the tossing muscle rising on its great neck as it slowly
took stock of its surroundings.

The banderillero to my left stepped out from behind his shelter and showed himself to the bull. The reaction was immediate.
Like a bolt, the bull charged across the ring and as it did so the
banderillero slipped back to his hiding place. The bull pulled up
sharply at the barrier and hooked at the planking with its horns.
I could see the chips of wood flying at each blow.

I sensed rather than saw Fernando leave my side, and run out
into the ring, calling the bull as he did so. The bull by this time
had realised the futility of hooking at the barrier and now stood
with its tail swishing, looking for something else to attack. It
spotted Fernando and immediately charged towards him. Fernando stood his ground and as the bull arrived, swung the cape
out with one hand in a wide sweeping arc. The animal followed the
cloth perfectly. "He is good on that horn," I thought to myself.

The bull, furious at not having hit anything solid, turned and
came at Fernando again on the other side and once more my
banderillero swung his cape out in a wide arc and once more the
bull followed it perfectly.

He was good on both horns and I realised that Miguel and
Adolfo hadn't exaggerated after all. At least not as far as this bull
was concerned.

Fernando snatched his cape away from under the bull's nose
and left the animal looking bewildered and wondering where its
target had disappeared to. I stepped out of my shelter and advanced towards the bull. Fernando grinned at me as he passed.
His teeth positively flashed in the sunlight as he did so and I
realised for the first time that they were all gold.

"It's an animal in a million, *jefe*," he whispered. "If you don't get yourself awarded an ear with this one, you never will. Just take it calmly."

I opened my cape and profiled to the horns. The bull watched me intently with his black beady eyes. I stepped nearer and shook my cape. The tension and silence in the ring were very noticeable. Not a murmur came from the crowd.

I moved a little nearer and called to the bull, "*Aha torito, toma bonito.*" He started for me. I swung the cape out and keeping my hands low I led him past in a *veronica*. Suddenly the bullring exploded with the shout of "Olé" from ten thousand voices.

The bull wheeled and came at me again and I made another *veronica,* and again ten thousand voices shouted as one man. indeed was the stimulation I needed. I did a third *veronica* and then a *media veronica* to fix the bull in one place. Turning my back on the bull I faced up to the crowd. The applause was deafening and, as is the custom, I took off my hat to acknowledge it. I then decided to do some *chicuelinas*, passes where the bullfighter pulls the cape back on to himself and spins between the horns as the bull turns on him. I called the bull and executed a *chicuelina* and then, as the bull turned and came at me again, I started another. The next thing I knew I was flying through the air. There was a rapid kaleidoscopic view of sand, faces, and blue sky, and then I was laying on my back in the sand.

As rapidly as possible I rolled over on to my stomach and covered my head with my hands as I had seen other bullfighters do when tossed. The bull was trampling on me now and any moment I expected to feel the horn thrust into my body. It was not, however, and for a second the trampling stopped. I uncovered my head. In that brief instant I was hit in the mouth by what felt like a sledgehammer. The impact of the blow rolled me completely over and I felt my mouth fill with blood from a gash the horn had made in my lip and on the inside of my cheek and gum. Luckily I must have had my mouth open, otherwise the horn would have smashed through my teeth.

It had all happened in a split second and now my banderilleros, together with Miguel Campos and Pepe Chapi, were around me calling the bull off.

Fernando helped me to my feet and over to the barrier where my swordhandler wiped my mouth and gave me a glass of water so that I could swill out some of the blood. Miguel, my manager, was looking worried.

"You'd better get along to the *enfermería* and get that fixed, Vicente," he said.

"*Mierda*! It's nothing," I replied. "Pedro, give me another cape, quickly," I shouted at my swordhandler.

"It was your own fault, *jefe*," said Fernando; "you kept your elbows into your sides and pulled the bull on to yourself. Don't forget he will go where you send him."

I turned away quickly and rudely. I did not want to start having lessons on bullfighting at this stage.

After completing a couple more passes, the trumpet sounded for the banderillas to be placed and I retired to the barrier. Pedro handed me a towel to wipe the sweat from my face and I took a swig of water to rinse my mouth. I spat the water into the sand and watched as the globules of liquid turned into dust balls which rolled in all directions from the point of impact. My banderilleros made short work of placing the darts and the trumpet sounded for the last act to begin. Pedro handed me my folded *muleta* and sword, and crossing them I held both in my left hand as I had practised. I then removed my hat and advanced towards the president's box to go through the formality of asking his permission to kill the bull. Stopping before his box I raised my hat towards him and said, "Good afternoon, sir. With your permission?" He smilingly nodded his assent.

At this moment I happened to look down and noticed a bottle-cap lying in the sand. The ring of the bottle had broken off and I could see the circle of glass gleaming inside the metal cap. For some reason it annoyed me and I knew that I would have to remove it from the sand before I began the final act.

Having received the president's permission to go ahead, I walked over to where Mr. Gomez, the British Vice-Consul, was sitting in the front row, to dedicate the bull to him. Mr. Gomez stood up as I arrived before him, and raising my arm holding my hat in his direction I said, "I have the honour to dedicate the death of this bull, the first I shall kill in my life as a professional bullfighter, to you, Mr. Gomez, as representative of my country in La Linea." I then tossed up my hat to him. Catching it, he smiled in acknowledgment and sat down.

Turning to where Fernando was keeping the bull's attention whilst all this was going on I motioned to him to bring the animal to just the other side of the presidential box. I could read the look of mystification on his face as if to say, "It's all right here, why bother to take it over there." But it is a banderillero's obligation to obey the matador at all times and to take the bull wherever the matador chooses to fight it. Fernando obeyed immediately and caped the bull to the position I had indicated. He still looked quizzical as he passed me on his way back to the barrier.

Walking towards the bull I kept glancing down on the ground and then I spotted it again. That offending bottle top. With the point of the sword I flicked the circle of metal under the barrier. Now I could carry on. It never occurred to me that it was a silly thing to worry about, or that the onlookers would wonder what on earth I was doing. It was something that just had to be done.

Waiting until I was about six paces from the bull, I let the *muleta* fall open and spread the cloth over the sword. I would begin with a *pase de la muerte*. The bull watched interestedly, wondering what his new adversary might be. I shook the cloth gently and called to him. He charged and I waited for him with my feet together, firmly planted in the sand. His horns arrived at the cloth of the *muleta*, I raised my hands and he passed underneath, his nearside horn grazing my chest. He went through and quickly turning came at the *muleta* again. I did not move a muscle until he was up to the *muleta*. Again the horn passed a few inches from my body. I repeated this four times and I was conscious of the cries of "Olé" from the crowd. The band struck up with a *pasa doble*. I continued with the right hand, then the left, and then went through my repertoire of fancy passes. At one point I stretched out my hand and held the bull's horn to show how close I was fighting. Twice more I was tossed, fortunately without serious consequences, but by this time I was too intoxicated by this new experience to care what happened. All the time I was remembering Pajarero's instructions, like those of an old sweat to a recruit: "If you get your guts ripped out, hold them in with one hand and keep on fighting with the other." This was exaggerating a bit but I knew what he meant by it. The important thing was to keep on fighting.

The time had now come for me to kill. I lined the bull up and making sure that his forefeet were in line, I raised my sword, sighted along the blade, and fell on the bull. The blade of the sword disappeared into the beast's body and only the red hilt showed between its shoulders. It staggered, coughed, and crashed to the sand, dead!

After saluting the president I went over to Mr. Gomez, who returned my hat. The crowd went wild and Beaty grabbed my hand and shook it madly. "You've done it. You've done it, Vicente. It was terrific," he said.

The seats were a mass of white handkerchiefs and I knew that the public were asking the president to award me the ears. My banderilleros were standing by the carcase of the bull awaiting the president's signal, and in readiness to cut off what he had decided was to be my award.

Pedro handed me a towel and I wiped my hands and face. "We were good, *jefe*," he said. I smiled at him and his pleasure. It was a triumph for the whole cuadrilla.

Suddenly Fernando came up behind me. "Here you are, *jefe*, look what they have given us." Saying this he handed me the two ears and the tail of the bull. I was speechless. This was beyond my wildest expectations.

Taking the ears in one hand and the tail in the other I turned to the president and held the trophies aloft. He nodded his confirmation of the award and I bowed my thanks to him before starting off on a circuit of the ring. The crowd were wild with excitement and standing up in their seats they showered the ring with articles of apparel, flowers, wine-skins and cigars. The latter my cuadrilla pocketed, the rest they threw back.

Having once been right the way round the ring, Fernando insisted that I went to the *enfermería* to have my mouth attended to. This was to be my first but no means my last journey to a bullring's "hospital." This time I was, at least, able to walk there. The doctor swabbed the lacerated part and strapped it together. I refused to have stitches as I didn't wish the wound to leave a scar. It was a matter of minutes before I returned to the ring; Miguel Campos has just finishing killing his second bull and Pepe Chapi was preparing for his.

Pedro, my swordhandler, started to sew up the tears in my breeches. He made a first-class job of them and finished just in time for me to slip into the ring and await my second bull.

Taking my place beside my banderillero I watched intently as the door to the bull-pens was swung open. Would my next bull be as good as the first? That would be too much to hope for, I thought. I had already had more luck than I deserved.

"The gate of the big fear" opened to reveal the tunnel from which the bull would be loosed, and almost immediately he burst into the ring. He positively hurtled in and spotting his shadow on the barrier, immediately began to attack it. He did a half-circuit of the ring in this manner, attacking his own shadow with ferocity.

"*Es muy bravo*," said Fernando, "It is very wild."

It looked as if Adolfo and my manager had been right about both bulls after all. Fernando stepped out and ran the bull first on one side then on the other. The animal followed perfectly. Fernando then stopped it about seven yards from where I was standing and without hesitation I stepped out from behind the barrier.

As before, I started with *veronicas*, finishing with a half *veronica*. Again the "Olés" cracked out like pistol shots from the crowd and I started another series of passes called *gaoneras*, in which the bullfighter holds the cape behind his body. The bull was passing so close that his shoulder bumped my chest each time, and later Pedro showed me the black hairs that he had picked out of the embroidery on the front of my jacket.

The banderilleros placed the darts quickly and efficiently and the time came for the last act. This time I decided to dedicate the bull to the crowd.

After receiving the sword and *muleta* from Pedro, I took off my hat and going out to the centre of the ring I held it at arm's length and slowly turning, I described a circle which embraced every part of the public in the bullring. This signified that everyone present was included in the dedication. They were appreciative of this gesture and let me know it by their applause.

My *faena* this time followed closely on the pattern of the previous one and culminated in a single sword thrust. The reaction of the audience was as before and again I was awarded the ears and the tail of the bull.

Whilst I was making the circuit of the ring several enthusiasts climbed down on to the sand and lifted me on their shoulders and carried me round and round the ring to the accompaniment of wild cheers. "This is indeed an honour," I thought; but it was not finished. They carried me out into the street and down towards the Calle Real. All the way, people who had not been to the fight came out on to their balconies and cheered loudly. Down the Calle Real we went and men sitting in the bars there came out and gave me glasses of wine. Round and round the streets they carried me and so great was my elation that I didn't give a thought to my uncomfortable, even perilous, position. Still the people kept cheering and pressing drinks on me, and it was some time before I could persuade my enthusiastic bearers to carry me back to my room.

The house in which I was living stood in a square which was now packed with people. The noise from their acclamation was terrific and my manager made me go out on to the balcony to acknowledge them. I felt like royalty.

After two or three appearances on the balcony I told Pedro to close the shutters. I was worn out and could hardly stand. Pedro helped me to undress and after taking a shower bath I lay on the bed.

Until then I hadn't realised how tired I was. The nervous exhaustion that always follows a bullfight hit me and I fell into a sound sleep. However, I wasn't allowed to rest for long. My manager came into the room and waking me told me that his father's bar was full of people who were wanting to congratulate me and that I must go there. The bar was packed, and there followed a mad evening of drinking, hand-shaking and autograph-signing.

Time passed quickly and it was ten o'clock when Miguel took me into the parlour to listen to the bullfight reports on the radio. They gave my appearance precedence over all the other bullfights that had taken place in Spain that day, and it was then that I fully appreciated the extent of my achievements. The hardships I had suffered had been worthwhile. Bullfighting was my life.

The Crazy One

Norman Mailer

NORMAN MAILER *(b. 1923), the brilliant, unpredictable, Pulitzer Prize-winning writer whose interests range across a whole variety of subjects from film making to politics, first encountered bullfighting in Mexico, and from his early casual interest has grown what he calls "a small size obsession." He crystallizes a lot of what he has come to understand and feel in this remarkable article centered on a matador who could alternately be the best or the very worst bullfighter you ever saw in the ring.*

In Mexico, the hour before the bullfight is always the best hour of the week. It would be memorable not to sound like Hemingway, but in fact you would get happy the night before just thinking of that hour next day. Outside the Plaza Mexico, cheap cafés open only on Sunday, and huge as beer gardens, filled with the public (us tourists, hoodlums, pimps, pickpurses and molls, Mexican variety—which is to say the whores had headdresses and hindquarters not to be seen elsewhere on earth, for their hair rose vertically 12 inches from the head, and their posteriors projected horizontally 12 inches back into that space the rest of the whore had just marched through). The *mariachis* were out with their romantic haunting caterwauling of guitar, violin, song of carnival and trumpet, their song told of hearts which were true and hearts which were broken, and the wail of the broken heart went right into the trumpet until there were times, when drunk the right way on tequila or Mexican rum, it was perhaps the best sound heard this side of Miles Davis.

You see, my friends, the wild hour was approaching. The horrors of the week in Mexico were coming to term. Indeed, no week in Mexico is without its horrors for every last Mexican alive—it is a city and a country where the bones of the dead seem to give the smell of their char to every desert wind and auto exhaust and frying *tortilla*. The mournfulness of unrequited injustice hangs a shroud across the centuries. Every Mexican is gloomy until the instant he becomes happy, and then he is a maniac. He howls, he whistles, smoke of murder passes off his pores, he bullies, he beseeches friendship, he is a clown, a brigand, a tragic figure suddenly merry. The intellectuals and the technicians of Mexico abominate their national character because it is always in the way. It puts the cracks in the plaster of new buildings, it forgets to cement the tiles, it leaves rags in the new pipes of new office buildings and forgets to put the gas cap back on the tank. So the intellectuals and the technicians hate the bullfight as well. You cannot meet a socialist in Mexico who approves of the running of the bulls. They are trying to turn Mexico into a modern country, and thus the same war goes on there that goes on in three quarters of the world—the battlefront is the new highways to the suburbs, and the corporation's office buildings, the walls of hospital white and the myopic sheets of glass. In Mexico, like everywhere else, it is getting harder and harder to breathe in a mood through the pores of the city because more and more of the city is being covered with corporation architecture, with surgical dressing. To the vampires and banshees and dried blood on the cactus in the desert is added the horror of the new technology in an old murder-ridden land. And four o'clock on Sunday is the beginning of release for some of the horrors of the week. If many come close to feeling the truth only by telling a lie, so Mexicans come close to love by watching the flow of blood on an animal's flanks and the certain death of the bull before the bravery and/or humiliation of the bullfighter.

I could never have understood it if someone tried to explain ahead of time, and in fact, I came to love the bullfight long before I comprehended the first thing about why I did. That was very much to the good. There are not too many experiences a radical American intellectual could encounter in those days (when the youngest generation was called the silent generation) which invaded his sure sense of his own intellectual categories. I did not like the first bullfights I saw, the formality of the ritual bored me, the fights appeared poor (indeed they were) and the human content of the spectacle came out atrocious. Narcissistic matadors, vain when they made a move, pouting like a girl stood up on Saturday night when the crowd turned on them, clumsy at killing, and the crowd, brutal to a man. In the Plaza Mexico, the Indians in the cheap seats buy a paper cup of beer and when they are done drinking, the way to the w.c. is miles away, and besides they are usually feeling sullen, so they urinate in their paper cup and hurl it down in a cascade of harvest gold, Indian piss. If you are an American escorting an American girl who has blonde hair, and you have tickets in *sol*, you buy your girl a cheap sombrero at the gate, for otherwise she will be a prime target of attention. Indeed, you do well not to sit near an American escorting a blonde whose head is uncovered, for the aim of a drunken Indian is no better than you when your aim is drunk. So no surprise if one's early detestation of the bullfight was fortified in kidney brew, Azteca.

Members of a minority group are always ready to take punishment, however, and I was damned if I was going to be excluded from still another cult. So I persisted in going to bullfights, and they were a series of lousy bullfights, and then the third or fourth time I got religion. It was a windy afternoon, with threats of rain, and now and then again ten minutes of rain, poisonous black clouds overhead, the chill gloom of a black sky on Sundays in Mexico, and the particular torero (whose name I could not recall for anything) was a clod. He had a nasty build. Little spindly legs, too big a chest, a butt which was broad and stolid, real peasant ass, and a vulgar worried face with a gold tooth. He was engaged with an ugly bull who kept chopping at the *muleta* with his horns, and occasionally the bull would catch the *muleta* and fling it in the air and trample it and wonder why the object was either dead or not dead, the bull smelling a hint of his own blood (or the blood of some cousin) on the blood of the *muleta,* and the crowd would hoot, and the torero would go over to his sword-handler at the *barrera,* and shake his head and come out with a new *muleta,* and the bull would chop, and the wind would zig the *muleta* out of control, and then the matador would drop it and scamper back to the *barrera,* and the crowd would jeer and the piss would fly in yellow arcs through the rain all the way down from the cheap seats, and the whores would make farting sounds with their spoiled knowledgeable mouths, while the aficionados would roll their eyes, and the sound of Mexican laughter, that operative definition of the echo of total disgust, would shake along like jelly-gasoline through the crowd.

I got a look at the bullfighter who was the center of all this. He was not a man I could feel something for. He had a cheap pimp's face and a dull thoroughgoing vanity. His face, however, was now in despair. There was something going on for him more humiliating than humiliation—as if his life was going to take a turn into something more dreadful than anything it had encountered until now. He was in trouble. The dead dull fight he was giving was going to be death for certain hopes in his psyche. Somehow it was going to be more final than the average dead dull fight to which he was obviously all too accustomed. I was watching the despair of a profoundly mediocre man.

Well, he finally gave up any attempts to pass the bull, and he worked the animal forward with jerks of his *muleta* to left and right, a competent rather than a beautiful technique at best, and even to my untutored eye he was a mechanic at this, and more whistles, and then desperation all over that vain incompetent pimp's face, he profiled with his sword, and got it halfway in, and the animal took a few steps to one side and the other and fell over quickly.

The art of killing is the last skill you learn to judge in bull-fighting, and the kill on this rainy afternoon left me less impressed than the crowd. Their jeers were replaced by applause (later I learned the crowd would always applaud a kill in the lung

—all audiences are Broadway audiences) and the approbation continued sufficiently for the torero to take a tour of the ring. He got no ears, he certainly didn't deserve them, but he had his tour and he was happy, and in his happiness I found there was something likable about him. So this bad bullfight in the rain had given a drop of humanity to a very dry area of my heart, and now I knew a little more and had something to think about which was no longer altogether in category.

We have presented the origin of an addiction. For a drug's first appeal is always existential—our sense of life (once it is made alert by the sensation of its absence) is thereupon so full of need as the desire for a breath of air. The sense of life comes alive in the happy days when the addict first encounters his drug. But all histories of addiction are the same—particularly in the beginning. They fall into the larger category of the history of a passion. So I will spare each and every one of us the titles of the books I read on the running of the bulls, and I will not reminisce about the great bullfighters I saw, of the majesties of Arruza and the *machismo* of Procuna, the liquidities of Silverio and the solemnity of César Girón; no, we will not micturate the last of such memory. The fact is that I do not dwell on Arruza and Procuna and Silverio and Girón, because I did not see them that often and in fact most of them I saw but once. I was always in Mexico in the summer, you see, and the summer is the *temporada de novillos,* which is to say it is the time when the *novilladas* are held, which is to say it is the time of the novices.

Now the fellow who is pushing up this article for you is a great lover of the bullfight—make on it no mistake. For a great bullfight he would give up just about any other athletic or religious spectacle—the World Series in a minute, a pro football championship, a Mass at the Vatican, perhaps even a great heavy-weight championship—which, kids, is really saying it. No love like the love for four in the afternoon at the Plaza Mexico. Yet all the great matadors he saw were seen only at special festivals when they fought very small bulls for charity. The *novil-*

lada is, after all, the time of the *novilleros,* and a *novillero* is a bullfighter approximately equal in rank to a Golden Gloves fighter. A very good *novillero* is like a very good Golden Gloves finalist. The Sugar Ray Robinson and the Rocky Marcianos of the bullfighting world were glimpsed by me only when they came out of retirement long enough to give the equivalent of a snappy two-round exhibition. My love of bullfighting and my experience of it as a spectator was founded then by watching *novilleros* week after week over two separate summers in Mexico City.

After a while I got good at seeing the flaws and virtues in *novilleros,* and in fact I began to see so much of their character in their style, and began to learn so much about style by comprehending their character (for nearly everything good or bad about a novice bullfighter is revealed at a great rate) that I began to take the same furious interest and partisanship in the triumph of one style over another that is usually reserved for literary matters (is Philip Roth better than John Updike?—you know) or that indeed average Americans and some not so average might take over political figures. To watch a bullfighter have an undeserved triumph on Sunday afternoon when you detest his style is not the worst preparation for listening to Everett Dirksen nominate Barry Goldwater or hearing Lyndon Johnson give a lecture on TV about Amurrican commitments to the free universe. Everything bad and god-awful about the style of life got into the style of bullfighters, as well as everything light, delightful, honorable and good.

About the time I knew a lot about bullfighting, or as much as you could know watching nothing but *novilleros* week after week, I fell in love with a bullfighter. I never even met this bullfighter, I rush to tell you. I would not have wanted to meet him. Meeting him could only have spoiled the perfection of my love, so pure was my affection. And his name—not one in a thousand of you out there, dear general readers, can have heard of him—his name was El Loco. El Loco, the Crazy One. It is not a term of endearment in Mexico, where half the populace is crazy. To amplify the power of nomenclature, El Loco came from the provinces, he was God's own hick, and his real name was Amado Ramírez, which is like being a boy from Hicksville, Georgia, with a name like Beloved Remington. Yet there was a time when I thought Beloved Remington, which is to say Amado Ramírez, would become the greatest bullfighter in the whole world, and there were critics in Mexico City hoary with afición who held the same opinion (if not always in print). He came up one summer like a rocket, but a rocket with one tube hot and one tube wet and he spun in circles all over the bullfighting world of Mexico City all through the summer and fall.

But we must tell more of what it is like to watch *novilleros*. You see, novice bullfighters fight bulls who are called *novillos*, and these bulls are a year younger and 200 to 400 pounds lighter than the big fighting bulls up around 1,000 pounds which matadors must face. So they are less dangerous. They can still kill a man, but not often does that happen—they are more likely to pound and stomp and wound and bruise a *novillero* than to catch him and play him in the air and stab him up high on the horns the way a terrible full-grown fighting bull can do. In consequence, the analogy to the Golden Gloves is imperfect, for a talented *novillero* can at his best look as exciting, or more exciting, than a talented matador—the novice's beast is smaller and less dangerous, so his lack of experience is compensated for by his relative comfort—he is in less danger of getting killed. (Indeed, to watch a consummate matador like Carlos Arruza work with a new young bull is like watching Norman Mailer box with his three-year-old son— absolute mastery is in the air.)

Novilleros possess another virtue. Nobody can contest their afición. For every *novillero* who has a manager, and a rich man to house and feed him, and influential critics to bring him along on the sweet of a bribe or two, there are a hundred devoted all but unknown *novilleros* who hitch from *poblado* to *poblado* on back dirt roads for the hint of a chance to fight at some fiesta so small the results are not even phoned to Mexico City. Some of these kids spend years in the provinces living on nothing, half-starved in the desire to spend a life fighting bulls and they will fight anything—bulls who are overweight, calves who are under the legal limit, beasts who have fought before and, so, are sophisticated and dangerous. These provincial *novilleros* get hurt badly by wounds which show no blood, deep bruises in the liver and kidney from the flat of a horn, deep internal bleedings in the gut, something lively taken off the groin. A number of them die years later from malnutrition and chronic malfunctions of some number of those organs; their deaths get into no statistics on the fatalities of the bullfight.

A few of these provincial *novilleros* get enough fights and enough experience and develop enough talent, however, to pick up a reputation of sorts. If they are very lucky and likable, or have connections or hump themselves—as some will—to rich homosexuals in the capital, then they get their shot. Listen to this. At the beginning of the *novillada*, six new bullfighters are brought in every Sunday to fight one bull each in the Plaza Mexico. For six or eight weeks this goes on. Perhaps 50 fighters never seen before in Mexico have their chance. Maybe ten will be seen again. The tension is enormous for each *novillero*. If he fails to have a triumph or attract outstanding attention, then his years in the provinces went for nothing. Back again he will go to the provinces as a punishment for failing to be superb. Perhaps he will never fight again in the Plaza Mexico. His entire life depends on this one fight. And even this fight depends on luck. For any *novillero* can catch a poor bull, a dull mediocre cowardly bull. When the animal does not charge, the bullfighter, unless possessed of genius, cannot look good.

Once a *novillero* came into the Plaza on such an occasion, was hit by the bull while making his first pass, a *verónica*, and the boy and the cape sailed into the air and came down together in such a way that when the boy rolled over, the cape wrapped around him like a *tortilla,* and one wit sitting in *sol,* full of the harsh wine of Mexico's harsh grapes, yelled out, "*Suerte des enchiladas.*" The young bullfighter was named The Pass of the Enchiladas. His career could never be the same. He went on to fight that bull, did a decent honorable job—the crowd never stopped laughing. El Suerte des Enchiladas. He was branded. He walked off in disgrace. The one thing you cannot be in any land where Spanish is spoken is a clown. I laughed with the rest. The bullfight is nine tenths cruelty. The bullfight brews one's cruelty out of one's pores —it makes an elixir of cruelty. But it does something else. It reflects the proportion of life in Latin lands. For in Mexico it does not seem unreasonable that a man spend years learning a dangerous trade, be rapped once by a bull and end up ruined, a Suerte des Enchiladas. It is unfair, but then life is monstrously unfair, one knows that, one of the few gleams in the muck of all this dubious Mexican majesty called existence is that one can on occasion laugh bitterly with the gods. In the Spanish-Indian blood, the substance of one's dignity is found in sharing the cruel vision of the gods. In fact, dignity can be found nowhere else. For courage is seen as the servant of the gods' cruel vision.

On to Beloved Remington. He arrived in Mexico City at the end of the beginning of the *novillada* several years back. He was there, I think, on the next to last of the early Sundays when six bulls were there for six *novilleros*. (In the full season of the *novillada*, when the best new young men have been chosen, there are six bulls for only three toreros—each kid then has two bulls, two chances.) I was not yet in Mexico for Amado Ramírez's first Sunday, but I heard nothing else from my bullfighting friends from the day I got in. He had appeared as the last of six *novilleros*. It had been a terrible day. All of the *novilleros* had been bad. He apparently had been the last and the worst, and had looked so clumsy that the crowd in derision had begun to applaud him. There is no sign of displeasure greater among the Mexican bullfighting public than to turn their ovations upside down. But Ramírez had taken bows. Serious solemn bows. He had bowed so much he hardly fought the bull. The Plaza Mexico rang with merriment. It took him forever to kill the beast—he received a tumultuous ovation. He gave a turn of the ring. A wit shouted

"Olé. El Loco." He was named. When they cheer incompetence, they are ready to set fire to the stadium.

El Loco was the sensation of the week. A clown had fought a bull in the Plaza Mexico and gotten out alive. The promoters put him on the following week as a seventh bullfighter, an extra added attraction. He was not considered worth the dignity of appearing on the regular card. For the first time that season, the Plaza was sold out.

Six young *novilleros* fought six mediocre bulls that day, and gave six mediocre fights. The crowd grew more and more sullen. When there is no good bullfight, there is no catharsis. One's money has been spent, the drinks are wearing down, and there has been no illumination, no moment to burn away all that spiritual sewer gas from the horrors of the week. Dull violence breeds, and with it, contempt for all bullfighters.

Out came the clown, El Loco. The special seventh bullfighter. He was an apparition. He had a skinny body and a funny ugly face with little eyes set close together, a big nose and a little mouth. He had very black Indian hair and a tuft in the rear of his head stood up like the spike of an antenna. He had very skinny legs and they were bent at the knee so that he gave the impression of trudging along with a lunch box in his hand. He had a ludicrous butt. It went straight back like a duck's tail feathers. His suit fit poorly. He was some sort of grafting between Ray Bolger and Charlie Chaplin. And he had the sense of self-importance to come out before the bull, he was indeed given a turn of the ring before he even saw the bull. An honor granted him for his appearance the week before. He was altogether solemn. It did not seem comic to him. He had the kind of somber extravagant ceremoniousness of a village mayor in a mountain town come out to greet the highest officials of the government. His knees stuck out in front and his buttocks in back. The Plaza rocked and rocked. Much applause followed by circulating zephyrs of laughter. And under it all, like a croaking of frogs, the beginnings of the biggest, thickest Bronx raspberry anybody ever heard.

Amado Ramírez went out to receive the bull. His first pass was a yard away from the animal, his second was six feet. He looked like a 55-year-old peon ready to retire. The third pass caught his cape, and as it flew away on the horns, El Loco loped over to the *barrera* with a gait like a kangaroo. A thunderstorm of boos was on its way! He held out his arm horizontally, an injunction to the crowd, fingers spread, palm down, a mild deprecatory pleasant gesture, as if to say, "Wait, you have seen nothing yet." The lip-farters began to smack. Amado went back out. He botched one pass, looked poor on a basic *verónica*. Boos, laughter, even the cops in every aisle were laughing. *Que payaso!*

Then, it happened. His next pass had a name, but few even of the afición knew it, for it was an old-fashioned pass of great intimacy which spoke of the era of Belmonte and El Gallo and Joselito. It was a pass of considerable danger, plus much formal content (for a flash it looked like he was inclining to kiss a lady's hand, his cape draped over his back, while the bull went roaring by his unprotected ass). If I remember, it was called a *Gallecina,* and no one had seen it in five years. It consisted of whirling in a reverse *serpentina* counterclockwise into the bull so that the cape was wrapped around your body just like the Suerte des Enchiladas, except you were vertical, but the timing was such that the bull went by at the moment your back was to him and you could not see his horns. Then the whirling continued, and the cape flared out again. Amado was clumsy in his approach and stepped on his cape when he was done, but there was one moment of lightning in the middle when you saw clear sky after days of fog and smelled the ozone, there was an instant of heaven—finest thing I had yet seen in the bullfight—and in a sob of torture and release, "Olé!" came in a panic of disbelief from one parched Mexican throat near to me. El Loco did the same pass one more time and then again. On the second pass, a thousand cried "Olé." And on the third, the Plaza exploded and 50,000 men and women gave up the word at the same time. Something merry and corny as a gypsy violin flowed out of his cape.

After that, nothing but comedy again. He tried a dozen fancy passes, none worked well. They were all wild, solemn, courtly, and he was there with his peasant bump of an ass and his knobby knees. The crowd laughed with tears in their eyes. With the *muleta* he looked absurd, a man about to miss a train and so running with his suitcase. It took him forever to kill and he stood out like an old lady talking to a barking dog, but he could do no wrong now for this crowd—they laughed, they applauded, they gave him a tour of the ring. For something had happened in those three passes which no one could comprehend. It was as if someone like me had gotten in the ring with Cassius Clay and for 20 seconds had clearly outboxed him. The only explanation was divine intervention. So El Loco was back to fight two bulls next week.

He did little with either bull, and killed the second one just before the third *aviso*. In a good season, his career would have been over. But it was a dreadful season. A couple of weeks of uneventful bullfights and El Loco was invited back. He looked awful in his first fight, green of face, timid, unbelievably awkward with the cape, morose and abominably prudent with the *muleta*. He killed badly. So badly in fact that he was still killing the bull when the third *aviso* sounded. The bull was let out alive. A dull sullen silence riddled with Mexican whistles. The crowd had had a bellyful of laughs with him. They were now getting very bored with the joke.

But the second bull he liked. Those crazy formal courtly passes, the *Gallecinas*, whirled out again, and the horns went by his back six inches away. Olé! He went to put the banderillas in himself and botched the job, had to run very fast on the last pair to escape the bull and looked like a chicken as he ran. The catcalls tuned up again. The crowd was like a bored lion uncertain whether to eat entrails or lick a face. Then he came out with the *muleta* and did a fine series of *derechazos*, the best seen in several weeks, and to everyone's amazement, he killed on the first *estocada*. They gave him an ear. He was the *triunfador* of the day.

This was the afternoon which confirmed the beginning of a

career. After that, most of the fights are mixed in memory because he had so many, and they were never without incident. All through that summer, he fought just about every week, and every week something happened which shattered the comprehension of the most veteran bullfighting critic. They decided after this first triumph that he was a mediocre *novillero* with nothing particular to recommend him except a mysterious flair for the *Gallecina*, and a competence with the *derechazo*. Otherwise, he was uninspired with the cape and weak with the *muleta*. So the following week he gave an exhibition with the *muleta*. He did four *pases de pecho* so close and luminous (a pass is luminous when your body seems to lift with breath as it goes by) that the horns flirted with his heart. He did *derechazos* better than the week before, and finished with *manoletinas*. Again he killed well. They gave him two ears. Then his second bull went out alive. A *fracaso*.

Now the critics said he was promising with the *muleta* but weak with the cape. He could not do a *verónica* of any value. So in one of the following weeks he gave five of the slowest, most luminous, most soaring *verónicas* anyone had ever seen.

Yet, for three weeks in a row, if he had cut ears on one bull, he let the other go out alive. A bullfighter is not supposed to let his animal outlive three *avisos*. Indeed, if the animal is not killed before the first *aviso*, the torero is in disgrace already. Two *avisos* is like the sound of the knell of the bell in the poorhouse, and a bullfighter who hears the third *aviso* and has to let his bull go out alive is properly ready to commit a Mexican variety of hara-kiri. No sight, you see, is worse. It take something like three to five minutes from the first *aviso* to the last, and in that time, the kill becomes a pigsticking. Because the torero has tried two, three, four, five times, even more, to go in over the horns, and he has hit bone, and he has left the sword half in but in some abominable place like the middle of the back or the flank, or he has had a perfect thrust and the bull does not die and minutes go by waiting for it to die and the peons run up with their capes and try to flick the sword out by swirling cloth around the pommel guard and giving a crude Latin yank—nothing is cruder than a peon in a sweat for his boss. Sometimes they kick the bull in the nuts in the hope it will go down, and the crowd hoots. Sometimes the bull sinks to its knees and the *puntillero* comes in to sever its neck with a thrust of his dagger, but the stab is off-center, the spinal cord is not severed. Instead, it is stimulated by the shock, and the dying bull gets up and wanders all over the ring looking for its *querencia* while blood drains and drips from its wounds and the bullfighter, looking ready to cry, trots along like a farmer accompanying his mule down the road. And the next *aviso* blows. Such scenes are a nightmare for the torero. The average torero can afford less than one occasion a year when three *avisos* are heard. El Loco was allowing an average of one bull a week to go out unkilled.

For a period, criticism of El Loco solidified. He had brilliant details, he was able on occasion to kill with inspiration, he had huge talent, but he lacked the indispensable ingredient of the bullfighter, he did not know how to get a good performance out of a bad bull. He lacked tenacity. So Ramírez created the most bizarre *faena* in anyone's memory, a fight which came near to shattering the rules of bullfighting. For on a given Sunday, he fought a very bad bull and worked with him in all the dull, technical, unaesthetic ways a bullfighter has to work with an unpromising beast, and chopped him to left and to right, and kept going into the bull's *querencia* and coaxing him out, and this went on for minutes, while the public demonstrated its displeasure. And El Loco paid no attention and kept working with the bull, and then finally got the bull to charge and he made a few fine passes. But then the first *aviso* sounded and everyone groaned. Because finally the bull was going good, and yet Amado would have to kill him now. But Amado had his bull in shape and he was not going to give him up yet, and so with everyone on the scent of the loss of each second, he made *derechazos* and the pass with the *muleta* which looks like the *gaonera* with the cape, and he did a deliberate *adorno* or two and the second *aviso* sounded and he made an effort to kill and failed, but stayed very cool and built up the crowd again by taking the bull through a series of *naturales,* and with 20 seconds left before the third *aviso* and the Plaza in pandemonium he went in to kill and had a perfect *estocada* and the bull moved around softly and with dignity and died about ten seconds after the third *aviso,* but no one could hear the trumpet for the crowd was in a delirium of thunder, and every white handkerchief in the place was out. And Amado was smiling, which is why you could love him, because his pinched ugly little peasant face was full of a kid's decent happiness when he smiled. And a minute later there was almost a riot against the judges, for they were not going to give him the tail or two ears or even an ear—how could they if the bull had died after the third *aviso?* And yet the tension of fighting the bull on the very edge of his time had given a quality to this fight which had more than a hint of the historic, for new emotions had been felt.

Amado was simply unlike any bullfighter who had ever come along. When he had a great fight, or even a great pass, it was unlike the passes of other fine *novilleros*—the passes of El Loco were better than anything you had ever seen. It was as if you were looking at the sky and suddenly a bird materialized in the air. And a moment later disappeared again. His work was frightening. It was simple, lyrical, light, illumined, but it came from nowhere and then was gone. When El Loco was bad, he was not mediocre or dull, he was simply the worst, most inept and most comical bullfighter anyone had ever seen. He seemed to have no technique to fall back on. He would hold his cape like a shroud, his legs would bend at the knees, his sad ass seemed to have an eye for the exit, his expression was morose as Fernandel and his feet kept tripping. And when he was afraid, he had a nerveless incapacity to kill which was so hopeless that the moment he stepped out to face his animal you knew he could not go near this particular bull. Yet when he was good, the comic body suddenly straightened, the back took on the camber of the best back any Spanish aristocrat ever chose to display, the buttocks retired into themselves like a masterpiece of poise, and the cape and the *muleta* moved slowly as full sails, or whirled like the wing of that mysterious bird. It was as if El Loco came to be every comic Mexican who ever breathed the finest Spanish grace into his pores. For five odd minutes he was as completely transformed as Charlie Chaplin's tramp doing a consummate impersonation of the one and only Valentino, the long-lost Rudolph.

Let me tell then of Amado's best fight. It came past the middle of that fine summer when he had an adventure every week in the Plaza and we had adventures watching him, for he had fights so mysterious that the gods of the bulls and the ghosts of dead matadors must have come with the mothers and the witches of the centuries, homage to Lorca!, to see the miracles he performed. Listen! One day he had a sweet little bull with nice horns, regular, pleasantly curved, and the bull ran with gaiety, even abandon. Now we have to stop off here for an imperative explanation: it is essential to discuss the attitude of afición to the *natural*. To them the *natural* is the equivalent of the full parallel turn in skiing or a scrambling T-formation quarterback or a hook off a jab—it cannot be done well by all athletes, no matter how good they are in other ways, and the *natural* is a dangerous pass, perhaps the most dangerous there is. The cloth of the *muleta* has no sword to extend its width. Now the cloth is held in the left hand, the sword in the right, and so the target of the *muleta* which is presented for the bull's attraction is half as large as it was before and the bullfighter's body is thus so much bigger and so much more worthy of curiosity to the beast—besides the bull is wiser now, he may be ready to suspect it is the man who torments him and not the swirling sinister chaos of the cloth in which he would bury his head. Moreover—and here is the mystique of the *natural* —the bullfighter has a psychic communion with the bull. People who are not psychic do not conceive of fighting bulls. So the torero fights the bull from his psyche first. And with the *muleta* he fights him usually with his right hand from a position of authority. Switching the cloth to the left hand exposes his psyche as well as his body. He feels less authority—in compensation his instinct plays closer to the bull. But he is so vulnerable! So a *natural* inspires a bullfighting public to hold their breath, for danger and beauty come closest to meeting right here.

It was *naturales* Amado chose to perform with this bull. He had not done many this season. The last refuge of his detractors was that he could not do *naturales* well. So here on this day he gave his demonstration. Watch if you can.

He began his *faena* by making no exploratory pass, no *pase de la muerte*, no *derechazos*, he never chopped, no, he went up to this sweet bull and started his *faena* with a series of *naturales*, with a series of five *naturales* which were all linked and all beautiful and had the Plaza in pandemonium because where could he go from there—how does Jack E. Leonard top himself?—and Amado came up sweetly to the bull, and did five more *naturales* as good as the first five, and then did five more without moving from his spot— they were superb—and then furled his *muleta* until it was the size of this page, and he passed the bull five more times in the same way, the horns going around his left wrist. The man and the bull looked in love with each other. And then after these 20 *naturales*, Amado did five more with almost no *muleta* at all, five series of five *naturales* had he performed. It is not much easier than making love 25 times in a row, and then he knelt and kissed the bull on the forehead he was so happy, and got up delicately, and went to the *barrera* for his sword, came back, profiled to get ready for the kill. Everyone was waiting on a fuse. If he managed to kill on the first *estocada* this could well be the best *faena* anyone had ever seen a *novillero* perform, who knew, it was all near to unbelievable, and then just as he profiled, the bull charged prematurely, and Amado, determined to get the kill, did not skip away but held ground, received the charge, stood there with the sword, turned the bull's head with the *muleta*, and the bull impaled himself on the point of the torero's blade which went right into the proper space between the shoulders, and the bull ran right up on it into his death, took several steps to the side, gave a toss of his head at heaven, and fell. Amado had killed *recibiendo*. He had killed standing still, receiving the bull while the bull charged. No one had seen that in years. So they gave him everything that day, ears, tail, *vueltas* without limit—they were ready to give him the bull.

He concluded the summer in a burst of honors. He had great fights. Afterward they gave him a day where he fought six bulls all by himself, and he went on to take his *alternativa* and become a full-fledged matador. But he was a Mexican down to the bones. The honors all turned damp for him. I was not there the day he fought six bulls, I had had to go back to America and never saw him fight again. I heard about him only in letters and in bullfighting newspapers. But the day he took on the six bulls, I was told, he did not have a single good fight, and the day he took his *alternativa* to become a matador, both his bulls went out alive, a disgrace too great even for Amado. He fought a seventh bull. Gypsy magic might save him again. But the bull was big and dull and El Loco had no luck and no magic and just succeeded in killing him in a bad difficult dull fight. It was obvious he was afraid of the big bulls. So he relinquished his *alternativa* and went back to the provinces to try to regain his reputation and his nerve. And no one ever heard much of him again. Or at least I never did, but then I have not been back to Mexico. Now I suspect I'm one of the very few who remember the happiness of seeing him fight. He was so bad when he was bad that he gave the impression you could fight a bull yourself and do no worse. So when he was good, you felt as if you were good, too, and that was something no other torero ever gave me, for when they were good they looked impenetrable, they were like gods, but when Beloved Remington was good, the whole human race was good—he spoke of the great distance a man can go from the worst in himself to the best, and that finally is what the bullfight could be all about, for in dark bloody tropical lands possessed of poverty and desert and swamp, filth and treachery, slovenliness, and the fat lizards of all the worst lust, the excretory lust to shove one's own poison into others, the one thing which can keep the sweet nerve of life alive, is the knowledge that a man cannot be judged by what he is every day, but only in his greatest moment, for that is the moment when he shows what he was intended to be. It is a romantic self-pitying impractical approach to the 20th Century's demand for predictable ethics, high production, dependability of function and categorization of impulse, but it is the Latin approach. Their allegiance is to the genius of the blood. So they judge a man by what he is at his best. By that logic, I will always have love for El Loco because he taught me how to love the bullfight, which is to say he taught me something about the mystery of form. And where is a writer or a lover without a knowledge of what goes on behind that cloth where shapes are born? Olé, Amado!

The Spanish Temper

V. S. Pritchett

V. S. PRITCHETT (*b.* 1900) *as a young man was fortunate enough to be able to travel abroad and settle wherever the fancy took him. In the twenties he discovered Spain and remained there for over two years absorbing the life around him. His recollections from this period form the basis of his book,* The Spanish Temper, *and from it I have taken this superb piece on bullfighting in which he examines the Spanish attitudes toward the ritual, the bulls, the horses, and the men.*

The high moment of Seville is at Easter, when, after a week of the most ornate and pagan processions in Europe, in an atmosphere of theatrical piety and picturesque remorse, the Fair begins and the Andalusian riders in their high hats and leather trouser-facings go by. This is the moment of street parties, pride and ceremony, the supreme moment of display for the women of the city. There is a heavy, torpid beauty. And it is the time of the great bullfights.

Not all the bullrings of Spain are fine. Many of them rise like great red gasworks outside the cities, but the bullring in Seville by the wide slow river is one of the prettiest in Spain. Seville is the city of the bull. The very day when Fernando VII closed the university in Seville, he opened a school for bullfighters there—a characteristic gesture of Spanish reaction. Outside the city are the estates where the fighting bulls are bred. In any Spanish town it is common to see boys playing at bullfighting. One sees them waving their shirts at dogs, pretending they are bulls, and the thing to notice is that they are neither playing nor fighting in any violent sense, but going through the stances, the passes, the exhibitions of the national ritual. Outside Seville it is common, at some noisy fair, for someone to shout out: "The bulls!" and for the boys to race down the hill, clamber over the stone walls, and jump down among the bulls to drive them away or to bait them. There is a respect for the bulls. There is admiration of them, but there is no fear, and indeed, in their herds, the bulls are not dangerous. All the same, the Spaniards never lack the courage to make the heroic gesture. The bull is admired, almost worshipped, as the horse is in Ireland. He is admired because he is great and capable of fury, and the Spaniard requires that furious force against which to display his singularity—the most precious of his possessions—and his courage. Always an extremist, he likes to test his courage and his whole personality to the utmost, and he has so contrived the phases of the bullfight that each one has the crisis of decorative perfection that he loves.

But the horses? This is a question which has been explained and argued many times since Hemingway became the first Anglo-Saxon apologist of the bullfight. To most people who are sensitive to spectacle and are capable of pleasure in strong feeling, the sight of these wretched nags blindfolded and weighed down by absurd cushions is grotesque. Before this protection six thousand horses were killed every year. They creak stiffly in like old people, ghastly in their bandaged eyes, repellent in their suggestion of a public hypocrisy. If the bull is killed in hot blood and at the supreme moment of his raging life, the horse is generally injured, and though he might have gone to the knackers the day before, his last moments are ones of terror. To Hemingway, the horse introduced the grotesque note, the necessary element of parody in the spec-tacle, the counterpoise of low comedy and calamity to the tragic intention of the ritual, for the picador is traditionally an absurd and clumsy fellow, the poor man of the ring. This is an ingenious literary argument; when we consult our reactions at the time we do not find that they confirm Hemingway's definition. Is it really low comedy such as Shakespeare pushed into his tragedies to catch the attention of the low audience? The elegance of the ritual is broken up by these ghastly buffoons, who are lifted up bodily by the enormous shoulders of the charging bull. Even when we are told by sound authorities—and I would refer the reader to John Marks's excellent book *To the Bullfight*—that horses are indispensable, for only a rider has the reach, the strength, and the position for paralysing the formidable neck muscles of the bull, and that, until he does that, the man on foot has no chance of handling the beast—even when we know this, we squirm at the sight of the pitiful and absurd cavalcade, which now looks like the man-horse of the comic circus. And for myself, Hemingway makes the great error of thinking this comic even in the macabre sense. It is merely ghastly, a mess; and now that the horses are cushioned, a cruel and hypocritical mess. Yet Hemingway has this on his side: the Spanish devotees of the bullfight—the aficionados—have never objected to the horses, cushioned or uncushioned: the mass of Spaniards have a rage for tradition; and the bullfighting public is "the people" par excellence. The objections have come from abroad.

There is in Spain a static indifference to animal suffering, or at any rate a passive, unperturbed regard of it which, after the primitive barbarities of the Civil War, cannot be denied. In the days of the *autos de fe*, it was the foreign guests at the court who turned their heads from the terrible ceremony in Valladolid and other cities; the Spaniards, either with passions roused or with their customary emptiness of mind, their capacity to experience with their senses, their limited imagination, looked on. I think we must say that the world has not been wrong about the Spaniards: they are, many of them, cruel or undisturbed by cruelty. Either their cruelty is forced up by passion or it is the kind of wayward, unchecked habit of people who have little curiosity, who have long periods of inertia and formlessness in their lives, who do not care to be made to become anything else. A spiritual indolence dwells inside the hard shell of the stoic.

In saying this, one has to recall the very large number of Spaniards who have no taste for the bullfight.

"I went once. I didn't like it," the shopkeeper says.

"Foreigners keep it alive," says the waiter contemptuously.

"I have never been to one. Complete barbarism," says a famous writer.

"Football is killing it," says a football fan.

"Reactionary," says a politician. "It represents everything we have been fighting for generations."

In the last thirty years a puritan opposition to the bullfight has certainly grown up in Spain. It began with the intellectuals who refused to have anything to do with the fights, and spread especially among the Left-wing groups. The typical Left-wing, anticlerical professor of the Spanish revival in the 1920's and early '30's would say: "The Jesuits told us to go to as many bullfights as we liked, but to avoid the theatre where one picks up dangerous ideas." The liberals and socialists, those engaged in educational, social, and religious reform, thought of the bullfight as the opium of the people.

In the last twenty years very much has been written about the decadence of the art. The public complains that the bulls are smaller and safer, that they are fought too young, before their terrible horns have spread wide. There are too many small fast bulls, not enough ferocious monsters. I have seen many dull and monotonous bullfights. A foreigner who is not a fan cannot judge these public criticisms. He can only record that many people regard this period as a poor one and, like so many enthusiasts, think the great bullfights took place in their youth. The opinion of Belmonte—whose autobiography, written with the aid of a journalist, is an excellent book, and is likely to have a lasting place among the curiosities of Spanish literature—is worth quoting, for Belmonte revolutionized bullfighting.

The fighting bull of today [he says, writing however in 1937] is a product of civilization, a standardized, industrial article like Coty perfume or Ford cars. The bull is manufactured according to popular demand . . . . The bull is just the same fierce and well-armed wild animal that it was before, but its development has been one-sided towards making the fight more pleasing to the eye. It is not true that it has lost courage. The modern bull charges much more often than the old one, although it is true that it does less damage. I doubt whether one of the bulls which were fought years ago could stand the strenuous *faenas* of today. [*Faena* is the general name for the collection of passes with the cape.]

Belmonte goes on to say that the public wants a bull that is easy to play because they want a fight that "is pretty to see and full of accurate and consistent fancy fighting . . . fancy figures and marvellous patterns." He would have liked to go back to the old tricky, savage, unplayable bulls. Yet when he was fighting the "easy" bulls in 1936, Belmonte fought over thirty corridas and was gored fourteen times.

I would not describe Belmonte as a typical matador—if there is such a thing. He was born a slum child in the Triana, the other side of the bridge in Seville, the gipsy quarter, and he picked up his training as an urchin going out into the fields at night and stripping off his shirt to harry the animals in their pasture. It was a form of poaching, and against the law. The urchins often played the bulls naked. Small, stunted by early poverty, often very ill, and without great physical strength, Belmonte developed a terrible, almost suicidal intensity, working so close to the bull that after one corrida he found his dress covered with the hairs of the animal. He became the intellectual artist of the bullring and was known for years as "the earthquake." He was spiritually rather than physically ambitious. His short, slightly stooping figure with the wide shoulders, the pale face with deep sunken eyes, and the powerful jaw, which seems to belong to another man, are familiar in the streets of Seville. He has made a lot of money and, with peasant prudence, has saved it, invested it in bull-breeding. His intellectual temperament attracted writers and artists, and Belmonte's passion for excellence, for seeing a disadvantage and making something of it, turned him to education. He was a distinctive figure in that intellectual movement which arose in Spain

in the generation before the Civil War and which went to pieces
when that war was lost.

The last time I was in Seville I was being pestered by one of
those little street arabs who are longing to earn a penny for clean-
ing your boots, and who, worse still, when you fall for them, begin
hammering a rubber sole on them while you read the paper. The
first thing I knew about it was a nail going into my foot. After
stopping the boy, I asked him his name. He told me and said: "I
am Belmonte's secretary."

I thought this was the usual Andalusian joke, and said: "If you
are his secretary where does he live?" He pointed to the flat I
knew. "And what are your duties?"

"To report first thing in the morning. And to go to school."

"Where is he now?"

"He left his house for his café at eleven. He is going to his farm
this afternoon. He will return at seven."

The boy was not making this up. Belmonte had taken an interest in the boy, given him odd jobs, appointed him "secretary"
—and insisted on his education. The boy was an orphan. Belmonte has the reputation of one who prudently watches his
money—Hemingway has stories of this—and in this shows himself a true, pretty tight-fisted Andalusian; but his admiration for
intelligence and determination, which the boy had, must have
made him think of his own half-starved childhood. Belmonte's
insistence on schooling is typical. When he first went to France,
as an ignorant young man, he did not come back repelled, and
chauvinistic about French civilization as many Spaniards do; on
the contrary, he was quick, like all the best of his generation, to
see the superior ease and refinement of European life.

El Cordobés—and Tremendismo

Kenneth Tynan

KENNETH TYNAN (b. 1927) *is equally fascinated by drama and bullfighting. His early life after studying at Oxford was devoted to the theater, where he acted, directed, and produced. In 1955* Bull Fever *was published. There are probably few other works that examine toreo so objectively and that have done so much to explain to the unconvinced a little of what the aficionado enthuses about. Today Tynan sees grave developments in bullfighting and writes of them here with particular reference to "El Cordobés."*

The bullfight today is not ruled by serious matadors. It is ruled by something the Spanish call *tremendismo* and we would call sensationalism. The matador who extends the red serge to the bull with his left hand, holding the sword right-handed behind his back, and takes the charge slowly around his motionless body in a gentle arc is behaving seriously. The matador who kneels with his back to the bull and lets it charge uncontrolled under his outstretched arm is a *tremendista*. He has courage, but no grace and mastery, which are the prerequisites of the art; he looks permanently unsafe, whereas art always looks secure. The embodiment of *tremendismo*—and arguably the highest-paid individual performer in European history—is a twenty-eight-year-old matador, christened Manuel Benitez but known wherever Spanish is spoken as "El Cordobés"—the Cordoban.

I first saw him in 1961, the season in which he began his subjugation of Spain: a wild, unteachable youth, his body already crisscrossed with horn scars and his hair an unmanageable mop, so much so that he had to brush it out of his eyes after each series of passes. (Spain regarded the gesture as effeminate, and snickered whenever he used it.) Instead of approaching the bull with grave, majestic tread and *muleta* correctly proffered, he shambled toward it with a cheery grin, trailing the *muleta* behind him in the sand. At that time he put in his own banderillas(because of a shoulder injury, he no longer does so); but rather than run at the charging bull in the classic quarter circle, he preferred to break the sticks in half and await the charge on his knees, leaping up at the last moment to jab them in as the animal lumbered past. He killed atrociously, never going in straight and slowly, but veering away from the horns and shoving the sword ignobly into the lung; his eyes would be tightly shut, so that he looked like a blindfold child in the old English game of pinning the tail on a painted donkey. Yet he showed abnormal valour in all the other skills of bullfighting, and it was valour that his publicity stressed. The words of a famous nineteenth-century matador were prominently quoted: "Without valour the art of bullfighting is like the sky without the sun: it is still the sky, but without radiance and beauty. The beginner must demonstrate three things: valour, valour and valour. Art can be learned, but valour is innate, like seductiveness in the eyes of beautiful women." The publicists failed to mention that in killing, the supreme test of valour, El Cordobés was nowhere. But a safe kill in the lung often drops a bull more quickly than a brave one between the shoulder blades; and modern crowds love quick kills.

In 1961 El Cordobés was still a *novillero*; even so, he was earning more than the best of the fully-fledged stars. He was beginning to price his betters out of the ring. It was no accident that Ordónez, who had sworn never to appear with a torero earning more than himself, decided to retire in 1962.

To the Spanish, El Cordobés was a startling novelty; but I recognized him as soon as I saw him. This cool uncaring boy, with his disdain for tradition and dignity and balletic "line," was a Spanish embodiment of something I had already met under several other names. In France, the *blouson noir*; in Britain, the Mod;

and in America, the hipster. Nonchalance, love of danger for kicks, casual contempt for conformity: these were the attributes that made El Cordobés the first hip bullfighter. He would attempt tricks so outlandish and graceless that his fans would laugh even as they applauded; and he would grin back at them, conscious that, although he had injected an element of comedy into an art formerly held to be tragic, they would pay even higher prices to laugh at him tomorrow. He had mastered several clever and seriously employable technical devices; he knew, for example, how to magnetise the bull by focusing the attention of its offside eye on the outstretched tip of the *muleta*, so that when it has passed him he could make it swing and recharge without having to run after it; but there was no artistic emotion in the use to which he put his knowledge. There was simply fun and hazard.

After one of the Cordoban's *faenas*, anyone who attempted a series of pure, commanding, unflamboyant left-handed passes—the keystones of classic bullfighting—would be lucky if he did not bore the crowd to distraction. The Spanish have always revered any performer who possesses the untranslatable quality they call *duende*, which means the power to convey profound emotion without fuss or frills. It is what separates great matadors and flamenco singers from merely good ones. In American terms, Billie Holiday had it, but not Ella Fitzgerald; Ernest Hemingway, but not John O'Hara. El Cordobés ostentatiously lacked it, but went on to prove that, alone among the top matadors of history, he did not need it. It was as if a great musician were to demonstrate that he could get along perfectly well without a sense of pitch.

I saw El Cordobés again in 1962. The bulls he faced were underweight insects, and when he made his début in Malaga, the horned midget that scampered into the ring provoked even that notoriously tolerant audience to cover the sand with a protesting hail of cushions and smashed bottles of beer. He fought it imperviously, earning more than ever. In 1963, when our paths next crossed, he had taken the alternativa and become the idol of Spain, a national treasure whose daily fee had risen to £3,500. In

Pamplona he was cool to the point of inertia, and a jeering mob chased him to his hotel. The two bulls he had fought were cowardly weaklings, lacking the frank, unhesitating charge he needs to bring off his effects; but what nettled the customers was that he had not even tried. Yet I discerned, in the noise of their outrage, something I had never heard in Spain before, something new and alien—a note of a cynical admiration, almost of envy. Even as they booed him, they were envying his ability to get away with such enormities; they could barely resist congratulating him on having pulled off such a tremendous confidence trick.

After all, had not Juan Belmonte said that the best bullfighter was the one they paid the most? Nineteen sixty-three was the year when every novice grew his hair, went down on his knees and tried to look swingingly indifferent, like the Cordoban. It was also the year in which I realised that the era of Dominguín and Ordónez had been a golden age. Any gutsy beginner could ape El Cordobés; but nobody could look like Ordónez.

In the winter of 1963–64 the Cordoban rode in triumph across Mexico, fighting almost every day and picking up $25,000 per corrida. Like the Spanish, the Mexicans were mesmerized into tearing up the rules of bullfighting: tow-haired tremendismo ousted classical standards. I returned to Spain in 1964 hoping that the vogue would have evaporated: but no. El Cordobés was now pocketing a million pesetas every time he appeared, and he appeared five or six afternoons a week. Before going to see him, I consulted Orson Welles, one of the few Anglo-Saxon aficionados whose opinions the Spanish take seriously. He filled in a little historical background.

"When Louis XIV's grandson became king of Spain, Louis said that the Pyrenees had ceased to exist. He was wrong." (Thus Orson, genially booming.) "It was El Cordobés who abolished the Pyrenees. Europe used to end at the French border; now it covers Spain. He's a symbol of the way the whole peninsula has been Europeanized. The tourists adore him. He's a beatnik from anywhere; he's taken the Spanishness out of bullfighting and made it a by-product of the beat revolution. And he's the first great figure in bullfighting who could have succeeded in other performing arts—singing, for instance, or acting. He's already made two movies, and he plays himself in both of them. The first was called *Learning to Die*, although some people say they ought to call it *Learning to Die Rich*. He never forgets the future, and he cares about self-improvement. He has a cultural instructor who travels around with him and tells him about Spanish history—who the *reyes catolicos* were, and so on. If you measure his income against the time he takes to earn it—say forty minutes a day—I'd say he was the highest paid performer of all time, with the possible exception of Elizabeth Taylor. As a bullfighter, he's a comedian. But make no mistake about it: he's a star. He's the greatest tremendista since Manolete. He can't walk like a matador, because he has flat feet—I know because I have them, too. But he's a genuine star." I asked Orson if he had ever met El Cordobés. "Sure, and he told me he had no aficion. He said he disliked the bulls and was only interested in success." I thought of Sid Caesar's dying matador bit in one of his early TV shows: "I do not hate the bulls, and the bulls do not hate me. They're just making a living like anybody else."

In May 1964, Orson took Ordónez and his wife to see the Cordoban's début in Madrid. The day was wet and windy, but the demand for tickets was such that one American tourist traded a station wagon for two seats in the third row. Orson challenged his guests to bet on the afternoon's awards. Ordónez said the Cordoban would cut three ears; his wife voted for two. Orson plumped for a horn wound. Before that audience, he felt, in an atmosphere of such expectation, El Cordobés had no alternative but to be gored.

He won the bet. After caping his first bull and kissing it three times on the flank—a repulsive piece of showmanship—El Cordobés mistimed a pass and took six inches of horn in his left thigh, together with a nasty jab in the scrotum. He was whisked off to the bullring infirmary, leaving the animal to be killed by one of his colleagues. In clear defiance of the taurine regulations —which insist that trophies must be awarded only to those who

have actually killed their bulls—the president granted him an
ear. It was duly delivered to his hospital bed. "All over Spain,"
said Orson, summing up, "you can buy little printed cards to
give to your friends. You hand them to your host when you go
out to dinner. They bear a simple message—'Kindly Do Not
Talk About El Cordobés.' "

From Madrid I flew to Valencia, where the idol was due to
appear in the July feria. There I talked to his manager, a tall,
attractive, long-faced man in his thirties named Chopera, who
owns—with his father—some 20 important bullrings in Spain,
10 in South America, several in Mexico, and a select stable of
Spanish matadors, of whom El Cordobés is king. With Chopera's
help I pieced together the facts of the Cordoban's life.

He was born in Palma del Rio, a village 30-odd miles from
Cordoba, on 4 May 1936. His father was a waiter in a local bar,
and the household was desperately poor: "I've stolen more
chickens than a gypsy," he nowadays recalls. That summer the
Spanish Civil War broke out, and hardship increased for the
Benitez children—three girls and two boys, of whom Manuel
was the youngest. When the war ended three years later, the
family could not feed him, and he was sent to an orphanage. In
1941 real orphanhood befell him: his parents died within a few
months of each other, and his eldest sister took over his up-
bringing. (Like many bullfighters, he grew up in a suffocatingly
feminine *ambiente*.) Necessity and opportunity drew him toward
the bulls. Southern Spain breeds the best bulls and the most
poverty: then, as now, the quickest way to conquer the latter is
to fight the former. So Manuel stole by night into the pastures
of neighbouring bull ranches and caped the moonlit animals. At
any rate, that is the official story, and it may very well be true—
although the same legend has been told of almost every top
matador since Juan Belmonte, who actually did indulge in such
nocturnal rehearsals.

In his teens Manuel took part in small-town bullfights, amateur scrambles held in village squares between improvised barri-
cades. In both Madrid and Barcelona (how he got there, God

knows) he was an *espontaneo,* which means a young fanatic who leaps into the ring from a cheap seat with a smuggled *muleta* and gets in as many passes as he can before being gored or dragged off to jail. Between exploits like this he worked on a building site in Madrid and taught himself to read. In a recent interview he said: "I'm not afraid of the bulls. Of *life,* yes . . . ." Given his background, the statement rings true.

In August 1959, with scant success, he made his first appearance in the suit of lights. A month later he and Manuel Gomez, a fellow novillero, faced seven-year-old bulls in a village called Loeches. Both were wounded and sent to hospital in Madrid, where they occupied adjoining beds. During the night Gomez died. It was not until the next season that the new star began to rise; he met, and acquired as manager, a paunchy publicist named El Pipo, who persuaded him to call himself "El Cordobés" and fixed a fight for him in Cordoba. The local critics adored his crazy, carefree valour, and by the end of the year he had killed 72 bulls, cutting 90 ears, 31 tails and 13 hoofs. In 1961 he began to conquer the big ferias; Valencia, where he was twice badly gored, especially warmed to him; and his tally for the summer was 67 *novilladas,* from which—tackling the usual quota of two bulls per engagement—he garnered 111 ears, 27 tails and 13 hoofs. (To average more than one ear per fight is a feat that only the best achieve.) The unique, unprecedented year was 1962, in which the Cordoban broke all records by fighting 111 times— more than anyone else had ever fought in a single season—and bagging a total of 167 ears and 28 tails. (It was also the year in which the cutting of hoofs was officially prohibited.) In May 1963, to hysterical acclamation, he took his alternativa in Cordoba, and that winter he paid his first visit to Mexico, where the big money is. He swept it into his souvenir collection, along with 60 ears and 7 tails. It was hereabouts that he changed managers, switching from El Pipo, who owned only bullfighters, to Chopera, who owned bullrings as well.

He had still not appeared in Madrid, where a single disaster can tarnish a hundred golden afternoons elsewhere. He took the crucial plunge on 20 May 1964, getting himself gored (as Welles pre-dicted) and cutting an undeserved ear. But he returned to face the Madrid public a month later at an annual charity fight that is always attended by Franco (who hates the bulls) and the serious aficionados. The day before the event he was interviewed by a bullfight weekly. The reporter spoke with awe of his almond-coloured eyes, his schoolboy laugh, his armies of friends and the single red rose that is delivered to his apartment every day by an unknown admirer. How did he feel when facing the bulls? "For me," the Cordoban said, "the bull is pure joy, like a wine that fills my heart and makes me drunk. You don't know what it's like to have a triumph in the bullring. It is delirium. You can't learn bullfighting. When you are before the bull, it's as if already in another world someone had taught you to fight it." Next day he drove to the big ring; the handkerchiefs waved like a snow-storm and won him two ears. As always, he stood with his feet together and wound the bull's charge around his body like a tourniquet; these circular passes look highly impressive until you study them and realise that as soon as the horns have passed the thighs the danger ceases. "His *muleta* was like a magnet!" exulted the mayor of his home town, who had come to Madrid for the occasion. Antonio Diaz Canabate, the leading bullfight critic, was less enthusiastic: "With the feet together, you cannot fight bulls, you can merely simulate passes. Only the body as a whole, not the wrist alone, can control a bull. And without con-trol there cannot be a good pass." He added that the applause for the Cordoban "verged on the supernatural—something never before seen or heard."

That was a month before Valencia. Since Madrid (Chopera told me) El Cordobés had flown to Mexico, where a special summer season of corridas had been staged for his benefit. I asked Chopera whether the Cordoban phenomenon could be com-pared in any way with the Beatles. "I suppose there's a connec-nection," he said. "Manolo's hair is long and he causes sensations wherever he goes. And I expect he's heard their records, although he's never seen them in person. But there's one big difference.

When Manolo performs, there's always the possibility of death."

I went upstairs to meet the maestro. It was ninety minutes before he was due to walk into the Valencian ring. The hotel lobby was jammed and the street outside impassable. *"Madre de Dios!"* said the elevator man. "The end of the world will be like this." Chopera showed me into a still-darkened bedroom: El Cordobés had fought in France the day before, and it had taken a plane trip and an overnight journey by car to get him to Valencia that morning. He sat grinning on the unmade bed, naked except for a jockstrap and a gold medallion around his neck. I learned afterwards that it was reversible, with a Spanish Virgin on one side and a Mexican Virgin on the other, thus usefully combining supernatural propitiation with good Hispano-American relations. He was chattering noisily to two other journalists, and laughing a lot —a derisive urchin's laugh, full of mischief and complicity. In the background his dresser was laying out his costume.

There was talk about habits and hobbies. He said he drank wine with meals, smoked a little, sang a lot at his guitar, and went shooting when he wanted to be alone. He owned two Mercedes, a private plane, an estate near Cordoba, apartments in Madrid and Jaen, and he was about to buy a bull ranch. (Already Chopera hand-picks the bulls he fights, owns many of the plazas in which he fights them, and virtually dictates terms to the matadors who fight with him: when El Cordobés starts fighting his own bulls, the circle will be complete. M.C.A., I reflected, never had it so good.) Somebody asked whether he planned to marry. A wide smile and a vigorous headshake. "But you're pestered by thousands of girls," said one of the journalists. "Haven't you a favourite?" "Yes," said El Cordobés, winking, "the bull." Then who was his favourite movie actor? *"El Cordobés!"* shouted El Cordobés, laughing like a monkey.

I now came nervously weaving in with sombre traditional questions about the bulls. What matadors had influenced him? *"Pues"*—a huge shrug—"Manolete." (Ask a traditional question and you get a traditional answer.) Had he ever seen Manolete fight? "No." Then how . . . ? "He saw movies," said Chopera quickly. What were his best and worst days in the ring? "The best was my alternativa in Cordoba. The worst—that's still to come." I asked him what books he read, a question to which most matadors have two set answers: either "Comics and thrillers" or "The great works of Spanish literature and philosophy." El Cordobés came up with a third: "Nothing."

It was almost time for him to dress. He was still attentive, but infectiously restless, like a jazz drummer late for a set. Before leaving I put a final question, embarrassing myself by its portentousness. "Outside the bullring," I said, "are you afraid of death?" He looked bewildered for a moment. "I never think of it," he said. Then, in a sudden outburst of glee: "I shall live forever!"

That afternoon—Friday, 24 July 1964—six bulls from the ranch of Samuel Flores were killed in the Valencian ring. The corrida was televised throughout Spain, and thousands of people started work at five in the morning in order to be free to switch on their sets at 6:30 P.M. They got their labour's worth. With the sixth bull—having failed with the third—El Cordobés had the greatest triumph not only of his life, but conceivably (I am choosing my words with care) of bullfight history. I speak in terms of audience reaction, not of art. "Collective madness," said one critic next day; another wrote that under the Cordoban spell, "eccentric unorthodoxy was miraculously converted into a fundamental source of artistic creation." A typical review summed up the occasion:

"During his *faena* with the last bull of Don Samuel Flores, the general paroxysm exceeded all limits. Cushions by the hundred, articles of clothing, and screams mingled with rapturous ovations filled the ring and the air. Circular passes, with effortless flexure of arms and legs; long, rhythmical *naturales*—all of these he performed in his own casual manner, the new orthodoxy from Cordoba. And if he lacks great artistic grace, he has the inexplicable gift of authority over the masses—the gift called empathy. When he killed with a single stroke, closing his eyes to administer it, hundreds of spectators poured into the ring to carry him shoulder-high. They flung themselves upon him, so that a squad of policemen had to be summoned to protect him from the explosion of enthusiasm. Only with their aid was he able to receive the ears and tail of his dead enemy, to make a triumphal circuit of the ring, and get back to his hotel, which he quitted an hour later to fight next day on the other side of the country he had conquered . . . ."

And what was the fight really like? Intensely exciting, but totally unmoving; plenty of risk, but little artistry; an apotheosis of the comic bullfights you can see at night in provincial plazas, with clown matadors dressed like Chaplin's tramp. It was no more, in essence, than a superlative circus turn. But it marked a revolution, even a *coup d'état*. After Valencia, it was clear beyond denying that the art of bullfighting had surrendered to the cult of personality, and that El Cordobés was its absolute emperor. The revolution also extended to audience behaviour. Before Valencia, spectators threw cushions only to indicate disgust, and police protection was reserved for matadors in serious danger of being lynched. El Cordobés changed all that in a single afternoon.

When at last he escaped to the Hotel Astoria, thousands of fans gathered in the square outside, many of them chanting his name. Eventually he appeared on a balcony, beaming beneath a vast sombrero, and flung into the crowd handful after handful of big, coarse 1,000-peseta bank notes, each of them worth about £6. It was a stupefying sight: the monarch of commercial bullfighting repaying his investors.

The following day, those who attended the bullfights in Valencia were handed a printed slip as they entered the plaza. It bore an admonition in several languages. The English version read: "To throw the seat cushions into the bull ring is not correck. Please to abandon oneself in the seat." The authorities need not have worried. Not a cushion was flung, and no one abandoned himself. The Cordoban was fighting three hundred miles away.

But do not despair. Help came in the late spring of 1965; to be precise, on 30 May, when Ordónez reappeared in Madrid in the sixteenth and last fight of the feria of San Isidro. The Cordoban had fought three times in the same fair, steering his usual erratic course from cheers to boos and back again. By confining himself to a single corrida, Ordónez took an enormous risk; he had only two chances to prove himself, against the Cordoban's six. If he failed, if the bulls proved unworkable, his reputation would lie in ruins; for the Spanish have no patience with gamblers who bet high and lose.

The bulls were his favourite Pablo Romeros. He dispatched the first well but without distinction; after taking six replendent *verónicas*, it ran out of breath and stumbled throughout the *faena*. With his second bull (551 kilos), in a high wind, he cut two ears, put the Cordoban to shame, and restored to bullfighting the honour and prestige of which fashion had threatened to rob it. He played the Pablo Romero like a Stradivarius, said a leading bullfight weekly, adding that his skill should be preserved as a national monument: "*Ave Maria Purisima!*" By unanimous vote, the taurine critics elected Ordónez the *triunfador* of the feria. "You won't see anything much better than that," said Orson Welles as we left the ring. I agreed that it would do to be going on with.

The Greatest Bullfight Ever

Barnaby Conrad

BARNABY CONRAD (b. 1922) studied in Mexico and subsequently served as an American vice-consul in Málaga, Seville, and Barcelona. Leaving the diplomatic service, he took up the study of bullfighting with Juan Belmonte and even fought for a period himself. Among his books on toreo are Matador, The Death of Manolete, La Fiesta Brava, Gates of Fear, and the exhaustive Encyclopedia of Bullfighting. In this article he describes the immortal corrida at Málaga in 1945 when Carlos Arruza was awarded—for the first time in bullfighting history—two ears, the tail, and two hoofs.

I had a pretty nice big house in Malaga and I was a friend of Carlos Arruza, the matador, so that's why the Town Council came to me. *"Mire, Señor Vice Consul,"* they said. "We are going to present a gorgeous diamond medal to the torero who gives the best performance at the bullfights during our annual fair. It is an exquisite thing, made especially in Madrid at a cost of 5,000 pesetas, and we should enjoy the honor of presenting it to your friend Arruza in your house."

"The honor will be mine," I said. "And I shall plan a party for that date. But how can you be sure Arruza will give the best show?"

"He cannot fail," they said. "First he is fighting both Friday and Sunday; if he is out of form or the bulls are bad on Friday, he will have another chance on Sunday. And secondly, Manolete, Arruza's only real competition, has been wounded and will not be able to fight."

"And thirdly," spoke up a member of the Council uneasily,

"he *has* to be the best for we already have his name engraved on the medal."

On Friday Carlos arrived for the first fight and Malaga was agog, for he had become the most sensational thing in bullfighting. Most people defended the classic purity of Manolete's style but for sheer brute courage, this young Mexican was unchallenged.

Then too, the señors and señoritas weren't oblivious to that beautiful physique, and the unruly brown hair that topped his shy handsome face. Arruza had donated the entire proceeds of his first fight of the season, $7,000, to the mother of a bullfighter killed in the ring. After that he was the most popular matador in Spain.

This season Arruza was contracted for the staggering number of 140 fights in 180 days! This meant fighting in Madrid one day, Barcelona the next, going to Lisbon, Bilbao, Mallorca, in planes, cars, trains, snatching a meal and a bit of sleep when he could, and every day leaving thousands of people thrilled by his skill and courage.

When I went to see him this afternoon before the fight his face was pale and drawn and I could see that the ninety fights he had already fought under this regime had aged him.

"*Chiquillo*," he said after we'd talked awhile and as he wiggled into the gold brocaded pants, "what's this about a medal?"

I explained.

"*Caracoles!*" exclaimed Carlos. "They have put my name on it already! But anything can happen in a bullfight! How can they know if I feel like fighting? Or what about the wind? Or what about the bulls, eh? That slight detail must be considered—the bulls."

At four o'clock they paraded into the brilliant sun and the band blared forth with the *paso doble, Carlos Arruza*. Carlos grinned nervously and threw his dress cape up to me.

His first bull was a bad one, but he did pretty well, and the *presidente* let him take a lap around the ring to receive the crowd's applause. The second bull was Estudiante's and he did a very good job, being conceded two ears from the dead animal as an evaluation of his bravery and skill. Morenito de Talavera felt the pressure of the two good fights that had gone before him, and surpassed by far his natural ability, cutting one ear and taking a lap around the ring.

Arruza, seemingly unconcerned by this competition as he waited for his second bull to come out, looked around, hugging his big red and yellow cape to him and smiling his little-boy smile at friends.

His bull skidded out of the *toril* and brought boos from the crowd because it was so small. But the boos switched to "Olés!" when Arruza passed the bull closely three times, the lethal horns inches away from his knees. Few people objected when, after he had placed three beautifully executed banderillas and one sword thrust, the *presidente* granted him both ears and the tail for his brilliant fight. Women threw down roses to him and men threw cigars, hats, even overcoats. A few people booed, though, saying he didn't deserve the tail since the bull was so small.

However, the medal seemed cinched, especially after Estudiante and Morenito de Talavera were bad on the last two bulls, and I left the plaza jubilantly. The next day the program was Estudiante and Morenito again plus a little Mexican Indian named Cañitas. Nothing to fear, we thought, for the bulls were giants; we had seen what Estudiante and Morenito had to offer and who ever heard of Cañitas?

None of the three fighters was anything but discreet on his first bull. But then—the trumpet sounded for Cañitas' second, and out it came—a black and white Villamarta weighing 750 kilos!

Cañitas went pale when he saw the creature rip part of the wooden barrier apart, but he set his Indian jaw and you could see him telling himself, "If I'm going to die I'll die in a blaze of glory." The bull ran around the empty ring twice looking for something to kill, and then Cañitas stepped out and dropped to his knees, letting it go by with a *whoosh*, as the great horns passed his head. A gasp of surprise went up from the crowd who had expected him to play the bull as safely as possible. Then when he passed the bull even closer, they set up a continuous roar. After

numerous fancy passes with the cape, he placed three sets of banderillas with the arrogance of a gipsy, with the *muleta* he accom-
plished a *faena* that bullfighters dream about, then drew back
and dropped the bull with a sword thrust almost to the hilt. The
crowd went wild and insisted upon his getting both ears, tail and
a hoof, the most you can get. I left the plaza for the day, feeling
a little sick.

The next day was Sunday, and the Town Council came to see
me with long faces. "Now what do we do?" they asked reproachfully, as though it were my fault. "Order another medal," was all
I could suggest.

Arruza arrived at six in the morning after having fought in
Cadiz the afternoon before and driving all night to Malaga. I
went to the hotel to wake him at three, and the Idol of Spain was
a mess; he looked green and staggered as he got up to go to bathe.

"I'm exhausted." The words tumbled out. "I've got a fever of
102, I can't go on like this every day. I never want to fight again.
I'm going to go to bed for ten years when the season is over. How
was the fight yesterday?" he continued wearily while putting on
his frilled shirt. "I haven't seen the papers as yet."

"Cañitas turned in the best fight of the season," I said.

Carlos stopped tying his tie. "Are you joking?"

He and Cañitas had always hated each other.

"No," I said. "He got inspired—fought as he's never fought
before—cut ears, tail and a hoof." I cleared my throat. "But—uh
—you'll come up to the house for the ceremony anyway, won't
you?"

Arruza regarded me quietly and said: "I'll be there, *chiquillo*."

I made the error of taking two women to the last fight. Carlos
was first on the program, and when he got to his knees and let the
bull pass by him four times so close that it removed part of his
embroidered jacket, the girl on my right passed out; the other
girl was just about to faint too, but she was too busy reviving her
friend. Carlos did every pass in the book plus two of his own invention, and the girls couldn't stand any more; they left just
about the time he dropped the bull with one thrust. The crowd

went wild, and the *presidente* signalled with his handkerchief for the banderillero to cut one ear, two ears, two ears and tail, two ears, tail and a hoof, and Arruza circled the ring, triumphantly holding his prizes aloft.

It was a wonderful fight, but we all knew Cañitas had been just a bit more graceful, more daring, more suicidal, the day before.

After Arruza came Parrita and Andaluz, both good bull-fighters, but people were still limp from the first fight and didn't pay much attention to them. When Arruza came out and stood waiting for his second bull people applauded wildly, but we really didn't expect him to do anything more; it's rare when a bull-fighter puts up a good performance on both bulls.

The bull was a monstrous creature, and Arruza studied it from behind the fence for a few moments. Then he stepped out shakily into the ring and stood there swaying and putting his hand up to his feverish head and pressing his hot temples with his fingers, but as the bull drew near he collected himself, let the cape unfurl in front of the animal's nose and passed it by in a series of classic *verónicas* that drew great "Olés!" from the crowd. Then in a few moments they were yelling "No! No!" as he passed the bull in the graceful butterfly pass, letting it come so close each time it seemed he would be caught and spitted on one of the huge needlelike horns.

Time for the banderillas. One of history's great *banderilleros*, he placed three pairs of sticks superbly, running at an angle at the bull as it charged, and sticking them in the withers with his arms high and finally spinning to one side to let the bull hurtle by. Then he begged permission from the *presidente* to risk his life in still another pair. It was granted and Carlos picked an impossible way to place them: with his back against the fence, he incited the bull, "Uh-huh Toro! Uh-huh-huh!" and stood there calmly watching it bear down on him. When the enraged animal was two feet away, Carlos raised his arms, dropped the banderillas in place ducked to the side, the left horn grazing his chest as the bull crashed into the fence.

The trumpet blew for the death; with the scarlet rag and the curved sword in his hand, Carlos dedicated the bull, facing the crowd with exhausted, unseeing eyes. Then he went out for the last round.

His first pass with the *muleta* was the classic "Pass of Death," so called because so many bullfighters have been killed doing it. Carlos called the bull from twenty feet away, and as it *whooshed* by he remained absolutely motionless and straight, letting the bull choose whether he was going to crash into the cloth or into his legs. Still motionless, he let the bull wheel and charge three times. Then Arruza decided to try a pass of his invention—the *arrucina*. The *muleta* is held behind the back so that only a tiny portion of the deceptive cloth shows, leaving the entire body open as a target for the bull.

When he put the *muleta* in back and people realized what he was going to do they screamed "No! No!" again, but the bull had already charged and somehow the horns missed Carlos by centimeters. But when he tried it again from the other side, the right horn went around Arruza's leg and the bull hurled him high into the air. He somehow spun around on the horn so that when his body slapped the ground he was stretched out under the bull, the length of his body between the animal's front legs, and his head between the wicked horns. People hid their eyes, yet before the needle points could find the inert form, Carlos had reached up and locked his arms around the bull's neck in an iron grip. The bewildered bull spun around and around. Finally he gave his neck a mighty snap, flung the man from him like a rag doll to the ground ten feet away, but before he could charge, Arruza's men were between them and had attracted the bull's attention. Arruza lurched drunkenly to his feet and stood there swaying, bruised and dazed, his uniform in ribbons, but miraculously not wounded. He picked up his sword and the rag.

"*Fuera!*" he yelled at his banderilleros. "Get out of the ring."

The amazed men retreated several feet behind him.

Arruza whirled on them and snarled: "*Fuera*, I said! Leave me alone with him!"

When they had all left the ring, the matador calmly turned to the bull, who was pawing the ground and studying him ten feet away, got to his knees and inched forward toward the animal. The bull shifted his feet and the crowd gasped, sure that he would charge. But he didn't; it was as though he were hypnotized and cowed by the enormous brute courage of this man-thing on its knees and Arruza kept coming, staring fixedly at the bull until he arrived in its very face.

Then, with the muzzle of the bull almost touching him, he leaned forward and rested his elbow on the bull's forehead!

He turned around and stared up at the crowd with the bull's nose against his back. We were afraid to scream for fear the noise would make the bull charge, but when he faced the bull again and, still on his knees, made it pass by four times, spinning it against the shoulder each time, a great roar burst from our throats. And then suddenly Carlos rose to his feet, and hurling himself on top of the horns, he sank the sword in between the shoulders to the hilt, the bull reeling and its hulk crashing over backwards to the sand.

Delirium took over the plaza, and the *presidente* waved his handkerchief for one ear, again for two ears, again for the tail, again for a hoof—*and still again for another hoof, for the first time in bullfighting's long history!*

Still the crowd chanted "more, more, more!" And the *presidente* shrugged as though to say: hell, take the whole, then.

So Arruza got the medal and we had the party, but our honored guest left early. He had to hurry to Valencia for a fight the following day.

The Aficionados

James A. Michener

JAMES A. MICHENER (b. 1907), best-selling author of numerous books, such as Hawaii, The Source, and Iberia, first visited Spain as a cabin boy in 1932—and by his own admission has returned as often as possible ever since. He has written extensively on many aspects of the country and this includes bullfighting. He is particularly interested in the breeding of the fighting bulls and in those people—like himself—who are irresistibly drawn to the plaza de toros each year.

One of the side attractions of bullfighting is the bizarre gang of fans addicted to the art. Everyone who has followed the bulls has known the epicene who drives his Hispano-Suiza back and forth across Spain, enamored of some young man whom he attends slavishly and without regard to the pathetic figure he is cutting before his friends. He doesn't care. He has bull fever interlaced with sex, and few diseases are more virulent.

One also gets to know the American widow of forty-six whose husband left her several hundred thousand dollars and a passport, and with these she travels from feria to feria, passionately in love with some matador who has not yet spoken to her, for he does not know that she exists. If I were to describe faithfully even one of these women, and I have known several dozen, American readers would be incensed and would claim that I was burlesquing the species. "Such women couldn't exist!" my friends have protested on the few occasions when I have tried to describe them orally, but they do exist and some of them are dear friends whom I regard with affection. They happen to be nutty about bullfighting, and some of my other good friends are nutty about other things.

One hears much of integrity these days, and I have indicated that I prefer El Viti among the current crop of matadors because of his integrity. Once when the crowd had petitioned for, and the judge had awarded, an ear, El Viti turned it back, saying, "Today I did not deserve an ear." But no one connected with the art ever exhibited such integrity as an American woman I know who pined for one of the leading matadors. She followed him about Spain as if she were a puppy and he a wise old bulldog. At the arena she showered him with roses; at his hotel she would stand for hours waiting for him to make an appearance; she suffered humiliations by the score; and then one day when she had already paid for a ticket to a good fight in Madrid she heard belatedly that her idol was to fight that afternoon in Aranjuez, some thirty miles to the south.

She thereupon gave away her ticket to the fight in Madrid, paid a scalper's price for a ticket to the new fight, bought an armful of roses for her matador and hired a taxicab to take her to Aranjuez, where she found as she was about to enter the plaza that her beloved, to whom she had so far not spoken a word, had been injured the day before in another town and would not fight this day. His place was being taken by a matador of higher category, so that the fight was probably going to be better than the one scheduled, but to her this was inconsequential; if the object of her passion was not going to perform, the fight was not worth her attendance. She handed her ticket to a young man hanging about the entrance in hopes of just such a miracle, gave her roses to an old woman selling flowers and climbed into her taxi, announcing with a certain grandeur, "Take me back to Madrid."

The aficionado from whom I have learned most is Angus Macnab, who has been described as "the Scotsman's Scotsman." To hear him explain, in Scottish accents, the merits of a particular fight is to enjoy language and emotions at its best: "Mind you, I'm not one to question the judgment of Ernest Hemingway, nor of matador John Fulton, but when I hear people assure me that in the great hand-to-hand at the Málaga feria in 1959 Antonio Ordóñez and Dominguín presented between them the fight of the century . . . some even claim the fight of the ages with six bulls killed by six single sword strokes, etcetera. Well, when sensible men tell me this with their smiles on straight and I'm expected to believe them, I keep my mouth shut and ask myself one question. 'Has no one bothered to read what Alberto Vera, who wrote under the name of "Areva," said about this so-called magisterial fight?' Have you bothered to read it, Michener? No? Then I'll quote: 'This afternoon we saw two famous matadors fight six bulls, and each animal had two distinctions. It was barely three years old and was therefore more truly a calf. And what horns it did have were mercilessly shaved.' Michener, if you want to select one afternoon as an example of what bullfighting can be, at least choose one in which bulls were fought and not calves with their horns removed." Even the most trivial of Macnab's opinions on matadors and bulls are expressed with similar force. "Biggest bull I ever saw was at Pamplona one year. A Miura of nearly fifteen hundred pounds. Can you imagine how big that was? Killed two horses just by running into them. But the best man-and-bull-together I've ever seen was Domingo Ortega and a runty animal of admirable courage to whom he had given a great fight. At the end he dropped on his knees before the fine animal, then turned his back to the horns and remained so with the bull's right horn in the middle of his spine. Still on his knees he crawled away to pick up a hat that an admirer had thrown in the ring and this he placed on the bull's shoulder. Then, standing back, he sighted with his sword, moved forward and pushed the sword right through the hat and into the proper spot. The bull took one step and dropped dead."

The addict with whom it is most fun to attend a fight is Kenneth Vanderford, who has a sardonic wit and a dry skepticism concerning everything. At his apartment in Madrid, where all writers interested in the fiesta brava sooner or later converge to check facts, he has a modest library of taurine material, including complete files of most of the bullfight journals for the past eight years. Apart from the nonsense of looking like Hemingway, from which he derives much amusement, Vanderford is unusually erudite, with a Ph.D. in Spanish from the University of Chicago. When I last saw him he was engaged in a newspaper duel with a learned Spaniard who had written an essay lamenting the fact that the Spanish language does not permit words to begin with the letter *s* followed by a consonant, so that English words like scarp, spume and stupid became in Spanish *escarpa, espuma* and *estupido*. This meant, the essayist had pointed out, that the two radically different English words, eschatology, which means the philosophical analysis of ultimate goals, especially those religious, and scatology, which means preoccupation with or study of excrement, had each to be translated by the Spanish *escatalogía*. Vanderford, a remarkably irreligious man (he calls himself a humanist), humorously proposed that since no intelligent man really believed in the future life any more and since there was not much to be gained by continuing to talk about it, maybe it would be better to drop the first meaning and cling to the second, which is concerned with an inescapable fact of life that is always with us. He continued with the suggestion that on second thought neither meaning need be dropped, since further study of the conflict had revealed an intimate relationship between the two meanings of the word, psychologically if not etymologically. He pointed out that the famous ascetics of history, who have always been interested in eschatology, have also notoriously been interested in scatology, since the French Catholic writer Vicomte Maxime de Montmorand, in his *Psychologie des Mystiques Catholiques Orthodoxes*, hold that nearly all Christian ascetics have been scatophagous. Vanderford holds equally recondite and stubborn views on bullfight matters.

"You say it. Hemingway says it. Tynan says it and Macnab says it, so I suppose I can't fight you all. But to say that at the kill a matador 'goes over the horn' is pure nonsense. Let him go in that way and he'll get a horn in the gut every time. What he does is to trick the bull into charging one way while he slides in on a curving trajectory the other way, thus avoiding the horn. Over the horn? Never."

It is Vanderford's opinion that "the best-informed and most dedicated foreign bullfight expert of either sex is Alice Hall." This tall, slim gray-haired spinster was, until her recent retirement, a teacher of Spanish in a fancy private school in Atlanta, Georgia. She came originally to Spain for the laudable purpose of improving her pronunciation, little aware of what was in store. Like any dutiful tourist she went routinely to a bullfight, had the good fortune of seeing César Girón on one of his great days, and promptly surrendered. Year after year she returned during her vacations and applied to bullfighting the tenacious scholarship which had made her a fine teacher. A friend says, "Alice feels intuitively what the bull and the man are going to do next . . . what they must do . . . and she is in the ring with them when they do it." "Each autumn when I go back to Atlanta and face my first class of girls," she says quietly, "I feel as if I have been sentenced to exile, that I am in a strange land surrounded by strangers. My heart was left behind in Andalucia."

My favorite aficionado was a Frenchman. On the afternoon of the first fight at Pamplona, which is quite near to France and therefore attracts many Frenchmen, this doughty little bourgeois, with mustache, close-buttoned black suit and lunch in a briefcase, became so enraptured with the performance of Paco Camino that as the matador took a turn of the plaza he threw his *bota* of wine into the ring, and Camino drank from it. The crowd applauded. Later my Frenchman did the same for Diego Puerta, and again the crowd cheered.

It was not until the fourth day that I was close enough to see why the crowd kept cheering this modest Frenchman, but on this day, when he tossed his *bota* at the feet of Miguelín, his section of the plaza rose *en masse* and accorded him a round of applause usually reserved for generals or generalísimos. Why? Because when this prudent fellow tossed his *bota* into the ring he kept it attached to a long length of French fishing cord, so that when the matador finished taking his drink, the valuable leather bottle, worth about forty cents, could be reeled back to its owner.

The aficionado who best exemplifies the emotional hold that bullfighting can exert is a man I have not met. George Smith, a retired high school Spanish teacher from Los Angeles, saw his first fight in Mexico and subsequently came to Spain on vacation, developing an intense interest in the bulls. He began to acquire a bullfight library, and with the help of a former matador who in retirement became an expert on old books, has built up what many call the finest library of its kind in the United States. He intends leaving it to the Los Angeles public library. Sudden and protracted illness has prevented him from returning to Spain but he is so infatuated with the ambiente that each spring, during San Isidro, he sends his matador-bibliophile a substantial check in order to assemble in Salvador's taurine restaurant a group of aficionados to partake of the feast that he would like to give in person. In 1967 Nicanor Villalta, one of the finest and bravest of the old-time matadors, attended. Also present was the critic who wears the gold watch that once belonged to Manolete: "The mother of Manolete to Antonio Bellón, loyal and unselfish friend of her son." Vanderford was there and several others who appreciate the bulls, and as the meal drew to an end, Vicente Molina, the book dealer, proposed the toast, "To a man who truly loves our crazy world."

Some travelers in Spain, seeing the crowds of such tourists at bullfights, conclude that it is only the thrill-seeking foreigner who keeps the art alive, and it is true that along the Mediterranean coast the rings are populated mainly by travelers from northern countries who understand little of what they are seeing. I remember the last fight of the season in Barcelona, when more than two-thirds of the meager audience consisted of white-hatted sailors from the visiting American fleet. In Mallorca foreigners constitute a majority of the audience, and standards have degenerated so badly that a local impresario has rigged up his private plaza and keeps a tame bull therein for tourists to "fight" at five dollars a throw. For two dollars they rent gaudy matador suits, and for an additional two dollars they can have their photographs taken facing the bull. When they get back into street clothes for another dollar they can purchase from the Plaza Mallorca a colorful poster showing their name printed between that of Manolete and El Cordobés.

"We call that animal El Toro de Oro, the Golden Bull," Bartolomé Bestard, honorary American consul in Mallorca, told me. "He's so smart that when he sees a camera he shows the one-day matadors where to stand. But don't laugh! That bull personally has paid for those three apartment houses over there. A fabulous animal."

The Decline of Bullfighting

Robert Graves

ROBERT GRAVES (*b.* 1895) *is one of the great men of English letters whose associations with Spain are long and devoted. Author of some of the most distinguished historical novels of this century—including the prize-winning* I, Claudius—*Graves has in recent years turned toward social commentary and here writes of his own disappointments in the art of bullfighting.*

The years between the outbreak of World War I and that of the Spanish Civil War in 1936 will go down in history as the Golden Age of Bullfighting. Matadors were courageous, audiences responsive, bulls heavy and fierce. Besides Belmonte and Joselito, we had the temperamental El Gallo, the classically elegant Bienvenida brothers, the resourceful Barrera, the daredevil Mexicans Carnicerito and El Soldado. Also Marcial Lalanda, who perfected the mariposa, an attractive feat of running backwards and moving the cape behind his body from side to side so that the bull constantly changes direction. And the greatest of them all: Dominga Ortega, once an illiterate young valienta, of Borax, near Toledo. He would dominate his bulls by talking to them as he fought, telling them what he expected of them, until the moment came for ritual sacrifice. So far from being the slender, handsome type of matador, Ortega was ungainly, chubby-faced, round-shouldered, and walked with a slouch. Yet he persuaded difficult and evil-hearted bulls to play around him like poodles. Though his jealous rivals said, "What luck he has in drawing easy bulls!" it happened too often for coincidence. A foreign aficionado once shouted, just as Ortega was about to kill: "Stop, fool! You can sell that beast for a million pesetas as a performing animal!"

By the time that World War II ended, the Silver Age had begun. Its leading figure, Manolete, performed exquisitely with cape and *muleta* until gored to death at Linares in 1947. Under his rule, graceful passes, rather than the business of preparing a bull for slaughter and then dispatching him cleanly, became the matador's main preoccupation. Manolete was, to be frank, a bad matador, in the sense that he seldom killed at the first attempt. A popular refrain accused him of not being able to kill a bathroom cockroach. A more serious criticism was that he worked his bulls so close as to give them no room for manoeuvre, thus gaining safety by a pretence of recklessness.

Manolete performed coldly and unsmilingly, as a famous surgeon might show hospital internes the right way to remove an appendix, and semed to despise his audience. This broke a Golden Age tradition of warm friendship between the matador and his aficionados, who suffered and rejoiced with him, following the niceties of play as if in the ring themselves. Those Golden Age bulls were fighters, and though the required weight of a single beast was fixed fairly low, the average weight of an afternoon's six had always been far higher. During the early thirties I saw bulls scaling five hundred pounds above the legal minimum, and tall enough to look over a six-foot *barrera*. Hardy beasts, too, bred for courage and speed, with huge horns. By the late forties they were being bred as near the minimum as possible, and often confined to paddocks where they took insufficient exercise—so that their weight consisted of fat rather than muscle. When such bulls rush out of the toril, they appear formidable enough; but their legs and lungs are weak, and they come up for no more punishment once the banderillas have been well placed. Only a few good herds remain, to be used at special corridas.

Some years ago, Antonio Bienvenida publicly exposed the Silver Age trick of cutting four or five inches off a bull's horns and shaving the butt to a point again. This was done half an hour before the corrida began and, the horn tips being then at an unfamiliar angle to the bull's eye, he misjudged distances, much to the matador's benefit. Manolete had all his bulls doctored in this way, though the public never knew it. Among other unethical tricks were using false scales; giving a bull constipating fodder or tranquillizers; and allowing the picadors to cripple him with an illegally long lance-blade. When most of these abuses were officially banned, casualties rose and some matadors quit. But at Madrid, Seville and Barcelona alone can one still hope to see an honest fight.

A prominent matador clears six thousand dollars a performance, after paying his own squadron of picadors, banderilleros, capemen and the rest. He seldom contracts for fewer than eighty corridas a season, and may also undertake a winter programme in Mexico and South America. This means big money. And bullfighting is the one sure ladder from the gipsy camp or hovel to the ranks of Spanish society. Yet no more arduous profession exists, and by the time a *novillero* has been safely enrolled in the guild, he too often rests on his laurels and does as little as possible to earn his fees. He will have taken several bad gorings already, so why court danger? And why waste one's talents to amuse ignorant tourists?

This is the real trouble! The decline of bullfighting may be confidently ascribed to the immense tourist influx. Most of the annual millions would think ill of themselves if they omitted a corrida from their visit. They do not come to see sport; they cannot appreciate the art; they want to witness the spectacle. And, as a spectacle, a corrida remains superb: the well-mounted old alguazils wearing sixteenth century costume, the slender matadors in expensively braided jackets and tights, the burly picadors with their long boots and wide-brimmed hats, the coloured silk capes, the trumpets, the band playing *paso dobles*, and the black bull suddenly charging out across the sand . . . . Tourists have cash to spend, and it would be foolish to deny them this romantic vision of antique Spain.

The Spanish Government has helped the bullrings by banning

much of the barbarity which once attended corridas. First, the mastiffs were dropped; they had been trained to attack the bull's muzzle and genitals. Next, the gaunt, highly expendable hacks ridden by picadors were provided with thick quilted coats reaching to their knees. A disembowelled horse is a shocking sight, and three or four horses might be massacred by a single bull. But tourists never consider that the internal injuries suffered when a strong bull evades the lance, charges a quilted horse square, and then returns to the charge, may be crueller than a mortal horning. Nor are they encouraged to disbelieve in the protection afforded by the quilt; because if it were not for tourists, the rings would stay almost empty. Even at Seville, the home of bullfighting, not enough seats are sold after the Spring Fair had ended to attract expensive matadors.

Spaniards no longer wholeheartedly support the National Fiesta. From habit they attend certain corridas of prestige, where the bulls are the best obtainable, and the matadors on their mettle. Otherwise, they watch football matches and see keener sport for less money. The most depressing entertainment in the world is a bad bullfight. Thus, nine times out of ten, the small group of aficionados who react immediately to every turn of play with either acclamation or scorn, gets smothered by the vast, excited, but puzzled mass. Not that the aficionados are always reliable judges. Ortega has said sourly: "Many aficionados, but no experts! When I am in the ring, only two of us know what is happening: the bull and myself."

I saw Dominguin deal with two bad bulls at Palma de Mallorca, before twenty thousand English, French, German, Dutch, Swiss and Scandinavian tourists, reinforced by a detachment from the American Sixth Fleet. He good-humouredly squeezed the last ounce of fight out of these animals. Furthermore, he consented to amuse the visitors with perilous circus tricks: sitting on the lower ledge of the *barrera*, from where he waved the bull past him, and afterwards *telefoneando*, which means negligently leaning an elbow on the beaten bull's forehead, as if phoning an acquaintance.

Yet this is the same man who, in the ring with brave bulls and a warm, appreciative audience, fights as nobly and unostentatiously as Belmonte and Ortega ever did. Too many matadors are in the game merely to enrich themselves, and there are no *novilleros* of outstanding promise on the way. But miracles may still happen.

I Even Saw Manolete...

John Steinbeck

JOHN STEINBECK (1902–1969) *always wrote out of personal knowledge and involvement, evident in this article, written in the year before his death. Here he makes clear where he stands on the subject of bullfighting. He won a Pulitzer Prize in 1940 and the Nobel Prize for literature in 1962.*

I have always been interested in sports, but more as an observer than as a participant. It seems to me that any sport is a kind of practice, perhaps unconscious, for the life-and-death struggle for survival. Our team sports simulate war, with its strategy, tactics, logistics, heroism and/or cowardice. Individual competition of all kinds has surely ingredients of single combat, which was for millions of years the means of going on living.

The Greeks, who invented realism and pretty much cornered the market, began the training of a soldier by teaching him dancing. The rhythm, precision and co-ordination of the dance made the hoplite one hell of a lot better trooper.

The very word "sport" is interesting. It is a shortening of "disport" (OED: "disportare, to carry away, hence to amuse or to entertain"). From earliest times people played lightly at the deadly and serious things so that they could stand them at all— all, that is, except the Greeks, who in their competitions were offering the gift of their endurance, their strength and their spirits to the gods. Perhaps our values and our gods have changed.

My own participation in sports has been completely undistinguished. I once threw the javelin rather promisingly until my arm glassed up. Once I was fairly good at boxing, mainly because I hated it and wanted to get it over with and to get out. This is not boxing but fighting.

My feeling about hunting has made me pretty unpopular. I have nothing against the killing of animals if there is any need. I did, can and always will kill anything I need or want to eat, including relatives. But the killing of large animals just to prove we can does not indicate to me that we are superior to animals but arouses a kind of deep-down feeling that we are not. A room full of stuffed and glass-eyed heads always gives me a feeling of sadness for the man so unsure of himself that he has constantly to prove himself and to keep the evidence for others to see.

What I do admire and respect is our memory of a time when hunting was a large part of our economy. We preserve this memory intact even though we now have a larger mortality in hunters than in game.

I find the so-called blood sports like fox hunting charming and sometimes ravishingly beautiful. Besides, fox hunting serves the useful purpose of preventing population explosion in the gentry and increasing the number of fine horses. This fox population doesn't seem affected one way or another.

But there is one activity which only the Anglo-Saxons consider a sport and hate and attend in droves. That is bullfighting.

In this I have gone full course, read, studied, and watched and shared. From the first horror I went to the mortal beauty, the form and exquisiteness from *verónica* to *faena*.

I have seen a great many bullfights (its is only called a fight in English). I even saw Manolete fight a number of times, which is more than Ernest Hemingway did. And I have seen a few great and beautiful things in the bullring. There are only a few, and you must see very many fights to see the great one.

But I suppose there are very few great anythings in the world. How many great sonnets are there? How many great plays? For that matter, how many great vines?

I think I have been through most of the possible feelings about tauromachy, rising eventually to the sublime conception that the incomparable bravery of the matador somehow doled out courage to the audience.

Oh! this was not blind and ignorant celebration. I hung around the rings. I knew about the underweight bulls, the sand-bags on the kidneys, the shaved horns and sometimes the needle of baritu-rate in the shoulder as the gate swung open. But there was also that moment of what they call truth, a sublimity, a halo of the invincible human spirit and unspeakable, beautiful courage.

And then doubt began to creep in. The matadors I knew had souls of Toledo steel for the bull, but they were terrified of their impresarios, pulp in the hands of their critics and avaricious be-yond belief. Pehaps they gave the audience a little courage of a certain kind, but not the kind the audience and the world needed and needs. I have yet to hear of a bullfighter who has taken a dangerous political stand, who has fought a moral battle unless its horns were shaved.

It began to seem to me that his superb courage could be put to better uses than the ritual slaughter of bulls in the afternoon. One Ed Murrow standing up to take the charge of an enraged Mc-Carthy, one little chicken-necked Negro going into a voting booth in Alabama, one Dag Hammarskjold flying to his death and know-ing it—this is the kind of courage we need because in the end it is not the bulls that will defeat us, I am afraid, but our own miserable, craven and covetous selves.

II

Fiction

The Bullfight

Leigh Hunt

LEIGH HUNT (1784–1859), *a poet and essayist, was a champion of liberalism and from 1808 edited* The Examiner, *which attracted contributions from many now-famous literary figures, including Shelley, Lamb, Keats, and Byron. Imprisoned in 1813 for a libel on the Prince Regent, he later accepted an invitation from Shelley to Italy and there began the bulk of his writing. He returned to England in 1825 and his home in Hampstead became a center for contemporary men of letters. In prefacing the delightful tale that follows, which is taken from his* Treasure House of Tales, *Hunt expounds his views on "these detestable bullfights."*

Everybody has heard of the bullfights in Spain. The noble animal is brought into an arena to make sport, as Samson was among the Philistines. And truly he presents himself to one's imagination as a creature equally superior with Samson to his tormentors; for the sport which he is brought in to furnish is that of being murdered. The poor beast is actuated by a perverse will, and by a brutality which is deliberate. He does but obey to the last just feelings of his nature. He would not be forced to revenge himself if he could help it. He would fain return to the sweet meadow and the fresh air, but his tyrants will not let him. He is stung with arrows, goaded and pierced with javelins, hewn at with swords, beset with all the devilries of horror and astonishment that can exasperate him into madness; and the tormentors themselves feel he is in the right, if he can but give bloody deaths to his bloody assassins. The worst of it is, that some of these assassins, who are carried away by custom, are persons who are otherwise among the best in the kingdom. They err from that very love of sympathy, and of the admiration of their fellows, which should have been employed to teach them better.

The excuse for this diabolical pastime is, that it keeps up old Spanish qualities to their height, and prevents the nation from becoming effeminate. To what purpose? And in how many instances? Are not the Spanish nobility the most degenerate in Europe? Has not its court, for three generations, been a scandal and a burlesque? And would any other nation in Christendom consent to be made the puppets of such superiors? What could Spain have done against France without England? What have all its bullfights, and all its other barbarities, done for it, to save it from the shame of being the feeblest and most superstitious of European communities, and having no voice in the affairs of the world?

Poor foolish Matadore! Poor idle, illiterate, unreflecting *caballero!*—that is to say, "horseman!" which, by the noble power or privilege of riding a horse (a thing that any groom can do in any decent country), came to mean "gentleman," as distinguished from that of "centaur," can you risk your life for nothing better than this? Must you stake wife, children, mistress, father, and mother, friends, fortune, love, and all which all of them may bring you, at no higher price than the power of having it said you are a better man than the butcher? Is there no sacred cause of country to fight for? No tyrants to oppose? No doctrine worth martyrdom? —that you must needs, at the hazard of death and agony, set the only wits or the best qualities you possess on outdoing the greatest fools and ruffians in your city? And can you wonder that your country has no cause which it can stand to without help or to any purpose? That your tyrants are cruel and laugh at you? And that your very wives and mistresses (for the most part) think there is nothing better in the world than a flaring show and a brutal sensation?

Bullfights are going on now, and bullfights were going on in the wretched time of King Charles the Second, of the House of Austria, whose very aspect seemed ominous of the disasters about to befall his country; for his face was very long, his lip very thick, his mouth very wide, his nose very hooked, and he had no calves to his legs, and no brains in his skull. His clemency consisted in letting assassins go, because passion was uncontrollable; and his wit in sending old lords to stand in the rain, because they intimated that it would be their death. However, he was a good-natured man, as times went, especially for a king of Spain; and it is not of public disasters that we are to speak, but of the misery that befell two lovers in his day, in consequence of these detestable bullfights.

Don Alphonso de Melos, a young gentleman of some five-and-twenty years of age, was the son of one of those Titulados of Castile, more proud than rich, of whom it was maliciously said, that "before they were made lords, they didn't dine; and after they were made lords, they didn't sup." He was, however, a very good sort of man, not too poor to give his sons good educations; and of his second son, Alphonso, the richest grandee might have been proud; for a better or pleasanter youth, or one of greater good sense, conventionalisms apart, had never ventured his life in a bull-fight, which he had done half a dozen times. He was, more-over, a very pretty singer; and it was even said, that he not only composed the music for his serenades, but that he wrote verses for them equal to those of Garcilaso. So, at least, thought the young lady to whom they were sent, and who used to devour them with her eyes, till her very breath failed her, and she could not speak for delight.

Poor, loving Lucinda! We call her poor, though she was at that minute one of the richest as well as happiest maidens in Madrid; and we speak of her as a young lady, for such she was in breeding and manners, and as such the very grandees treated her, as far as they could, though she was only the daughter of a famous jeweller, who had supplied half the great people with carkanets and rings. Her father was dead; her mother too; she was under the care of guardians; but Alphonso de Melos had loved her more than a year; had loved her with a real love, even though he wanted her money; would, in fact, have thrown her money to the dogs, rather

than have ceased to love her; such a treasure he had found in the
very fact of his passion. Their marriage was to take place within
the month; and, as the lady was so rich, and the lover, however
noble otherwise, was only of the lowest or least privileged order
of nobility (a class who had the misfortune of not being able to
wear their hats in the king's presence, unless his majesty expressly
desired it), the loftiest grandees, who would have been too happy
to marry the lovely heiress, had her father been anything but a
merchant, thought that the match was not only pardonable in the
young gentleman, but in a sort of way noticeable, and even in
some measure to be smilingly winked at and encouraged; nay,
perhaps, envied; especially as the future husband was generous,
and had a turn for making presents, and for sitting at the head of
a festive table. Suddenly, therefore, appeared some of the finest
emeralds and sapphires in the world upon the fingers of counts
and marquises, whose jewels had hitherto been of doubtful
value; and no little sensation was made on the gravest and most
dignified of the old nobility, by a certain grandee, remarkable for
his sense of the proprieties, who had discovered "serious reasons
for thinking" that the supposed jeweller's offspring was a natural
daughter of a late prince of the blood.

Be this as it may, Don Alphonso presented himself one morning as usual before his mistress, and after an interchange of trans-
ports, such as may be imagined between two such lovers, about
to be joined for ever, informed her that only one thing more was
now remaining to be done, and then—in the course of three
mornings—they would be living in the same house.

"And what is that?" said Lucinda, the tears rushing into her
eyes for excess of adoring happiness.

"Only the bullfight," said the lover, affecting as much indifference as he could affect in anything when speaking with his eyes
on hers. But he could not speak it in quite the tone he wished.

"The bullfight!" scarcely ejaculated his mistress, turning pale.
"Oh, Alphonso! you have fought and conquered in a dozen; and
you will not quit me, now that we can be so often together? Besides"—And here her breath began already to fail her.

But Alphonso showed her, or tried to show her, how he must inevitably attend the bullfight. "Honour demanded it; custom; everything that was expected of him"; his mistress herself, who would "otherwise despise him."

His mistress fainted away. She fell, a death-like burden, into his arms.

When she came to herself, she wept, entreated, implored, tried even with pathetic gaiety to rally and be pleasant; then again wept; then argued, and for the first time in her life was a logician, pressing his hand, and saying with a sudden force of conviction, "But hear me;" then begged again; then kissed him like a bride; reposed on him like a wife; did everything that was becoming and beautiful, and said everything but an angry word; nay, would have dared perhaps to say even that, had she thought of it; but she was not of an angry kind, or of any kind but the loving, and how was the thought to enter her head? Entire love is a worship, and cannot be angry.

The heart of the lover openly and fondly sympathized with that of his poor mistress; and, secretly, it felt more even than it showed. Not that Don Alphonso feared for consequences, though he had not been without pangs and thoughts of possibilities, even in regard to those; for, to say nothing of the danger of the sport in ordinary, the chief reason of his being unpersuadable in the present instance was a report that the animals to be encountered were of more than ordinary ferocity; so that the caballeros who were expected to be foremost in the lists in general now felt themselves to be particularly called on to make their appearance, at the hazard of an alternative too dreadful for the greatest valour to risk.

The final argument which he used with his mistress was the very excess of that love, and the very position in which it stood at that bridal moment, to which he in vain appealed. He showed how it had ever and irremediably been the custom to estimate the fighter's love by the measure of his courage; the more "apparent" the risk (for he pretended to laugh at any real danger), the greater the evidence of passion and the honour done to the

lady; and so, after many more words and tears, the honour was
to be done accordingly, grievously against her will, and custom
triumphed. Custom! That "little thing," as the people called it
to the philosopher. "That great and terrible thing," as the philosopher justly thought it. To show how secure he was, and how
secure still it would render him, he made her promise to be there;
and she required little asking; for a thought came into her head,
which made her pray with secret and sudden earnestness to the
Virgin; and the same thought enabled her to give him final looks,
not only of resigned lovingness, but of a sort of cheered composure; for, now that she saw there was no remedy, she would not
make the worst of his resolve, and so they parted. How differently
from when they met! and how dreadfully to be again brought
together!

The day has arrived; the great square has been duly set out; the
sand, to receive the blood, is spread over it; the barricados and
balconies (the boxes) are all right; the king and his nobles are
there; Don Alphonso and his Lucinda are there also; he in his
place in the square, on horseback, with his attendants behind him,
and the door out of which the bull is to come in front; she where
he will behold her before long, though not in the box to which he
has been raising his eyes. All the gentlemen who are to fight the
bulls, each in his turn, and who, like Alphonso, are dressed in
black, with plumes of white feathers on their heads, and scarfs of
different colours round the body, have ridden round the lists a
quarter of an hour ago; they salute the ladies of their acquaintance; and all is still and waiting. The whole scene is gorgeous with
tapestries and gold and jewels. It is a theatre in which pomp and
pleasure are sitting in a thousand human shapes to behold a cruel
spectacle.
    The trumpets sound; crashes of other music succeed; the door
of the stable opens, and the noble creature, the bull, makes his
appearance, standing still a while, and looking as it were with a
confused composure before him. Sometimes when the animal first
comes forth, it rushes after the horseman who has opened the

door, and who has rushed away from the mood in which it has shown itself. But the bull on this occasion was one that, from the very perfection of his strength, awaited provoking. He soon has it. Light, agile footmen, who are there on purpose, vex him with darts and arrows, garnished with paper set on fire. He begins by pursuing them hither and thither, they escaping by all the arts of cloaks and hats thrown on the ground, and deceiving figures of pasteboard. Soon he is irritated extremely; he stoops his sullen head to toss; he raises it, with his eyes on fire, to kick and trample; he bellows; he rages; he grows mad. His breath gathers like a thick mist about his head. He gallops, amidst cries of men and women, frantically around the square, like a racer, following and followed by his tormentors; he tears the horses with his horns; he disembowels them; he tosses the howling dogs that are let loose on him; he leaps and shivers in the air like a very stag or goat. His huge body is nothing to him in the rage and might of his agony.

For Alphonso, who had purposely got in his way to shorten his Lucinda's misery (knowing her surely to be there, though he has never seen her), has gashed the bull across the eyes with his sword, and pierced him twice with the javelins furnished him by his attendants. Half blinded with the blood, and yet rushing at him, it should seem, with sure and final aim of his dreadful head, the creature is just upon him, when a blow from a negro who is helping one of the pages, turns him distractedly in that new direction, and he strikes down, not the negro, but the youthful, and, in truth, wholly frightened and helpless page. The page in falling loses his cap, from which there flows a profusion of woman's hair, and Alphonso knows it in the instant. He leaps off his horse, and would have shrieked with horror; but for something which seemed to wrench and twist round his very being, and in a sort of stifled and almost meek voice, he could only sobbingly articulate the word, "Lucinda!" But in an instant he rose out of that self pity into frenzy; he hacked wildly at the bull, which was now spurning as wildly round; and though the assembly rose, crying out, and the king bade the brute be despatched, which was done by a thrust in the spine by those who knew the trick (ah, why did they not do it before?), the poor youth had fallen, not far from his Lucinda, gored alike with herself to death.

As recovery was pronounced hopeless, and the deaths of the lovers close at hand, they were both carried into the nearest house, and laid, as the nature of the place required, on the same bed. And, indeed, as it turned out, nothing could be more fitting. Great and sorrowful was the throng in the room; some of the greatest nobles were there, and a sorrowing message was brought from the king. Had the lovers been princes, their poor insensible faces could not have been watched with greater pity and respect.

At length they opened their eyes, one after the other, to wonder —to suffer—to discover each other where they lay—and to weep from abundance of wretchedness, and from the difficulty of speaking. They attempted to make a movement towards each other, but could not even raise an arm. Lucinda tried to speak, but could only sigh and attempt to smile. Don Alphonso said at last, half sobbing, looking with his languid eyes on her kind and patient face—"She does not reproach me, even now."

They both wept afresh at this, but his mistress looked at him with such unutterable love and fondess, making, at the same time, some little ineffectual movement of her hand, that the good old Duke de Linares said, "She wishes to put her arm over him; and he too—see—his arm over her." Tenderly, and with the softest caution, were their arms put accordingly; and then, in spite of their anguish, the good Duke said, "Marry them yet"; and the priest opened his book, and well as he could speak for sympathy, or they seem to answer to his words, he married them; and thus —in a few moments, from excess of mingled agony and joy, with their arms on one another, and smiling as they shut their eyes— their spirits passed away from them, and they died.

A Motor in the Bullring

R. B. Townshend

R. B. TOWNSHEND (1831–1906) *was one of the many well-known and prolific Victorian writers who so enraptured readers of the* Strand Magazine, Blackwood's, *and similar periodicals. In his story, "A Motor in the Bullring," great care is taken so that "no gentle reader may be offended," and while death and injury do occur we are spared any gory details. Note, too, that even our foolhardy hero is not English but a "mad Americano!"*

"Ah, you do not like the sight?" said the marquesa, with a flash of her dark eyes. "You have no taste for our toreros."

There was a touch of supercilious coldness in her tone that stung the American. "It is the horses, marquesa," he said, briefly. "I can't stand that."

He was sitting in the marquesa's box in the bullring, envied of most men, for the marquesa was as difficult as she was beautiful, and her victims were more in number than those of the most celebrated torero. Perhaps it was a sort of fellow-feeling that made the beautiful woman so fond of her national sport. Perfect skill and perfect courage might win anything in the ring, and only such qualities could find favour in her eyes—and both in the bullring and in the marquesa's drawing-room it was *vae victis!*

The visitor turned to face her with his back to the plaza. Out there in the sunshine one of Spain's most distinguished *espadas*, with the red cloak in one hand and his long, straight sword in the other, was coolly luring a sullen bull to his death.

The marquesa put up her fan as if to shut off a view of a part of the bullring where three horses were lying.

"Oh," she answered indolently, "life is not long enough to let one dwell on the disagreeables. If you look for them," she shut her fan with a click, "you can find them in the house as well as out there—but why look for them?"

It was rumoured that the lady had learned philosophy during the life of the late lamented marquis, who had not been a model husband.

"But, my friend," she continued, "the skill and the courage of the man, can you not even admire them?"

"Oh, the men, of course," returned the American. "I'm not saying anything against them. They're all right. Besides, it's their trade, anyway; and I will say they're real smart—quick as cats, and their nerve just splendid."

"Well," she took him up quickly, "what more would you have? What is there more admirable than address and courage? And where can we see it as in the bull-fight?"

A thrill passed through him at the proud challenge in her eyes.

"What would I have?" he answered, quickly. "I'd have them show their courage by something better than forcing blindfolded plugs only fit for the knacker on to a bull's horns. I'd have them come in on fancy cow-ponies and beat the bull at his own game of twisting and turning. That's worth doing, and I guess our Texas cowboys could do it, too."

"Ah, I knew you were right at heart," she smiled, with a look that for the first time seemed to admit him to the secret intimacy of her soul. "You should have been here when our King was crowned. Then the proudest nobles in Spain themselves rode their best steeds into the ring and met the bull with the lance in full career. Ah! that was a truly splendid sight!"

"Did they, by gum?" said the Transatlantic millionaire. "Wal, I'd have given a thousand dollars to see that. Wish I'd been here. Why, if I'd only known it was on I'd have hired Colonel Cody's best vaqueros to enter for the show and keep our end up."

"You would not then have ridden in the ring yourself?" she

said, with a drop of her eyelids. "Before the King no one was allowed to ride but the nobility—no vaqueros could have entered. I suppose you great millionaires are the nobles of America?" she added, with a tinge of malice.

He flushed darkly. "No," he answered, "I'm no nobleman; we don't keep a nobility in my country. And I don't brag that I'd have ridden in the ring myself. I was raised in New York and didn't get much of a chance to ride when I was young. If I'd been raised a cowboy out in Texas, it would have been different with me. You see, I wasn't born rich, and I didn't inherit any millions. I had to rustle around and make them for myself, every solitary cent."

"It appears, then," she insinuated, "that in America the men who make the millions are too busy to be heroes, and so it is your cowboys who have the horsemanship and the—how do you call it?—nerve?"

"I guess in America a man without nerve don't gather many millions," he retorted. "And if our city folks don't ride much they kin drive. It takes some nerve to drive a two-twenty trotter, and heaps more to drive a sixty horse-power motor. Nerve!" he laughed, scornfully. "There's more kinds of nerve than one, but they all mean that a man's got grit."

"Someone said you had a stable full of motors," she observed. "Do you, then, guide them yourself, or sit beside your chauffeur and let him steer the teuf-teuf?"

"Wal, that's as may be," he returned. "Sometimes one drives and sometimes the other. But if you ask me what I really like it's a sixty horse-power Panhard, a clear track, and a mile every fifty-five seconds. And I prefer my own hand on the steering-wheel every time."

He was interrupted by a roar of cheers from all round the ring. The gaily-harnessed mule-team had already dragged out the carcass of the bull whom the *espada* had duly dispatched and also those of the three horses who had fallen in the fray. Was it not Théophile Gautier who said of the steeds slain in the bullring, "They are not carcasses; they are corpses"?

Ringing cheers greeted the advent of a second bull, full of fire, who dashed round the ring like a tornado, sending the gold-bespangled toreros flying to the barrier.

"Ah, what a lively bull!" cried the lady, her eyes sparkling. "He moves like a whirlwind. Even your Texas cowboys might find· it hard to evade his swift rush—that is, supposing they had the nerve to enter and challenge him." He met her eyes, as hard as steel and as bright, and found there a challenge to his nation. Was there a personal one to himself, too? A sudden inspiration darted through his mind.

"I can rack that little ten horse-power Daimler round and turn it on a blanket just as good as a cow-pony. And a golden key, they say, opens any gate in Spain, including even that of the toril. B'gosh, I believe a thousand dollars wadded at the man who keeps the door will let me inside, and, once in, I guess I can find the nerve for the rest of the show. 'Twill take lightning steering, but I reckon I can show her a thing or two, if I am a New Yorker." He was watching the sharp rushes of the bull as the toreros called him and played him with their dexterous turns and twists. "Anyway, there's no great chance of wheels skidding on that sandy surface, and I'll gamble I can do the quick turning and dodging as well as those fancy-dressed fellers." He turned to the lady. "Marquesa," he said, aloud, "I've got to ask you to excuse me a few minutes. See you again soon. What's the pretty phrase you have? '*Hasta otra vista*,' and '*Beso sus manos*.' " And like a flash he was gone.

Five bulls had entered one after another the floor of that wide amphitheatre, round which rose to the sky row upon row of eager faces and bright costumes, and after their brief madness of rage and desperate fighting had in turn sunk on the sand before the unerring thrust of the great *espada*.

But as the sixth and last bull bounded from the darkness of his pen into the bright arena and stood there a moment bewildered by the light, the circling crowd, and the cheering, a new thing happened. Another door was hastily half opened and then closed again, and through it in that half-second there darted in, not a gaily caparisoned torero on horseback, but a very small motor-car with a single occupant. The swiftly whirling wheels were so low, and the whole machine so tiny, that the man, who held a red flag in one hand and the guiding-wheel in the other, seemed almost as exposed as if he had been on a bicycle. As he rushed past the bull his hooter gave three loud, derisive toots, the motor swung round the centre of the arena, and then came back full speed straight at the astonished beast. A great clamour went up from the no less astonished audience, some shouting *"Fuera, fuera"* ("Out with him"), indignant at this most unheard-of innovation on the sacred traditions of the great national institution of Spain; while others yelled *"Olé! Bravo! Viva!"* ("Well done, bravo, hurrah!") cheering the novelty of this entirely unexpected turn given to the performance. The puzzled toreros ran this way and that, for they were more taken aback than the bull. They were used to bulls, but not to a wild motor driven by a mad American. An enraged banderillero made a spurt for the car as if actually meaning to plant his barbed darts in the bold charioteer; but avoiding him by a rapid swerve the American left him behind as if he were standing still, and the yells and cheers of the audience changed in a moment into a burst of laughter. It tickled the spectators to see how the skill of the torero, trained solely to baffle the bull, had been as skilfully baffled in turn by the adroitness of the intruder. And now again the laughter ceased and the audience held their breath as the little motor, heading for the bull, speeded straight on to what seemed certain destruction. It came close, the red flag shot out at arm's length to the left, the bull charged blindly at the flag, and with the least possible swerve to the right the motor sped triumphantly past, and again swung round in swift obedience to the guiding hand of the American, now safe in the rear of the outmanoeuvred bull.

Round the edge of the barrier were being held hasty and excited conferences of the toreros. Taken at a disadvantage like this they hardly knew what to do. The laws of the Spanish bullring have come down from antiquity as sacred and as inviolable as those of cricket in England; doubtless there may indeed have been certain variations tolerated in bygone days, such as the use of bulldogs, nay, even the lasso. But this dreadful intrusion of the motor-car was a thing utterly beyond precedent. What was to be done? It was all very well to say, "Arrest the intruder," but to run in between a motor going thirty miles an hour and a furious bull was like running in between the devil and the deep sea.

But while the toreros hesitated, the audience made up its mind. It had been used to seeing six bulls killed, in the regular fashion, once a week from time immemorial, and it had seen five so killed to-day. Now there was offered the novel chance of seeing an up-to-date motor demolished by a bull, and the audience rose to the occasion. Shouts of *"Bravo, motorero; bravo, motorero,"* rent the air. The childish pun in "motorero" caught their fancy, and their laughter was as loud as their cheers. The American *motorero* had succeeded in tickling the imagination of the people, and those ten thousand shouts spoke their decision in his favour. In Spain, above all places, it is a dangerous thing to thwart the fancy of the people, and the much and justly irritated authorities (authorities are always irritated by a change of programme) saw that the people must be allowed to have their way.

As the American swung his "teuf-teuf" round in a large circle on the far side of the arena he divined in a flash the new feeling towards him that had come over that great multitude of spectators, and steering for a moment with his left hand he took off his hat and bowed right and left. The cheers were redoubled, and he heard innumerable cries of *"Otra vez! que se repita!"* ("Encore, encore"), while the jesters of the audience encouraged his car with the Madrid cab man's cry of *"Arre, arre!"* ("Gee up!") Never before in his life had Mr. Elihu P. Hanks performed on the public stage, and the effect on him of these cries was curious. He suddenly was aware that he, by nature the most masterful, self-controlled, and independent of men, was rapidly becoming the mere slave of a crowd. He was conscious of an insane desire to obey!—yes, to please them, to do any mortal thing they wanted. Individually, he rather despised, or even disliked them—all but one; as a mass, they set alight in his heart a new fire—the love of applause; and he half-hated himself for feeling it.

Round swung the car till it once more headed straight for the bull and at its highest speed. The bull saw it coming, knew his enemy, and with a savage roar charged headlong forward to meet it. Swiftly the gap between them closed up, as the gap might close between two locomotives encountering on a single rail; but just before the crash came the motor-car slowed up, swerved, and curled away to the left. But the bull, not hampered this time by the flag in his face, turned almost as quickly, and in a moment was galloping right at the tail of the little car. The American, with one hasty glance over his shoulder, gave her full speed again, and a desperate race ensued. For fifty yards there was nothing in it and the bull, barely two feet behind was furiously trying to gore the petrol tank at the rear. The little car was one of those for only two people, where both sit right in front. But inch by inch the car drew away and the American signalized his success by a volley of derisive toot-toot-toots on his hooter. Nearing the barrier the car swerved sharp to the right and the bull dashed past it and almost into a stately but startled municipal guard who, hesitating between his duty as a public official and his extreme disgust at this monstrous irregularity, had ventured inside the barrier. He was absolutely grazed by the unexpected swerve of the car, but a quick leap aside saved him by a hair's breadth, and springing to the barrier he went up it like a lamp-lighter, having had quite enough of the unwonted combination, while the bull, who had suddenly turned after him, roared with disappointed rage as he dashed his horns against the solid wood just below the fugitive.

At this same instant the bull was astonished to find himself spanked from behind with a flag. The American had turned instantly to succour, if need be, the hunted official, and, seeing him already safe, dashed past the bull's heels and flapped him as he went by. A round of cheers greeted the neatness of the trick, which the American acknowledged by another volley of toots; to the bull it seemed as if those toots were the challenge of a rival, and, forgetful of the municipal guard, he sped once more after the motor. For a moment it seemed as if he must catch the audacious *motorero* this time. The motor was running in a circular course close to the barrier, and the bull, who cut straight across and ran on the inner circle, had the advantage of a shorter track, an advantage which practically more than equalized their speeds. Now, he was all but up with the motor, which was, as it were, penned between the bull and the barrier, when lo! on went the brake hard, the car stopped within twice its length, the bull shot helplessly past, and the car glided gracefully out behind him into the middle of the arena. The *motorero* had scored again.

Then at last the American ventured to take his eyes from the ring and glance up at the box where he had been sitting half an hour before. The marquesa had risen and come forward and was leaning over the edge of the box. He had interested her. She would not hint again that American millionaires had no nerve. And yet was she pleased?

Was not that look upon her beautiful face one of mere expectancy, as if she were waiting for the real business to begin? Could it mean that she was unsatisfied because the final business of the *espada*, the death of the bull, was lacking? Did she expect him to produce a weapon and thrust home with it to win her favour? If so, he would be no *matador*—she might expect.

But while he thus debated in his own mind other people were active. The *espada* himself in particular was furious at this invasion, and his first wrath had fallen upon the unlucky wight at the gate, on whom he fixed the responsibility of having admitted the stranger and whom he trounced soundly therefore. Now, followed by his whole cuadrilla, he sprang into the ring, determined at once to stop the unseemly performance and to take ample vengeance for what he looked on as an insult to himself and his profession. But before he and his men could reach the middle of the arena there was a startling change. Hanks had started off after the bull again and had been waltzing round him in a sort of secure ecstasy. He had now found out exactly how near he could shave a collision without being caught; the car flickered this way and that under his sure touch on the steering-wheel, and the exhibition of his amazing dexterity brought cheer after cheer from the crowd. He had skilfully drawn the bull to the far side of the arena just below where the marquesa sat, and proud of his success glanced up at her once more. But just in front of him there stood one of the sweepers, those humble servants of the arena whose inglorious duty it is to rake smooth the sand and hide the gory traces left by the last victim. Theirs is no fancy gold and velvet costume; they win no plaudits from the excited crowd. They only sweep the floor. The man sprang aside to avoid the car, and in so doing put himself right in the path of the bull.

In a moment the unhappy victim was tossed high in the air, and as he fell the furious animal turned, to gore him through and through as he lay. Hanks heard the stricken man's cry of despair and, whirling his car, took in the situation in a flash. The toreros, as he perfectly well understood, had entered the arena after him and not after the bull, and in any case they were too far off to be of any use for a rescue. There was only one thing to be done and he did it. Without an instant's hesitation he headed the car full speed at the bull, and this time there was no swerving aside. He had no sword, no lance in his hand; but to save the life of the poor *chulo*, imperilled by the American's rash action, he would dare the uttermost. Right headlong into the bull he drove the car full smash, just as the terrible horns were within a yard of the prostrate sweeper. There was a terrific thud as they collided. The bull's legs were knocked clean from under him, and his great body crashed heavily down upon the car and its occupant. The farce had ended in a tragedy. The petrol from the burst tank caught fire and a great tongue of flame and smoke went up as from a holocaust.

The toreros darted to the spot, eager now not to punish, but to save. Some bore away the unconscious sweeper, others hastened to put the crippled but struggling bull out of his pain with the puntilla or dagger before they were able to drag out from under him and from under the burning wreck of the shattered car a piteous figure.

As they disengaged the stricken man with careful swiftness and raised him from the ground, his hanging head and nerveless limbs filled them with dismay. These men had spent their lives in the bullring and were familiar with the presence of the King of Terrors. Was he not claiming this rash foreigner as his own? One man shook his head, another shrugged his shoulders, as they skilfully raised the senseless form to bear it out of the ring. "It is possible," said one to the other; "he is tough; he still breathes; by a miracle he may live. But I do not believe it. Look at his face"; for indeed the ghastly pallor that overspread it was but too like the ashen hue of death.

The marquesa watching from her box saw it, and the ring of admiring young Madrileños who were gazing at her feared for a moment that her cheek grew paler.

The she furled her fan languidly.

"I think, on the whole," she said, "that the old fashions please me best. They are more artistic."

Yet some people ventured to doubt the marquesa's artistic taste when, three months later, she petrified society by giving her hand to a bridegroom with a cork leg; but the disappointed gallants finally consoled themselves by swearing that she did it for the honour of Spain, for no one could doubt that it needed more daring to marry a mad Americano than even to take a motor into the bullring.

Montes the Matador

Frank Harris

FRANK HARRIS (1856–1931)—*the inclusion of a story by this notorious English writer will, no doubt, come as a surprise to many readers of this collection. Yet Harris was fascinated by the art of the matador and from his absorption grew this stirring novella, which, while it contains factual inaccuracies, is still a vivid portrait of the atmosphere of the bullring. "Montes the Matador" was written prior to* My Life and Loves *(1923–27) and perhaps because of this lacks the distortion that Harris invariably introduced into much of his work. As it has been out of print for a good many years, its republication will doubtless introduce numerous readers to a facet of Frank Harris's writing that they may never have realized existed.*

"Yes! I'm better, and the doctor tells me I've escaped once more—as if I cared! . . . And all through the fever you came every day to see me, so my niece says, and brought me the cool drink that drove the heat away and gave me sleep. You thought, I suppose, like the doctor, that I'd escape you, too. Ha! ha! And that you'd never hear old Montes tell what he knows of bull-fighting and you don't. . . . Or perhaps it was kindness; though why you, a foreigner and a heretic, should be kind to me, God knows. . . . The doctor says I've not got much more life in me, and you're going to leave Spain within the week—within the week, you said, didn't you? . . . Well, then, I don't mind telling you the story.

"Thirty years ago I wanted to tell it often enough, but I knew no one I could trust. After that fit passed, I said to myself I'd never tell it; but, as you're going away, I'll tell it to you, if you swear by the Virgin you'll never tell it to ayone, at least until I'm dead. You'll swear, will you? easily enough! they all will; but as

you're going away, it's much the same. Besides, you can do nothing now; no one can do anything; they never could have done
anything. Why, they wouldn't believe you if you told it to them,
the fools! . . . My story will teach you more about bull-fighting
than Frascuelo or Mazzantini, or—yes, Lagartijo knows. Weren't
there Frascuelos and Mazzantinis in my day? Dozens of them.
You could pick one Frascuelo out of every thousand labourers if
you gave him the training and practice, and could keep him away
from wine and women. But a Montes is not to be found every
day, if you searched all Spain for one. . . . What's the good of
bragging? I never bragged when I was at work: the deed talks—
louder than any words. Yet, I think, no one has ever done the
things I used to do; for I read in a paper once an account of a
thing I often did, and the writer said 'twas incredible. Ha, ha!
incredible to the Frascuelos and Mazzantinis and the rest, who
can kill bulls and are called *espadas*. Oh, yes! bulls so tired out
they can't lift their heads. You didn't guess when you were telling me about Frascuelo and Mazzantini that I knew them. I
knew all about both of them before you told me. I know their
work, though I've not been within sight of a ring for more than
thirty years. . . . Well, I'll tell you my story: I'll tell you my
story—if I can."

The old man said the last words as if to himself in a low voice,
then sank back in the arm-chair, and for a time was silent.

Let me say a word or two about myself and the circumstances
which led me to seek out Montes.

I had been in Spain off and on a good deal, and had taken
from the first a great liking to the people and country; and no one
can love Spain and the Spaniards without becoming interested in
the bull-ring—the sport is so characteristic of the people, and in
itself to enthralling. I set myself to study it in earnest, and when I
came to know the best bull-fighters, Frascuelo, Mazzantini and
Lagartijo, and heard them talk of their trade, I began to understand what skill and courage, what qualities of eye and hand and
heart, this game demands. Through my love of the sport, I came
to hear of Montes. He had left so great a name that thirty years

after he had disappeared from the scene of his triumphs, he was still spoken of not infrequently. He would perhaps have been better remembered had the feats attributed to him been less astounding. It was Frascuelo who told me than Montes was still alive:

"Montes," he cried out in answer to me; "I can tell you about Montes. You mean the old *espada* who, they say, used to kill the bull in its first rush into the ring—as if anyone could do that! I can tell you about him. He must have been clever; for an old aficionado I know swears no one of us is fit to be in his cuadrilla. Those old fellows are all like that, and I don't believe half they tell about Montes. I dare say he was good enough in his day, but there are just as good men now as ever there were. When I was in Ronda, fours years ago, I went to see Montes. He lives out of the town in a nice, little house all alone, with one woman to attend to him, a niece of his, they say. You know he was born in Ronda; but he would not talk to me; he only looked at me and laughed —the little lame, conceited one!"

"You don't believe then, in spite of what they say, that he was better than Lagartijo or Mazzantini?" I asked.

"No, I don't," Frascuelo replied. "Of course, he may have known more than they do, and that wouldn't be difficult, for neither of them knows much. Mazzantini is a good matador because he's very tall and strong—that's his advantage. For that, too, the women like him, and when he makes a mistake and has to try again, he gets forgiven. It wasn't so when I began. There were aficionados then, and if you made a mistake they began to jeer, and you were soon pelted out of the ring. Now the crowd knows nothing and is no longer content to follow those who do know. Lagartijo? Oh! he's very quick and daring, and the women and boys like that, too. But he's ignorant: he knows nothing about a bull. Why, he's been wounded oftener in his five years than I in my twenty. And that's a pretty good test. Montes must have been clever; for he's very small and I shouldn't think he was ever very strong, and then he was lame almost from the beginning, I've heard. I've no doubt he could teach the business to Mazzantini or Lagartijo, but that's not saying much. . . . He must have made a lot of money, too, to be able to live on it ever since. And they didn't pay as high then or even when I began as they do now."

So much I knew about Montes when, in the spring of 188–, I rode from Seville to Ronda, fell in love with the place at first sight, and resolved to stop at Polos' inn for some time. Ronda is built, as it were, upon an island tableland high above the sea-level, and is ringed about by still higher mountain ranges. It is one of the most peculiar and picturesque places in the world. A river runs almost all round it; and the sheer cliffs fall in many places three or four hundred feet, from the tableland to the water, like a wall. No wonder that the Moors held Ronda after they had lost every other foot of ground in Spain. Taking Ronda as my head-quarters, I made almost daily excursions, chiefly on foot, into the surrounding mountains. On one of these I heard again of Montes. A peasant with whom I had been talking and who was showing me a short cut back to the town, suddenly stopped and said, pointing to a little hut perched on the mountain-shoulder in front of us, "From that house you can see Ronda. That's the house where Montes, the great matador, was born," he added, evidently with some pride. Then and there the conversation with Frascuelo came back to my memory, and I made up my mind to find Montes out and have a talk with him. I went to his house, which lay just outside the town, next day with the *alcalde*, who introduced me to him and then left us. The first sight of the man interested me. He was short—about five feet three or four, I should think—of well-knit, muscular frame. He seemed to me to have Moorish blood in him. His complexion was very dark and tanned; the features clean-cut; the nose sharp and inquisitive; the nostrils astonishingly mobile; the chin and jaws square, bony—resolute. His hair and thick moustache were snow-white, and this, together with the deep wrinkles on the forehead and round the eyes and mouth, gave him an appearance of great age. He seemed to move, too, with extreme difficulty, his lameness, as he afterwards told me, being complicated with rheumatism. But when one looked at his eyes, the appearance of age vanished. They were large and brown, usually inexpressive, or rather impenetrable, brooding wells of unknown depths. But when anything excited him, the eyes would suddenly flash to life and become intensely luminous. The effect was startling. It seemed as if all the vast vitality of the man had been transmuted into those wonderful gleaming orbs: they radiated courage, energy, intellect. Then, as his mood changed, the light would die out of the eyes, and the old, wizened, wrinkled face would settle down to its ordinary, ill-tempered, wearied expression. There was evidently so much in the man—courage, melancholy, keen intelligence—that in spite of an anything but flattering reception I returned again and again to the house. One day his niece told me that Montes was in bed, and from her description I decided that he was suffering from an attack of malarial fever. The doctor who attended him, and whom I knew, confirmed this. Naturally enough I did what I could for the sufferer, and so it came about that after his recovery he received me with kindness, and at last made up his mind to tell me the story of his life.

"I may as well begin at the beginning," Montes went on. "I was born near here about sixty years ago. You thought I was older. Don't deny it. I saw the surprise in your face. But it's true: in fact, I am not yet, I think, quite sixty. My father was a peasant with a few acres of land of his own and a cottage."

"I know it," I said. "I saw it the other day."

"Then you may have seen on the further side of the hill the pasture-ground for cattle which was my father's chief possession. It was good pasture, very good. My mother was of a better class than my father; she was the daughter of the chemist in Ronda; she could read and write, and she did read, I remember, whenever she could get the chance, which wasn't often, with her four children to take care of—three girls and a boy—and the house to look after. We all loved her, she was so gentle; besides, she told us wonderful stories; but I think I was her favourite. You see, I was the youngest and a boy, and women are like that. My father was hard—at least, I thought him so, and feared rather than loved him; but the girls got on better with him. He never talked to me as he did to them. My mother wanted me to go to school and become a priest; she had taught me to read and write by the time I was six. But my father would not hear of it. 'If you had had three boys and one girl,' I remember him saying to her once, 'you could have done what you liked with this one. But as there is only one boy, he must work and help me.' So by the time I was nine I used to go off down to the pasture and watch the bulls all day long. For though the herd was a small one—only about twenty head—it required to be constantly watched. The cows were attended to in an enclosure close to the house. It was my task to mind the bulls in the lower pasture. Of course, I had a pony, for such bulls in Spain are seldom approached, and cannot be driven by a man on foot. I see you don't understand. But it's simple enough. My father's bulls were of good stock, savage and strong; they were always taken for the ring, and he got high prices for them. He generally managed to sell three *novillos* and two bulls of four years old each year. And there was no bargaining, no trouble; the money was always ready for that class of animal. All day long I sat on my pony, or stood near it, minding the bulls. If any of them strayed too far, I had to go and get him back again. But in the heat of the day they never moved about much, and that time I turned to use by learning the lessons my mother gave me. So a couple of years passed. Of course, in that time I got to know our bulls pretty well, but it was a remark of my father which first taught me that each bull had an individual character, and which first set me to watch them closely. That must have been in my twelfth year; and in that summer I learned more than in the two previous years. My father, though he said nothing to me, must have noticed that I had gained confidence in dealing with the bulls; for one night, when I was in bed, I heard him say to my mother, 'The little fellow is as good as a man now.' I was proud of his praise, and from that time on I set to work to learn everything I could about the bulls.

"By degrees I came to know every one of them—better far than I ever got to know men or women later. Bulls, I found, were just like men, only simpler and kinder; some were good-tempered and honest, others were sulky and cunning. There was a black one which was wild and hot-tempered, but at bottom good, while there was one almost as black, with light horns and flanks, which I never trusted. The other bulls didn't like him. I could see they didn't; they were all afraid of him. He was cunning and suspicious, and never made friends with any of them; he would always eat by himself, far away from the others—but he had courage too; I knew that as well as they did. He was sold that very summer with the black one for the ring in Ronda. One Sunday night, when my father and eldest sister (my mother would never go to *los toros*) came back from seeing the game in Ronda, they were wild with excitement, and began to tell the mother how one of our bulls had caught the matador and tossed him and how the *chulos* could scarcely get the matador away. Then I cried out, 'I know; 'twas Judas' (so I had christened him), and as I saw my father's look of surprise I went on confusedly, 'the bull with the white horns I mean. Juan, the black one, wouldn't have been clever enough.' My father only said, 'The boy's right'; but my mother drew me to her and kissed me, as if she were afraid. . . . Poor mother! I think even then she knew or divined something of what came to pass later. . . .

"It was the next summer, I think, that my father first found out how much I knew about the bulls. It happened in this way. There hadn't been much rain in the spring; the pasture, therefore, was thin, and that, of course, made the bulls restless. In the summer the weather was unsettled—spells of heat and then thunderstorms —till the animals became very excitable. One day, there was thunder in the air I remember, they gave me a great deal of trouble, and that annoyed me, for I wanted to read. I had got to a very interesting tale in the story-book my mother had given me on the day our bulls were sold. The story was about Cervantes—ah, you know who I mean, the great writer. Well, he was a great man, too. The story told how he escaped from the prison over there in Algiers and got back to Cadiz, and how a widow came to him to find out if he knew her son, who was also a slave of the Moors. And when she heard that Cervantes had seen her son working in

chains, she bemoaned her wretchedness and ill-fortune, until the
heart of the great man melted with pity, and he said to her,
'Come, mother, be hopeful, in one month your son shall be here
with you.' And then the book told how Cervantes went back to
slavery, and how glad the Bey was to get him again, for he was
very clever; and how he asked the Bey, as he had returned of his
free will, to send the widow's son home in his stead; and the Bey
consented. That Cervantes was a man! . . . Well, I was reading
the story, and I believed every word of it, as I do still, for no ordinary person could invent that sort of tale; and I grew very much
excited and wanted to know all about Cervantes. But as I could
only read slowly and with difficulty, I was afraid the sun would
go down before I could get to the end. While I was reading as
hard as ever I could, my father came down on foot and caught
me. He hated to see me reading—I don't know why; and he was
angry and struck at me. As I avoided the blow and got away from
him, he pulled up the picket line, and got on my pony to drive
one of the bulls back to the herd. I have thought since, he must
have been very much annoyed before he came down and caught
me. For though he knew a good deal about bulls, he didn't show
it then. My pony was too weak to carry him easily, yet he acted
as if he had been well mounted. For as I said, the bulls were hun-
gry and excited, and my father should have seen this and driven
the bull back quietly and with great patience. But no; he wouldn't
let him feed even for a moment. At last the bull turned on him.
My father held the goad fairly against his neck, but the bull came
on just the same, and the pony could scarcely get out of the way in
time. In a moment the bull turned and prepared to rush at him
again. My father sat still on the little pony and held the goad; but
I knew that was no use; he knew it too; but he was angry and
wouldn't give in. At once I ran in between him and the bull, and
then called to the bull, and went slowly up to him where he was
shaking his head and pawing the ground. He was very angry, but
he knew the difference between us quite well, and he let me come
close to him without rushing at me, and then just shook his head

to show me he was still angry, and soon began to feed quietly. In a moment or two I left him and went back to my father. He had got off the pony and was white and trembling, and he said:

" 'Are you hurt?'

"And I said, laughing, 'No he didn't want to hurt me. He was only showing off his temper.'

"And my father said, 'There's not a man in all Spain that could have done that! You know more than I do—more than anybody.'

"After that he let me do as I liked, and the next two years were very happy ones. First came the marriage of my second sister; then the eldest one was married, and they were both good matches. And the bulls sold well, and my father had less to do, as I could attend to the whole herd by myself. Those were two good years. My mother seemed to love me more and more every day, or I suppose I noticed it more, and she praised me for doing the lessons she gave me; and I had more and more time to study as the herd got to know me better and better.

"My own trouble was that I had never seen the bulls in the ring. But when I found my father was willing to take me, and 'twas mother who wanted me not to go, I put up with that, too, and said nothing, for I loved her greatly. Then of a sudden came the sorrow. It was in the late winter, just before my fifteenth birthday. I was born in March, I think. In January my mother caught cold, and as she grew worse my father fetched the doctor, and then her father and mother came to see her, but nothing did any good. In April she died. I wanted to die too.

"After her death my father took to grumbling about the food and house and everything. Nothing my sister could do was right. I believe she only married in the summer because she couldn't stand his constant blame. At any rate, she married badly, a good-for-nothing who had twice her years, and who ill-treated her continually. A month or two later my father, who must have been fifty, married again, a young woman, a labourer's daughter without a *duro*. He told me he was going to do it, for the house needed a woman. I suppose he was right. But I was too young then to take such things into consideration, and I had loved my mother. When I saw his new wife I did not like her, and we did not get on well together.

"Before this, however, early in the summer that followed the death of my mother, I went for the first time to see a bull-fight. My father wanted me to go, and my sister, too; so I went. I shall never forget that day. The *chulos* made me laugh, they skipped about so and took such extra-good care of themselves; but the banderilleros interested me. Their work required skill and courage, that I saw at once; but after they had planted the banderillas twice, I knew how it was done, and I felt I could do it just as well or better. For the third or fourth banderillo made a mistake! He didn't even know with which horn the bull was going to strike; so he got frightened, and did not plant the banderillas fairly—in fact, one was on the side of the shoulder and the other didn't even stick in. As for the picadores, they didn't interest me at all. There was no skill or knowledge in their work. It was for the crowd, who liked to see blood and who understand nothing. Then came the turn of the *espada*. Ah, that seemed splendid to me. He knew his work I thought at first, and his work evidently required knowledge, skill, courage, strength—everything. I was intensely excited, and when the bull, struck to the heart, fell prone on his knees and the blood gushed from his nose and mouth, I cheered and cheered till I was hoarse. But before the games were over, that very first day, I saw more than one matador make a mistake. At first I thought I must be wrong, but soon the event showed I was right. For the matador hadn't even got the bull to stand square when he tried his stroke and failed. Ah, I see you don't know what that means—'to stand square.'"

"I do partly," I replied, "but I don't see the reason of it. Will you explain?"

"Well," Montes answered, "it's very simple. You see, so long as the bull's standing with one hoof in front of the other, his shoulder-blades almost meet, as when you throw your arms back and your chest out; that is, they don't meet, but the space between them is not as regular, and therefore, not as large as it is when their front hooves are square. Now, the space between the shoulder-blades is none too large at any time, for you have to strike with force to drive the sword through the inch-thick hide, and through a foot of muscle, sinew, and flesh besides to the heart. Nor is the stroke a straight one. Then, too, there's always the backbone to avoid. And the space between the backbone and the nearest thick gristle of the shoulder-blade is never more than an inch and a half. So if you narrow this space by even half an inch you increase your difficulty immensely. And that's not your object. Well, all this I've been telling you, I divined at once. Therefore, when I saw the bull wasn't standing quite square, I knew the matador was either a bungler or else very clever and strong indeed. In a moment he proved himself to be a bungler, for his sword turned on the shoulder-blade, and the bull, throwing up his head, almost caught him on his horns. Then I hissed and cried 'Shame!' And the people stared at me. That butcher tried five times before he killed the bull, and at last even the most ignorant of the spectators knew I had been right in hissing him. He was one of your Mazzantinis, I suppose."

"Oh, no!" I replied. "I've seen Mazzantini try twice, but never five times. That's too much!"

"Well," Montes continued quietly, "the man who tries once and fails ought never to be allowed in a ring again. But to go on. That first day taught me I could be an *espada*. The only doubt in my mind was in regard to the nature of the bulls. Should I be able to understand new bulls—bulls, too, from different herds and of different race, as well as I understood our bulls? Going home that evening I tried to talk to my father, but he thought the sport had been very good, and when I wanted to show him the mistakes the *matadores* had made, he laughed at me, and, taking hold of my arm, he said, 'Here's where you need the gristle before you could kill a bull with a sword, even if he were tied for you.' My father was very proud of his size and strength, but what he said had reason in it, and made me doubt myself. Then he talked about the gains of the matadores. A fortune, he said, was given for a single day's work. Even the pay of the *chulos* seemed to me to be extravagant, and a banderillero got enough to make one rich for life. That night I thought over all I had seen and heard, and fell asleep and dreamt I was an *espada*, the best in Spain, and rich, and married to a lovely girl with golden hair—as boys do dream.

"Next day I set myself to practise with our bulls. First I teased one until he grew angry and rushed at me; then, as a *chulo*, stepped aside. And after I had practised this several times, I began to try to move aside as late as possible and only just as far as was needful; for I soon found out the play of horn of every bull we had. The older the bull the heavier his neck and shoulders become, and, therefore, the sweep of horns in an old bull is much smaller than a young one's. Before the first morning's sport was over I knew that with our bulls at any rate I could beat any *chulo* I had seen the day before. Then I set myself to quiet the bulls, which was a little difficult, and after I had succeeded I went back to my pony to read and dream. Next day I played at being a banderillero, and found out at once that my knowledge of the animal was all-important. For I knew always on which side to move to avoid the bull's rush. I knew how he meant to strike by the way he put his head down. To plant the banderillas perfectly would have been child's play to me, at least with our bulls. The matador's work was hard to practise. I had no sword, besides the bull I wished to pretend to kill, was not tired and wouldn't keep quiet. Yet I went on trying. The game had a fascination for me. A few days later, provided with a makeshift red *capa*, I got a bull far away from the others. Then I played with him till he was tired out. First I played as a *chulo*, and avoided his rushes by an inch or two only; then, as banderillero, I escaped his stroke, and, as I did so, struck his neck with two sticks. When he was tired I approached him with the *capa* and found I could make him do what I pleased, stand crooked or square in a moment, just as I liked. For I learned at once that as a rule the bull rushes at the *capa* and not at the man who holds it. Some bulls, however, are clever enough to charge the man. For weeks I kept up this game, till one day my father expressed his surprise at the thin and wretched appearance of the bulls. No wonder! The pasture ground had been a ring to them and me for many a week.

"After this I had to play matador—the only part which had any interest for me—without first tiring them. Then came a long series of new experiences, which in time made me what I was, a real *espada*, but which I can scarcely describe to you.

"For power over wild animals comes to man, as it were, by leaps and bounds. Of a sudden one finds he can make a bull do something which the day before he could not make him do. It is all a matter of intimate knowledge of the nature of the animal. Just as the shepherd, as I've been told, knows the face of each sheep in a flock of a thousand, though I can see no difference between the faces of sheep, which are all alike, stupid, to me, so I came to know bulls, with a complete understanding of the nature and temper of each one. It's just because I can't tell you how I acquired this part of my knowledge that I was so long-winded in explaining to you my first steps. What I knew more than I have told you, will appear as I go on with my story, and that you must believe or disbelieve as you think best."

"Oh," I cried, "you've explained everything so clearly, and thrown light on so many things I didn't understand, that I shall believe whatever you tell me."

Old Montes went on as if he hadn't heard my protestation:

"The next three years were intolerable to me: my stepmother repaid my dislike with interest and found a hundred ways of making me uncomfortable, without doing anything I could complain of and so get altered. In the spring of my nineteenth year I told my father I intended to go to Madrid and become an *espada*. When he found he couldn't induce me to stay, he said I might go. We parted, and I walked to Seville; there I did odd jobs for a few weeks in connection with the bull-ring, such as feeding the bulls, helping to separate them, and so forth; and there I made

an acquaintance who was afterwards a friend. Juan Valdera was
one of the cuadrilla of Girvalda, a matador of the ordinary type.
Juan was from Estremadura, and we could scarcely understand
each other at first; but he was kindly and careless and I took a
great liking to him. He was a fine man; tall, strong and handsome, with short, dark, wavy hair and dark moustache, and great
black eyes. He liked me, I suppose, because I admired him and
because I never wearied of hearing him tell of his conquests
among women and even great ladies. Of course, I told him I
wished to enter the ring, and he promised to help me to get a
placed in Madrid where he knew many of the officials. 'You may
do well with the *capa*,' I remember he said condescendingly, 'or
even as a banderillero, but you'll never go further. You see, to be
an *espada*, as I intend to be, you must have height and strength,'
and he stretched his fine figure as he spoke. I acquiesced hum-
bly enough. I felt that perhaps he and my father were right, and
I didn't know whether I should ever have strength enough for
the task of an *espada*. To be brief, I saved a little money, and
managed to get to Madrid late in the year, too late for the bullring. Thinking over the matter, I resolved to get work in a blacksmith's shop, and at length succeeded. As I had thought, the
labour strengthened me greatly, and in the spring of my twentieth
year, by Juan's help, I got employed on trial one Sunday as a
chulo.

"I suppose," Montes went on, after a pause, "I ought to have
been excited and nervous on that first Sunday—but I wasn't; I
was only eager to do well in order to get engaged for the season.
The blacksmith, Antonio, whom I had worked with, had advanced me the money for my costume, and Juan had taken me to
a tailor and got the things made, and what I owed Antonio and
the tailor weighed on me. Well, on that Sunday I was a failure at
first. I went in the procession with the rest, then with the others
I fluttered my *capa*; but when the bull rushed at me, instead of
running away, like the rest, I wrapped my *capa* about me and,
just as his horns were touching me, I moved aside—not half a

pace. The spectators cheered me, it is true, and I thought I had done very well, until Juan came over to me and said:

" 'You mustn't show off like that. First of all, you'll get killed if you play that game; and then you fellows with the *capa* are there to make the bull run about, to tire out so that we matadores may kill him.'

"That was my first lesson in professional jealousy. After that I ran about like the rest, but without much heart in the sport. It seemed to me stupid. Besides, from Juan's anger and contempt, I felt sure I shouldn't get a permanent engagement. Bit by bit, however, my spirits rose again with the exercise, and when the fifth or sixth bull came in I resolved to make him run. It was a good, honest bull; I saw that at once; he stood in the middle of the ring, excited, but not angry, in spite of the waving of the *capas* all round him. As soon as my turn came I ran forward, nearer to him than the others had considered safe, and waved the challenge with my *capa*. At once he rushed at it, and I gave him a long run, half round the circle, and ended it by stopping and letting him toss the *capa* which I held not quite at arm's length from my body. As I did this I didn't turn round to face him. I knew he'd toss the *capa* and not me, but the crowd rose and cheered as if the thing were extraordinary. Then I felt sure I should be engaged, and I was perfectly happy. Only Juan said to me a few minutes later:

" 'You'll be killed, my boy, one of these fine days, if you try those games. Your life will be a short one if you begin by trusting a bull.'

"But I didn't mind what he said. I thought he meant it as a friendly warning, and I was anxious only to get permanently engaged. And sure enough, as soon as the games were over, I was sent for by the director. He was kind to me, and asked me where I had played before. I told him that was my first trial.

" 'Ah!' he said, turning to a gentleman who was with him, 'I knew it, Señor Duque; such courage always comes from—want of experience, let me call it.'

" 'No,' replied the gentleman, whom I afterwards knew as the Duke of Medina Celi, the best aficionado, and one of the noblest men in Spain; 'I'm not so sure of that. Why,' he went on speaking now to me, 'did you keep your back turned to the bull?'

" 'Señor,' I answered, ' 'twas an honest bull, and not angry, and I knew he'd toss the *capa* without paying any attention to me.'

" 'Well,' said the Duke, 'if you know that much, and aren't afraid to risk your life on your knowledge, you'll go far. I must have a talk with you some day, when I've more time; you can come and see me. Send in your name; I shall remember.' And as he said this, he nodded to me and waved his hand to the director, and went away.

"Then and there the director made me sign an engagement for the season, and gave me one hundred *duros* as earnest money in advance of my pay. What an evening we had after that! Juan, the tailor, Antonio the blacksmith, and I. How glad and proud I was to be able to pay my debts and still have sixty *duros* in my pocket after entertaining my friends. If Juan had not hurt me every now and then by the way he talked of my foolhardiness, I should have told them all I knew; but I didn't. I only said I was engaged at a salary of a hundred *duros* a month.

" 'What!' said Juan. 'Come, tell the truth; make it fifty.'

" 'No,' I said; 'it was a hundred,' and I pulled out the money.

" 'Well,' he said, 'that only shows what it is to be small and young and foolhardy! Here am I, after six years' experience, second, too, in the cuadrilla of Girvalda, and I'm not getting much more than that.'

"Still, in spite of such little drawbacks, in spite, too, of the fact that Juan had to go away early, to meet 'a lovely creature,' as he said, that evening was one of the happiest I ever spent.

"All that summer through I worked every Sunday, and grew in favour with the Madrileños, and with the Madrileñas, though not with these in Juan's way. I was timid and young; besides, I had a picture of a woman in my mind, and I saw no one like it. So I went on studying the bulls, learning all I could about the different breeds, and watching them in the ring. Then I sent money to my sister and to my father, and was happy.

"In the winter I was a good deal with Antonio; every day I did a spell of work in his shop to strengthen myself, and he, I think, got to know that I intended to become an *espada*. At any rate, after my first performance with the *capa*, he believed I could do whatever I wished. He used often to say God had given him strength and me brains, and he only wished he could exchange some of his muscle for some of my wits. Antonio was not very bright, but he was good-tempered, kind, and hard-working, the only friend I ever had. May Our Lady give his soul rest!

"Next spring, when the director sent for me, I said that I wanted to work as a banderillero. He seemed to be surprised, told me I was a favourite with the *capa*, and had better stick to that for another season at least. But I was firm. Then he asked me whether I had ever used the banderillas, and where? The director always believed I had been employed in some other ring before I came to Madrid. I told him I was confident I could do the work. 'Besides,' I added, 'I want more pay,' which was an untruth; but the argument seemed to him decisive, and he engaged me at two hundred *duros* a month, under the conditions that, if the spectators wished it, I should work now and then with the *capa* as well. It didn't take me long to show the aficionados in Madrid that I was as good with the banderillas as I was with the *capa*. I could plant them when and where I liked. For in this season I found I could make the bull do almost everything. You know how the banderillero has to excite the bull to charge him before he can plant the darts. He does that to make the bull lower his head well, and he runs toward the bull partly so that the bull may not know when to toss his head up, partly because he can throw himself aside more easily when he's running fairly fast. Well, again and again I made the bull lower his head and then walked to him, planted the banderillas, and as he struck upwards swayed aside just enough to avoid the blow. That was an infinitely more difficult feat than anything I had ever done with the *capa*, and it gave me reputation among the aficionados and also with the *espadas*; but the ignorant herd of spectators preferred my trick with the *capa*. So the season came and went. I had many a carouse with Juan, and gave him money from time to time, because women always made him spend more than he got. From that time, too, I gave my sister fifty *duros* a month, and my father fifty. For before the season was half over my pay was raised to four hundred *duros* a month, and my name was put on the bills. In fact, I was rich and a favourite of the public.

"So time went on, and my third season in Madrid began, and with it came the beginning of the end. Never was anyone more absolutely content that I when we were told *los toros* would begin in a fortnight. On the first Sunday I was walking carelessly in the procession beside Juan, though I could have been next to the *espadas* had I wished, when he suddenly nudged me, saying:

" 'Look up! there on the second tier; there's a face for you.'

"I looked up, and saw a girl with the face of my dreams, only much more beautiful. I suppose I must have stopped, for Juan pulled me by the arm, crying, 'You're moonstruck, man; come on!' And on I went—lovestruck in heart and brain and body. What a face it was! The golden hair framed it like a picture, but the great eyes were hazel, and the lips scarlet, and she wore the *mantilla* like a queen. I moved forward like a man in a dream, conscious of nothing that went on round me, till I heard Juan say:

" 'She's looking at us. She knows we've noticed her. All right, pretty one! We'll make friends afterwards.'

" 'But how?' I asked stupidly.

" 'How!' he replied mockingly. 'I'll just send some one to find out who she is, and then you can send her a box for next Sunday, and pray for her acquaintance, and the thing's done. I suppose that's her mother sitting behind her,' he went on. 'I wonder if the other girl next to her is the sister. She's as good-looking as the fair-haired one, and easier to win, I'd bet. Strange how all the timid ones take to me.' And again he looked up.

"I said nothing; nor did I look up at the place where she was sitting; but I worked that day as I had never worked before. Then, for the first time, I did something that has never been done since by anyone. The first bull was honest and kindly: I knew the sort. So, when the people began to call for *El Pequeño* (the little fellow)—that was the nickname they had given me—I took up a *capa*, and, when the bull chased me, I stopped suddenly, faced him, and threw the *capa* round me. He was within six paces of me before he caught my look, and began to stop; but before he came to a standstill his horns were within a foot of me. He tossed his head once or twice as if he would strike me, and then went off. The people cheered and cheered as if they would never stop. Then I looked up at her. She must have been watching me, for she took the red rose from her hair and threw it into the ring towards me, crying, '*Bien! Muy bien! El Pequeño!*'

"As I picked up the rose, pressed it to my lips, and hid it in my breast, I realized all that life holds of triumphant joy! . . . Then I made up my mind to show what I could do, and everything I did that day seemed to delight the public. At last, as I planted the banderillas, standing in front of the bull, he tried twice in quick succession to strike me and failed, the crowd cheered and cheered and cheered, so that, even when I went away after bowing, and stood among my fellows, ten minutes passed before they would let the game go on. I didn't look up again. No! I wanted to keep the memory of what she looked like when she threw me the rose.

"After the games were over, I met her, that same evening. Juan had brought it about, and he talked easily enough to the mother and daughter and niece, while I listened. We all went, I remember, to a restaurant in the Puerta del Sol, and ate and drank together. I said little or nothing the whole evening. The mother told us they had just come from the north: Alvareda was the family name; her daughter was Clemencia, the niece, Liberata. I heard everything in a sort of fever of hot pulses and cold fits of humility, while Juan told them all about himself, and what he meant to do and to be. While Clemencia listened to him, I took my fill of gazing at her. At last Juan invited them all to *los toros* on the following Sunday, and promised them the best *palco* in the ring. He found out, too, where they lived, in a little street running parallel to the Alcala, and assured them of our visit within the week. Then they left, and as they went out of the door Liberata looked at Juan, while Clemencia chatted with him and teased him.

" 'That's all right,' said Juan, turning to me when they were gone, 'and I don't know which is the more taking, the niece or Clemencia. Perhaps the niece; she looks at one so appealingly; and those who talk so with their eyes are always the best. I wonder have they any money. One might do worse than either with a good portion.'

" 'Is that your real opinion?' I asked hesitatingly.

" 'Yes,' he answered; 'why?'

" 'Because, in that case leave Clemencia to me. Of course you could win her if you wanted to. But it makes no difference to you, and to me all the difference. If I cannot marry her, I shall never marry.'

" 'Jesus!' he cried, 'how fast you go, but I'd do more than that for you; and besides, the niece really pleases me better.'

"So the matter was settled between us.

"Now, if I could tell you all that happened, I would. But much escaped me at the time that I afterwards remembered, and many things that then seemed to me to be as sure as a straight stroke, have since grown confused. I only know that Juan and I met them often, and that Juan paid court to the niece, while I from time to time talked timidly to Clemencia.

"One Sunday after another came and went, and we grew to know each other well. Clemencia did not chatter like other women: I liked her the better for it, and when I came to know she was very proud, I liked that, too. She charmed me; why, I can scarcely tell. I saw her faults gradually, but even her faults appeared to me fascinating. Her pride was insensate. I remember one Sunday afternoon after the games, I happened to go into a restaurant, and found her sitting with her mother. I was in costume and carried in my hand a great nosegay of roses that a lady had thrown me in the ring. Of course, as soon as I saw Clemencia I went over to her and—you know it is the privilege of the matadores in Spain, even if they do not know the lady—taking a rose from the bunch I presented it to her as the fairest of the fair. Coming from the cold North, she didn't know the custom and scarcely seemed pleased. When I explained it to her, she exclaimed that it was monstrous; she'd never allow a mere matador to take such liberty unless she knew and liked him. Juan expostulated with her laughingly; I said nothing; I knew what qualities our work required, and didn't think it needed any defence. I believe in that first season, I came to see that her name Clemencia wasn't very appropriate. At any rate she had courage and pride, that was certain. Very early in our friendship she wanted to know why I didn't become an *espada*.

" 'A man without ambition,' she said, 'was like a woman without beauty.'

"I laughed at this and told her my ambition was to do my work well, and advancement was sure to follow in due course. For love of her seemed to have killed ambition in me. But no. She wouldn't rest content in spite of Juan's telling her my position already was more brilliant than that of most of the *espadas*.

" 'He does things with the *capa* and the banderillas which no *espada* in all Spain would care to imitate. And that's position enough. Besides, to be an *espada* requires height and strength.'

"As he said this she seemed to be convinced, but it annoyed me a little, and afterwards as we walked together, I said to her,

" 'If you want to see me work as an *espada*, you shall.'

" 'Oh no!' she answered half carelessly; 'if you can't do it, as Juan says, why should you try? To fail is worse than to lack ambition.'

" 'Well,' I answered, 'you shall see.'

"And then I took my courage in both hands and went on:

" 'If you cared for me I should be the first *espada* in the world next season.'

"She turned and looked at me curiously and said,

" 'Of course I'd wish it if you could do it.'

"And I said, 'See, I love you as the priest loves the Virgin; tell me to be as *espada* and I shall be one for the sake of your love.'

" 'That's what all men say, but love doesn't make a man tall and strong.'

" 'No; nor do size and strength take the place of heart and head. Do you love me? That's the question.'

" 'I like you, yes. But love—love, they say, comes after marriage.'

" 'Will you marry me?'

" 'Become an *espada* and then ask me again,' she answered coquettishly.

"The very next day I went to see the Duke of Medina Celi; the servants would scarcely let me pass till they heard my name and that the Duke had asked me to come. He received me kindly. I told him what I wanted.

" 'But,' he said, 'have you ever used the sword? Can you do it? You see we don't want to lose the best man with *capa* and banderillas ever known, to get another second-class *espada*.'

"And I answered him:

" 'Señor Duque, I have done better with the banderillas than I could with the *capa*. Believe me, I shall do better with the *espada* than with the banderillas.'

" 'You little fiend!' he laughed, 'I believe you; but now for the means. All the *espadas* are engaged; it'll be difficult. . . . But early in July the Queen has asked me to superintend the sports, and then I shall give you your chance. Will that do? In the meantime, astonish us all with *capa* and banderillas, so that men may not think me mad when I put your name first on the bill.'

"I thanked him from my heart, as was his due, and after a little more talk I went away to tell Clemencia the news. She only said:

" 'I'm glad. Now you'll get Juan to help you.'

"I stared at her.

" 'Yes!' she went on, a little impatiently; 'he has been trained to the work; he's sure to be able to teach you a great deal.'

"I said not a word. She was sincere, I saw, but then she came from the North and knew nothing. I said to myself, 'That's how women are!'

"She continued, 'Of course you're clever with the *capa* and banderillas, and now you must do more than ever, as the Duke said, to deserve your chance.' And then she asked carelessly, 'Couldn't you bring the Duke and introduce him to us some time or other? I should like to thank him.'

"And I, thinking it meant our betrothal, was glad, and promised. And I remember I did bring him once to the box and he was kind in a way, but not cordial as he always was when alone with me, and he told Clemencia that I'd go very far, and that any woman would be lucky to get me for a husband, and so on. After a while he went away. But Clemencia was angry with him and said he put on airs, and, indeed, I had never seen him so cold and reserved; I could say little or nothing in his defence.

"Well, all that May I worked as I had never done. The Director told me he knew I was to use the *espada* on the first Sunday in July, and he seemed to be glad; and one or two of the best *espadas* came to me and said they'd heard the news and should be glad to welcome me among them. All this excited me, and I did better and better. I used to pick out the old prints of Goya, the great painter—you know his works are in the Prado—and do everything the old matadores did, and invent new things. But nothing 'took' like my trick with the *capa*. One Sunday, I remember, I had done it with six bulls, one after the other, and the people cheered and cheered. But the seventh was a bad bull, and, of course, I didn't do it. And afterwards Clemencia asked me why I didn't, and I told her. For you see I didn't know then that women rate high what they don't understand. Mystery is everything to them. As if the explanation of such a thing makes it any easier. A man wins great battles by seizing the right moment and using it—the explanation is simple. One must be great in order to know the moment, that's all. But women don't see that it is only small men who exaggerate the difficulties of their work. Great men find their work easy and say so, and, therefore, you'll find that women underrate great men and over-praise small ones. Clemencia really thought I ought to learn the *espada's* work from Juan. Ah! women are strange creatures. . . . Well, after that Sunday she was always bothering me to do the *capa* trick with every bull.

" 'If you don't,' she used to say, 'you won't get the chance of being an *espada*.' And when she saw I laughed and paid no attention to that, she became more and more obstinate.

" 'If the people get to know you can only do it with some bulls, they won't think much of you. Do it with every bull, then they can't say anything.'

"And I said 'No! and I shouldn't be able to say anything either.

" 'If you love me you will do as I say!'

"And when I didn't do as she wished—it was madness—she grew cold to me, and sneered at me, and then urged me again, till I half yielded. Really, by that time I hardly knew what I couldn't do, for each day I seemed to get greater power over the bulls. At length a Sunday came, the first, I think, in June, or the last in May. Clemencia sat with her mother and cousin in the best *palco*; I had got it from the Director, who now refused me nothing. I had done my *capa* trick with three bulls, one after the other, then the fourth came in. As soon as I saw him, I knew he was bad, cunning I mean, and with black rage in the heart of him. The other men stood aside to let me do the trick, but I wouldn't. I ran away like the rest, and let him toss the *capa*. The people liked me, and so they cheered just the same, thinking I was tired; but suddenly Clemencia called out: 'The *capa* round the shoulders; the *capa* trick!' and I looked up at her; and she leaned over the front of the *palco*, and called out the words again.

"Then rage came into me, rage at her folly and cold heart; I took off my cap to her, and turned and challenged the bull with the *capa*, and, as he put down his head and rushed, I threw the *capa* round me and stood still. I did not even look at him. I knew it was no use. He struck me here on the thigh, and I went up into the air. The shock took away my senses. As I came to myself they were carrying me out of the ring, and the people were all standing up; but, as I looked towards the *palco*, I saw she wasn't standing up: she had a handkerchief before her face. At first I thought she was crying, and I felt well, and longed to say to her, 'It doesn't matter, I'm content'; then she put down the handkerchief and I saw she wasn't crying; there wasn't a tear in her eyes. She seemed surprised merely and shocked. I suppose she thought I could work miracles, or rather she didn't care much whether I was hurt or not. That turned me faint again. I came to myself in my bed, where I spent the next month. The doctor told the Duke of Medina Celi—he had come to see me the same afternoon—that the shock hadn't injured me, but I should be lame always, as the bull's horn had torn the muscles of my thigh from the bone. 'How he didn't bleed to death,' he said, 'is a wonder; now he'll pull through, but no more play with the bulls for him.' I knew better than the doctor, but I said nothing to him, only to the Duke I said:

" 'Señor, a promise is a promise; I shall use the *espada* in your show in July.'

"And he said, 'Yes, my poor boy, if you wish it, and are able to; but how came you to make such a mistake?'

" 'I made no mistake, Señor.'

" 'You knew you'd be struck?'

"I nodded. He looked at me for a moment, and then held out his hand. He understood everything, I'm sure; but he said nothing to me then.

"Juan came to see me in the evening, and next day Clemencia and her mother. Clemencia was sorry, that I could see, and wanted me to forgive her. As if I had anything to forgive when she stood there so lithe and straight, with her flower-like face and the appealing eyes. Then came days of pain while the doctors forced the muscles back into their places. Soon I was able to get up, with a crutch, and limp about. As I grew better, Clemencia came seldomer, and when she came, her mother never left the room. I knew what that meant. She had told her mother not to go away; for, though the mother thought no one good enough for her daughter, yet she pitied me, and would have left us alone—sometimes. She had a woman's heart. But no, not once. Then I set myself to get well soon. I would show them all, I said to myself, that a lame Montes was worth more than other men. And I got better, so the doctor said, with surprising speed. . . . One day, towards the end of June, I said to the servant of the Duke—he sent a servant every day to me with fruit and flowers—that I wished greatly to see his master. And the Duke came to see me, the very same day.

"I thanked him first for all his kindness to me, and then asked:

" 'Señor, have you put my name on the bills as *espada*?'

" 'No,' he replied; 'you must get well first, and, indeed, if I were in your place, I should not try anything more till next season.'

"And I said, 'Señor Duque, it presses. Believe me, weak as I am, I can use the sword.'

"And he answered my very thought: 'Ah! she thinks you can't. And you want to prove the contrary. I shouldn't take the trouble, if I were you; but there! Don't deceive yourself or me; there is time yet for three or four days: I'll come again to see you, and if you wish to have your chance you shall. I give you my word.' As he left the room I had tears in my eyes; but I was glad, too, and confident; I'd teach the false friends a lesson. Save Antonio, the blacksmith, and some strangers, and the Duke's servant, no one had come near me for more than a week. Three days afterwards I wrote to the Duke asking him to fulfill his promise, and the very next day Juan, Clemencia, and her mother all came to see me together. They all wanted to know what it meant. My name as *espada* for the next Sunday, they said, was first on the bills placarded all over Madrid, and the Duke had put underneath it— 'By special request of HM the Queen.' I said nothing but that I was going to work; and I noticed that Clemencia wouldn't meet my eyes.

"What a day that was! That Sunday I mean. The Queen was

in her box with the Duke beside her as our procession saluted them, and the great ring was crowded tier on tier, and she was in the best box I could get. But I tried not to think about her. My heart seemed to be frozen. Still I know now that I worked for her even then. When the first bull came in and the *capa* men played him, the people began to shout for me—'El Pequeño! El Pequeño! El Pequeño!'—and wouldn't let the games go on. So I limped forward in my *espada's* dress and took a *capa* from a man and challenged the bull, and he rushed at me—the honest one; I caught his look and he knew it was all right, so I threw the *capa* round me and turned my back upon him. In one flash I saw the people rise in their places, and the Duke lean over the front of the *palco*; then, as the bull hesitated and stopped they began to cheer, I handed back the *capa*, and, after bowing, went again among the *espadas*. Then the people christened me afresh—'El Cojo!' (The Cripple!)—and I had to come forward and bow again and again, and the Queen threw me a gold cigarette case. I have it still. There it is. . . . I never looked up at Clemencia, though I could see her always. She threw no rose to me that day. . . . Then the time came when I should kill the bull. I took the *muleta* in my left hand and went towards him with the sword uncovered in my right. I needed no trick. I held him with my will, and he looked up at me. 'Poor brute,' I thought, 'you are happier than I am.' And he bowed his head with the great, wondering, kindly eyes, and I struck straight through to the heart. On his knees he fell at my feet, and rolled over dead, almost without a quiver. As I put my sword in the *muleta* and turned away, the people found their voices, 'Well done, The Cripple! Well done!' When I left the ring that day I left it as the first *espada* in Spain. So the Duke said, and he knew —none better. After one more Sunday the sports were over for the year, but that second Sunday I did better than the first, and I was engaged for the next season as first *espada*, with fifty thousand *duros* salary. Forty thousand I invested as the Duke advised —I have lived on the interest ever since—the other ten thousand I kept by me.

"I had resolved never to go near Clemencia again, and I kept my resolve for weeks. One day Juan came and told me Clemencia was suffering because of my absence. He said:

" 'She's proud, you know, proud as the devil, and she won't come and see you or send to you, but she loves you. There's no doubt of that: she loves you. I know them, and I never saw a girl so gone on a man. Besides they're poor now, she and her mother; they've eaten up nearly all they had, and you're rich and could help them.'

"That made me think. I felt sure she didn't love me. That was plain enough. She hadn't even a good heart, or she would have come and cheered me up when I lay wounded—because of her obstinate folly. No! It wasn't worth while suffering any more on her account. That was clear. But if she needed me, if she were really poor? Oh, that I couldn't stand. I'd go to her. 'Are you sure?' I asked Juan, and when he said he was, I said:

" 'Then I'll visit them to-morrow.'

"And on the next day I went. Clemencia received me as usual: she was too proud to notice my long absence, but the mother wanted to know why I had kept away from them so long. From that time on the mother rather seemed to like me. I told her I was still sore—which was the truth—and I had had much to do.

" 'Some lady fallen in love with you, I suppose,' said Clemencia half scoffingly—so that I could hardly believe she had wanted to see me.

" 'No,' I answered, looking at her, 'one doesn't get love without seeking for it, sometimes not even then—when one's small and lame as I am.'

"Gradually the old relations established themselves again. But I had grown wiser, and watched her now with keen eyes as I had never done formerly. I found she had changed—in some subtle way had become different. She seemed kinder to me, but at the same time her character appeared to be even stronger than it had been. I remember noticing one peculiarity in her I had not remarked before. Her admiration of the physique of men was now keen and outspoken. When we went to the theatre (as we often did) I saw that the better-looking and more finely-formed actors had a great attraction for her. I had never noticed this in her before. In fact she had seemed to me to know nothing about virile beauty, beyond a girl's vague liking for men who were tall and strong. But now she looked at men critically. She had changed; that was certain. What was the cause? . . . I could not divine. Poor fool that I was! I didn't know then that good women seldom or never care much for mere bodily qualities in a man; the women who do are generally worthless. Now, too, she spoke well of the men of Southern Spain; when I first met her she professed to admire the women of the South, but to think little of the men. Now she admired the men, too; they were warmer-hearted, she said; had more love and passion in them, and were gentler with women than those of the North. Somehow I hoped that she referred to me, that her heart was beginning to plead for me, and I was very glad and proud, though it all seemed too good to be true.

"One day in October, when I called with Juan, we found them packing their things. They had to leave, they said, and take cheaper lodgings. Juan looked at me, and some way or other I got him to take Clemencia into another room. Then I spoke to the mother: Clemencia, I hoped, would soon be my wife; in any case I couldn't allow her to want for anything; I would bring a thousand *duros* the next day and they must not think of leaving their comfortable apartments. The mother cried and said I was good: 'God makes few such men,' and so forth. The next day I gave her the money, and it was arranged between us without saying anything to Clemencia. I remember about this time, in the early winter of that year, I began to see her faults more clearly, and I noticed that she had altered in many ways. Her temper had changed. It used to be equable though passionate. It had become uncertain and irritable. She had changed greatly. For now, she would let me kiss her without remonstrance, and sometimes almost as if she didn't notice the kiss, whereas before it used always to be a matter of importance. And when I asked her when she would marry me she would answer half-carelessly, 'Some time, I suppose,' as she used to do, but her manner was quite different. She even sighed once as she spoke. Certainly she had changed. What was the cause? I couldn't make it out, therefore I watched, not suspiciously, but she had grown a little strange to me—a sort of puzzle, since she had been so unkind when I lay wounded. And partly from this feeling, partly from my great love for her, I noticed everything. Still I urged her to marry me. I thought as soon as we were married, and she had a child to take care of and to love, it would be all right with both of us. Fool that I was!

"In April, which was fine, I remember, that year in Madrid—you know how cold it is away up there, and how keen the wind is; as the Madrileños say, 'twon't blow out a candle, but it'll kill a man'—Clemencia began to grow pale and nervous. I couldn't make her out! and so, more than ever, pity strengthening love in me, I urged her to tell me when she would marry me; and one days she turned to me, and I saw she was quite white as she said:

" 'After the season, perhaps.'

"Then I was happy, and ceased to press her. Early in May the games began—my golden time. I had grown quite strong again, and surer of myself than ever. Besides, I wanted to do something to deserve my great happiness. Therefore, on one of the first days when the Queen and the Duke and Clemencia were looking on, I killed the bull with the sword immediately after he entered the ring, and before he had been tired at all. From that day on the people seemed crazy about me. I couldn't walk in the streets without being cheered; a crowd followed me wherever I went; great nobles asked me to their houses, and their ladies made much of me. But I didn't care, for all the time Clemencia was kind, and so I was happy.

"One day suddenly she asked me why I didn't make Juan an *espada*. I told her I had offered him the first place in my cuadrilla; but he wouldn't accept it. She declared that it was natural of him to refuse when I had passed him in the race; but why didn't I go to the Duke and get him made an *espada*? I replied laughingly that the Duke didn't make men *espadas*, but God or their parents. Then her brows drew down, and she said she hadn't thought to find such jealousy in me. So I answered her seriously that I didn't believe Juan would succeed as an *espada*, or else I should do what I could to get him appointed. At once she came and put her arms on my shoulders, and said 'twas like me, and she would tell Juan; and after that I could do nothing but kiss her. A little later I asked Juan about it, and he told me he thought he could do the work at least as well as Girvalda, and if I got him the place, he would never forget my kindness. So I went to the Director and told him what I wished. At first he refused, saying Juan had no talent, he would only get killed. When I pressed him he said all the *espadas* were engaged, and made other such excuses. So at last I said I'd work no more unless he gave Juan a chance. Then he yielded after grumbling a great deal.

"Two Sundays later Juan entered the ring for the first time as an *espada*. He looked the part to perfection. Never was there a more splendid figure of a man, and he was radiant in silver and blue. His mother was in the box that day with Clemencia and her mother. Just before we all parted as the sports were about to begin Clemencia drew me on one side, and said, 'You'll see that he succeeds, won't you?' And I replied, 'Yes, of course, I will. Trust me; it'll be all right.' And it was, though I don't think it would have been, if she hadn't spoken. I remembered my promise to her, and when I saw that the bull which Juan ought to kill was vicious, I told another *espada* to kill him, and so got Juan an easy bull, which I took care to have tried out before I told him the moment had come. Juan wasn't a coward—no! but he hadn't the peculiar nerve needed for the business. The matador's spirit should rise to the danger, and Juan's didn't rise. He was white, but determined to do his best. That I could see. So I said to him, 'Go on, man! Don't lose time, or he'll get his wind again. You're all right; I shall be near you as one of your cuadrilla.' And so I was, and if I hadn't been, Juan would have come to grief. Yes, he'd have come to grief that very first day.

"Naturally enough we spent the evening together. It was a real *tertulia,* Señora Alvareda said; but Clemencia sat silent with the great, dark eyes turned in upon her thoughts, and the niece and myself were nearly as quiet, while Juan talked for every one, not forgetting himself. As he had been depressed before the trial so now he was unduly exultant, forgetting altogether, as it seemed to me, not only his nervousness but also that it had taken him two strokes to kill the bull. His first attempt was a failure, and the second one, though it brought the bull to his knees, never reached his heart. But Juan was delighted and seemed never to weary of describing the bull and how he had struck him, his mother listening to him the while adoringly. It was past midnight when we parted from our friends; and Juan, as we returned to my rooms, would talk of nothing but the salary he expected to get. I was out of sorts; he had bragged so incessantly I had scarcely got a word with Clemencia, who could hardly find time to tell me she had a bad headache. Juan would come up with me; he wanted to know whether I'd go on the morrow to the Director to get him a permanent engagement. I got rid of him, at last, by saying I was tired to death, and it would look better to let the Director come and ask for his services. So at length we parted. After he left me I sat for some time wondering at Clemencia's paleness. She was growing thin, too! And what thoughts had induced that rapt expression of face?

"Next morning I awoke late and had so much to do that I resolved to put off my visit to Clemencia till the afternoon, but in the meantime the Director spoke to me of Juan as rather a bungler, and when I defended him, agreed at last to engage him for the next four Sundays. This was a better result than I had expected, so as soon as I was free I made off to tell Juan the good news. I met his mother at the street door where she was talking with some women; she followed me into the patio saying Juan was not at home.

" 'Never mind,' I replied carelessly, 'I have good news for him, so I'll go upstairs to his room and wait.'

" 'Oh!' she said, 'you can't do that; you mustn't; Juan wouldn't like it.'

"Then I laughed outright. Juan wouldn't like it—oh no! It was amusing to say that when we had lived together like brothers for years, and had had no secrets from one another. But she persisted and grew strangely hot and excited. Then I thought to myself— there you are again; these women understand nothing. So I went away, telling her to send Juan to me as soon as he came in. At this she seemed hugely relieved, and became voluble in excuses. In fact, her manner altered so entirely that before I had gone fifty yards down the street, it forced me to wonder. Suddenly wonder changed to suspicion. Juan wasn't out! Who was with him I mustn't see?

"As I stopped involuntarily, I saw a man on the other side of the street who bowed to me. I went across and said:

" 'Friend, I am Montes, the matador. Do you own this house?'

"He answered that he did, and that every one in Madrid knew me.

"So I said, 'Lend me a room on your first-floor for an hour; *cosa de muier* (a lady's in the case), you understand.'

"At once he led me upstairs and showed me a room from the windows of which I could see the entrance to Juan's lodging. I thanked him, and when he left me I stood near the window and smoked and thought. What could it all mean? . . . Had Clemencia anything to do with Juan? She made me get him his trial as *espada*; charged me to take care of him. He was from the South, too, and she had grown to like Southern men: 'they were passionate and gentle with women.' Curses on her! Her paleness occurred to me, her fits of abstraction. As I thought, every moment fitted into its place, and what had been mysterious grew plain to me; but I wouldn't accept the evidence of reason. No! I'd wait and see. Then I'd—at once I grew quiet. But again the thoughts came—like the flies that plague the cattle in summer-time—and again I brushed them aside, and again they returned.

"Suddenly I saw Juan's mother come into the street wearing altogether too careless an expression. She looked about as haphazard as if she expected someone. After a moment or two of this she slipped back into the patio with mystery in her sudden decision and haste. Then out came a form I knew well, and, with stately, even step, looking neither to the right hand nor the left, walked down the street. It was Clemencia, as my heart had told me it would be. I should have known her anywhere even had she not—just below the window where I was watching—put back her *mantilla* with a certain proud grace of movement which I had admired a hundred times. As she moved her head to feel that the *mantilla* draped her properly I saw her face; it was drawn and set like one fighting against pain. That made me smile with pleasure.

"Five minutes later Juan swung out of the doorway in the full costume of an *espada*—he seemed to sleep in it now—with a cigarette between his teeth. Then I grew sad and pitiful. We had been such friends. I had meant only good to him always. And he was such a fool! I understood it all now; knew, as if I had been told, that the intimacy between them dated from the time when I lay suffering in bed. Thinking me useless and never having had any real affection for me, Clemencia had then followed her inclination and tried to win Juan. She had succeeded easily enough, no doubt, but not in getting him to marry her. Later, she induced me to make Juan an *espada*, hoping against hope that he'd marry her when his new position had made him rich. On the other hand he had set himself to cheat me because of the money I had given her mother, which relieved him from the necessity of helping them, and secondly, because it was only through my influence that he could hope to become an *espada*. Ignoble beasts! And then jealousy seized me as I thought of her admiration for handsome men, and at once I saw her in his arms. Forthwith pity, and sadness, and anger left me, and, as I thought of him swaggering past the window, I laughed aloud. Poor weak fools! I too, could cheat.

"He had passed out of the street. I went downstairs and thanked the landlord for his kindness to me. 'For your good nature,' I said, 'you must come and see me work from a box next Sunday. Ask for me, I won't forget.' And he thanked me with many words and said he had never missed a Sunday since he had first seen me play with the *capa* three years before. I laughed and nodded to him and went my way homewards, whither I knew Juan had gone before me.

"As I entered my room, he rose to meet me with a shadow as of doubt or fear upon him. But I laughed cheerfully, gaily enough to deceive even so finished an actor as he was, and told him the good news. 'Engaged,' I cried, slapping him on the shoulder. 'The Director engages you for four Sundays certain.' And that word 'certain' made me laugh louder still—jubilantly. Then afraid of overdoing my part, I sat quietly for some time and listened to his expressions of fatuous self-satisfaction. As he left me to go and trumpet the news from café to café, I had to choke down my contempt for him by recalling that picture, by forcing myself to see them in each other's arms. Then I grew quiet again and went to call upon my betrothed.

"She was at home and received me as usual, but with more kindness than was her wont. 'She feels a little remorse at deceiving me,' I said to myself, reading her now as if her soul were an open book. I told her of Juan's engagement and she let slip 'I wish I had known that sooner!' But I did not appear to notice anything. It amused me now to see how shallow she was and how blind I had been. And then I played with her as she had often, doubtless, played with me. 'He will go far, will Juan,' I said, 'now that he has begun—very far, in a short time.' And within me I laughed at the double meaning as she turned startled eyes upon me. And then, 'His old loves will mourn for the distance which must soon separate him from them. Oh yes, Juan will go far and leave them behind.' I saw a shade come upon her face, and therefore, added: 'But no one will grudge him his success. He's so good-looking and good-tempered, and kind and true.' And then she burst into tears, and I went to her and asked as if suspiciously, 'Why, what's the matter? Clemencia!' Amid her sobs, she told me she didn't know, but she felt upset, out of sorts, nervous: she had a headache. 'Heartache,' I laughed to myself, and bade her go and lie down; rest would do her good; I'd come again on the morrow. As I

turned to leave the room she called me back and put her arms
around my neck and asked me to be patient with her; she was
foolish, but she'd make it up to me yet. . . . And I comforted her,
the poor, shallow fool, and went away.

"In some such fashion as this the days passed; each hour—now
my eyes were opened—bringing me some new amusement; for, in
spite of their acting, I saw that none of them were happy. I knew
everything. I guessed that Juan, loving his liberty, was advising
Clemencia to make up to me, and I saw how badly she played her
part. And all this had escaped me a few days before; I laughed at
myself more contemptuously than at them. It amused me, too, to
see that Liberata had grown suspicious. She no longer trusted
Juan's protestations implicitly. Every now and then, with feminine bitterness, she thrust the knife of her own doubt and fear into
Clemencia's wound. 'Don't you think, Montes, Clemencia is getting pale and thin?' she'd ask; 'it is for love of you, you know. She
should marry soon.' And all the while she cursed me in her heart
for a fool, while I laughed to myself. The comedy was infinitely
amusing to me, for now I held the cords in my hand, and knew
I could drop the curtain and cut short the acting just when I
liked. Clemencia's mother too, would sometimes set to work to
amuse me as she went about with eyes troubled, as if anxious for
the future, and yet stomach-satisfied with the comforts of the
present. She too, thought it worth while, now and then, to befool
me, when fear came upon her—between meals. That did not
please me! When she tried to play with me, the inconceivable
stupidity of my former blind trust became a torture to me. Juan's
mother I saw but little of; yet I liked her. She was honest at least,
and deceit was difficult to her. Juan was her idol; all he did was
right in her eyes; it was not her fault that she couldn't see he was
like a poisoned well. All these days Juan was friendly to me as
usual, with scarcely a shade of the old condescension in his manner. He no longer showed envy by remarking upon my luck. Since
he himself had been tested, he seemed to give me as much respect
as his self-love could spare. Nor did he now boast, as he used to

do, of his height and strength. Once, however, on the Friday evening, I think it was, he congratulated Clemencia on my love for her, and joked about our marriage. Then I felt the time had come to drop the curtain and make an end.

"On the Saturday I went to the ring and ordered my *palco* to be filled with flowers. From there I went to the Duke of Medina Celi. He received me as always with kindness, though I looked ill, and asked me whether I felt the old wound still. 'No,' I replied, 'no, *Señor Duque*, and if I come to you now it is only to thank you once more for all your goodness to me.'

"And he said after a pause—I remember each word; for he meant well:

" 'Montes, there's something very wrong.' And then, 'Montes. One should never adore a woman; they all want a master. My hairs have grown grey in learning that. . . . A woman, you see, may look well and yet be cold-hearted and—not good. But a man would be a fool to refuse nuts because one that looked all right was hollow.'

" 'You are wise,' I said, '*Señor Duque*! and I have been foolish. I hope it may be well with you always; but wisdom and folly come to the same end at last.'

"After I left him I went to Antonio and thanked him, and gave him a letter to be opened in a week. There were three enclosures in it—one for himself, one for the mother of Juan, and one for the mother of Clemencia, and each held three thousand *duros*. As they had cheated me for money, money they should have—with my contempt. Then I went back to the ring, and as I looked up to my *palco* and saw that the front of it was one bed of white and scarlet blossoms, I smiled. "White for purity," I said, 'and scarlet for blood, a fit show!' And I went home and slept like a child.

"Next day in the ring I killed two bulls, one on his first rush, and the other after the usual play. Then another *espada* worked, and then came the turn of Juan. As the bull stood panting I looked up at the *palco*. There they all were, Clemencia with hands clasped on the flowers and fixed, dilated eyes, her mother half-asleep behind her. Next to Clemencia, the niece with flushed cheeks, and leaning on her shoulder his mother. Juan was much more nervous than he had been on the previous Sunday. As his bull came into the ring he asked me hurriedly, 'Do you think it's an easy one?' I told him carelessly that all bulls were easy, and he seemed to grow more and more nervous. When the bull was ready for him he turned to me, passing his tongue feverishly over his dry lips.

" 'You'll stand by me, won't you, Montes?'

"And I asked with a smile:

" 'Shall I stand by you as you've stood by me?'

" 'Yes, of course, we've always been friends.'

" 'I shall be as true to you as you have been to me!' I said. And I moved to his right hand and looked at the bull. It was a good one; I couldn't have picked a better. In his eyes I saw courage that would never yield and hate that would strike in the death-throe, and I exulted and held his eyes with mine, and promised him revenge. While he bowed his horns to the *muleta*, he still looked at me and I at him; and as I felt that Juan had levelled his sword, and was on the point of striking, I raised my head with a sweep to the side, as if I had been the bull; and as I swung, so the brave bull swung too. And then—then all the ring swam round with me, and yet I had heard the shouting and seen the spectators spring to their feet.

"I was in the street close to the Alvaredas's. The mother met me at the door; she was crying and the tears were running down her fat, greasy cheeks. She told me Clemencia had fainted and had been carried home, and Juan was dead—ripped open—and his mother distracted, and 'twas a pity, for he was so handsome and kind and good-natured, and her best dress was ruined, and *los toros* shouldn't be allowed, and—as I brushed past her in disgust—that Clemencia was in her room crying.

"I went upstairs and entered the room. There she sat with her elbows on the table and her hair all round her face and down her back, and her fixed eyes stared at me. As I closed the door and folded my arms and looked at her, she rose, and her stare grew wild with surprise and horror, and then, almost without moving her lips, she said:

" 'Holy Virgin! You did it! I see it in your face!'

"And my heart jumped against my arms for joy, and I said in the same slow whisper, imitating her:

" 'Yes; I did it.'

"As I spoke she sprang forward with hate in her face, and poured out a stream of loathing and contempt on me. She vomited abuse as from her very soul: I was low and base and cowardly; I was—God knows what all. And he was handsome and kind, with a face like a king. . . . And I had thought she could love me, me, the ugly, little, lame cur, while he was there. And she laughed. She'd never have let my lips touch her if it hadn't been that her mother liked me and to please him. And now I had killed him, the best friend I had. Oh, 'twas horrible! Then she struck her head with her fists and asked how God, God, God could allow me to kill a man whose finger was worth a thousand lives such as mine!

"Then I laughed and said:

" 'You mistake. You killed him. You made him an *espada*—you!'

"As I spoke her eyes grew fixed and her mouth opened, and she seemed to struggle to speak, but she only groaned—and fell face forwards on the floor.

"I turned and left the room as her mother entered it." After a long pause Montes went on:

"I heard afterwards that she died next morning in premature child-birth. I left Madrid that night and came here, where I have lived ever since, if this can be called living. . . . Yet at times now fairly content, save for one thing—Remorse! Yes!"—and the old man rose to his feet, while his great eyes blazing with passion held me—"Remorse! That I let the bull kill him.

"I should have torn his throat out with my own hands."

None of That

D. H. Lawrence

D. H. Lawrence (1885–1930) *is not generally known for his interest in bullfighting. Perhaps he was attracted by the spectacle while he was living in Mexico, away from the persecution his early novels had brought him in England—but this is mere speculation. His ability to probe human emotions is revealed in "None of That," the harsh story of a brutal Mexican matador. Few writers have revealed the underworld of bullfighting with more skill than Lawrence in this tale.*

I met Luis Colmenares in Venice, not having seen him for years. He is a Mexican exile living on the scanty remains of what was once wealth, and eking out a poor and lonely existence by being a painter. But his art is only a sedative to him. He wanders about like a lost soul, mostly in Paris or in Italy, where he can live cheaply. He is rather short, rather fat, pale, with black eyes which are always looking the other way, and a spirit the same, always averted.

"Do you know who is in Venice?" he said to me. "Cuesta! He is in the Hôtel Romano. I saw him bathing yesterday on the Lido."

There was a world of gloomy mockery in this last sentence.

"Do you mean Cuesta, the bullfighter?" I asked.

"Yes. Don't you know, he retired? Do you remember? An American woman left him a lot of money. Did you ever see him?"

"Once," said I.

"Was it before the revolution? Do you remember, he retired and bought a hacienda very cheap from one of Madero's
generals, up in Chihuahua? It was after the Carranzista, and I
was already in Europe."

"How does he look now?" I said.

"Enormously fat, like a yellow, round, small whale in the sea.
You saw him? You know he was rather short and rather fat always. I think his mother was a Mixtec Indian woman. Did you
ever know him?"

"No," said I. "Did you?"

"Yes, I knew him in the old days, when I was rich, and thought
I should be rich for ever."

He was silent, and I was afraid he had shut up for good. It was
unusual for him to be even as communicative as he had been. But
it was evident that having seen Cuesta, the toreador whose fame
once rang through Spain and through Latin America, had moved
him deeply. He was in a ferment, and could not quite contain
himself.

"But he wasn't interesting, was he?" I said. "Wasn't he just a—
bull-fighter—a brute?"

Colmenares looked at me out of his own blackness. He didn't
want to talk. Yet he had to.

"He was a brute, yes," he admitted grudgingly. "But not just
a brute. Have you seen him when he was at his best? Where did
you see him? I never liked him in Spain, he was too vain. But in
Mexico he was very good. Have you seen him play with the bull,
and play with death? He was marvellous. Do you remember him,
what he looked like?"

"Not very well," said I.

"Short, and broad, and rather fat, with rather a yellow colour,
and a pressed-in nose. But his eyes, they were marvellous, also
rather small, and yellow, and when he looked at you, so strange
and cool, you felt your inside melting. Do you know that feeling?
He looked into the last little place of you, where you keep your

courage. Do you understand? And so you felt yourself melting. Do you know what I mean?"

"More or less, perhaps," said I.

Colmenares' black eyes were fixed on my face, dilated and gleaming but not really seeing me at all. He was seeing the past. Yet a curious force streamed out of his face; one understood him by the telepathy of passion, inverted passion.

"And in the bullring, he was marvellous. He would stand with his back to the bull, and pretend to be adjusting his stocking, while the bull came charging on him. And with a little glance over his shoulder, he would make a small movement, and the bull had passed him without getting him. Then he would smile a little, and walk after it. It is marvellous that he was not killed hundreds of times, but I saw him bathing on the Lido to-day, like a fat, yellow, small whale. It is extraordinary! But I did not see his eyes. . . ."

A queer look of abstracted passion was on Colmenares' fat, pale, clean-shaven face. Perhaps the toreador had cast a spell over him, as over so many people in the old and the new world.

"It is strange that I have never seen eyes anywhere else like his. Did I tell you, they were yellow, and not like human eyes at all? They didn't look at you. I don't think they ever looked at anybody. He only looked at the little bit inside your body where you keep your courage. I don't think he could see people, any more than an animal can: I mean see them personally, as I see you and you see me. He was an animal, a marvellous animal. I have often thought, if human beings had not developed minds and speech, they would have become marvellous animals like Cuesta, with those marvellous eyes, much more marvellous than a lion's or a tiger's. Have you noticed a lion or a tiger never sees you personally? It never really looks at you. But also it is afraid to look at the last little bit of you, where your courage lives inside you. But Cuesta was not afraid. He looked straight at it, and it melted."

"And what was he like, in ordinary life?" said I.

"He did not talk, was very silent. He was not clever at all. He was not even clever enough to be a general. And he could be very brutal and disgusting. But usually he was quiet. But he was always *something*. If you were in the room with him, you always noticed him more than anybody, more than women or men, even very clever people. He was stupid, but he made you physically aware of him; like a cat in the room. I tell you, that little bit of you where you keep your courage was enchanted by him; he put over you an enchantment."

"Did he do it on purpose?"

"Well! It is hard to say. But he knew he could do it. To some people, perhaps, he could not do it. But he never saw such people. He only saw people who were in his enchantment. And of course, in the bullring, he mesmerized everybody. He could draw the natural magnetism of everybody to him—everybody. And then he was marvellous, he played with death as if it were a kitten, so quick, quick as a star, and calm as a flower, and all the time, laughing at death. It is marvellous he was never killed. But he retired very young. . . . And then suddenly it was he who killed the bull, with one hand, one stroke. He was very strong. And the bull sank down at his feet, heavy with death. The people went mad! And he just glanced at them, with his yellow eyes, in a cool, beautiful contempt, as if he were an animal that wrapped the skin of death round him. Ah, he was wonderful! And today I saw him bathing on the Lido, in an American bathing-suit with a woman. His bathing-suit was just a little more yellow than he is. . . . I have held the towel when he was being rubbed down and massaged, often. He had the body of an Indian, very smooth, with hardly any hair, and creamy-yellow. I always thought it had something childish about it, so soft. But also, it had the same mystery as his eyes, as if you could never touch it, as if, when you touched it, still it was not he. When he had no clothes on, he was naked. But it seemed he would have many, many more nakednesses before you really came to *him*. . . . Do you understand me at all? Or does it seem to you foolish?"

"It interests me," I said "And women, of course, fell for him by the thousand?"

"By the million! And they were mad because of him. Women went mad, once they felt him. It was not like Rudolph Valentino, sentimental. It was madness, like cats in the night which howl, no longer knowing whether they are on earth or in hell or in paradise. So were the women. He could have had forty beautiful women every night, and different ones each night, from the beginning of the year to the end."

"But he didn't naturally?"

"Oh, no! At first, I think, he took many women. But later, when I knew him, he took none of those that besieged him. He had two Mexican women whom he lived with, humble women, Indians. And all the others he spat at, and spoke of them with terrible, obscene language. I think he would have liked to whip them, or kill them, for pursuing him."

"Only he must enchant them when he was in the bullring," said I.

"Yes. But that was like sharpening his knife on them."

"And when he retired—he had plenty of money—how did he amuse himself?"

"He was rich, he had a big *hacienda,* and many people like slaves to work for him. He raised cattle. I think he was very proud to be *hacendado* and *patrón* of so many people, with a little army of his own. I think he was proud, living like a king. . . . I had not heard of him for years. Now, suddenly, he is in Venice with a Frenchwoman, a Frenchwoman who talks bad Spanish. . . ."

"How old is he?"

"How old? He is about fifty, or a little less."

"So young! And will you speak to him?"

"I don't know. I can't make up my mind. If I speak to him, he will think I want money."

There was a certain note of hatred now in Colmenares' voice.

"Well, why shouldn't he give you money? He is still rich, I suppose?"

"Rich, yes! He must always be rich. He has got American money. An American woman left him half a milion dollars. Did you never hear of it?"

"No. Then why shouldn't he give you money? I suppose you often gave him some, in the past?"

"Oh, that—that is *quite* the past. He will never give me any-thing—or a hundred francs, something like that! Because he is mean. Did you never hear of the American woman who left him half a million dollars, and committed suicide?"

"No. When was it?"

"It was a long time ago—about 1914, or 1913. I had already lost all my money. Her name was Ethel Cane. Did you never hear of her?"

"I don't think I did," I said, feeling it remiss not to have heard of the lady.

"Ah! You should have known her. She was extraordinary. I had known her in Paris, even before I came back to Mexico and knew Cuesta well. She was almost as extraordinary as Cuesta: one of those American women, born rich, but what we should call provincial. She didn't come from New York or Boston, but some-where else. Omaha or something. She was blonde, with thick, straight, blonde hair, and she was one of the very first to wear it short, like a Florentine page-boy. Her skin was white, and her eyes very blue, and she was not thin. At first, there seemed something childish about her—do you know that look, rather round cheeks and clear eyes, so false-innocent? Her eyes especially were warm and naïve and false-innocent, but full of light. Only sometimes they were bloodshot. Oh, she was extraordinary! It was only when I knew her better I noticed how her blonde eyebrows gathered together above her nose, in a diabolic manner. She was much too much a personality to be a lady, and she had all that terrible American energy! Ah! energy! She was a dynamo. In Paris she was married to a dapper little pink-faced American who got yellow at the gills, bilious, running after her when she would not have him. He painted pictures and wanted to be modern. She knew all the people, and had all sorts come to her, as if she kept a human menagerie. And she bought old furniture and brocades; she would go mad if she saw someone get a piece of velvet brocade with the misty bloom of years on it, that she coveted. She coveted such

things with lust, and would go into a strange sensual trance, looking at some old worm-eaten chair. And she would go mad if someone else got it, and not she: that nasty old wormy chair of the
quattrocento! Things! She was mad about 'things'. . . . But it was
only for a time. She always got tired, especially of her own en-
thusiasms.

"That was when I knew her in Paris. Then I think she divorced
that husband, and, when the revolutions in Mexico became
quieter, she came to Mexico. I think she was fascinated by the
idea of Carranza. If ever she heard of a man who seemed to have
a dramatic sort of power in him, she must know that man. It was
like her lust for brocade and old chairs and a perfect aesthetic
setting. Now it was to know the most dangerous man, especially
if he looked like a prophet or a reformer. She was a socialist also,
at this time. She no longer was in love with chairs.

"She found me again in Mexico: she knew thousands of people,
and whenever one of them might be useful to her, she remembered him. So she remembered me, and it was nothing to her that
I was now poor. I know she thought of me as 'that little Luis
Something,' but she had a certain use for me, and found, perhaps,
a certain little flavour in me. At least she asked me often to dinner, or to drive with her. She was curious, quite reckless and a
dare-devil, yet shy and awkward out of her own *milieu*. It was only
in intimacy that she was unscrupulous and dauntless as a devil
incarnate. In public, and in strange places, she was very uneasy,
like one who has a bad conscience towards society, and is afraid of
it. And for that reason she could never go out without a man to
stand between her and all the others.

"While she was in Mexico, I was that man. She soon discovered
that I was satisfactory. I would perform all the duties of a husband without demanding any of the rights. Which was what she
wanted. I think she was looking round for a remarkable and
epoch-making husband. But, of course, it would have to be a
husband who would be a fitting instrument for her remarkable
and epoch-making energy and character. She was extraordinary,

but she could only work through individuals, through others. By herself she could accomplish nothing. She lay on a sofa and mused and schemed, with the energy boiling inside her. Only when she had a group, or a few real individuals, or just one man, then she could start something, and make them all dance in a tragiocomedy, like marionettes.

"But in Mexico, men do not care for women who will make them dance like puppets. In Mexico, women must run in the dust like the Indian women, with meek little heads. American women are not very popular. Their energy, and their power to make other people do things, are not in request. The men would rather go to the devil in their own way, than be sent there by the women, with a little basket in which to bring home the goods.

"So Ethel found not a cold shoulder, but a number of square, fat backs turned to her. They didn't want her. The revolutionaries would not take any notice of her at all. They wanted no woman interfering. General Isidor Garabay danced with her, and expected her immediately to become his mistress. But, as she said, she was having *none of that*. She had a terrible way of saying 'I'm having none of that'—like hitting a mirror with a hammer. And as nobody wanted to get into trouble over her, they were having none of her.

"At first, of course, when the generals saw her white shoulders and blonde hair and innocent face, they thought at once: 'Here is a *type* for us!' They were not deceived by her innocent look. But they were deceived by what looked like helplessness. The blood would come swelling into her neck and face, her eyes would go hot, her whole figure would swell with repellent energy, and she would say something very American and very crushing, in French, or in American. None of *that*! Stop *that*!

"She, too, had a lot of power. She could send out of her body a repelling energy, to compel people to submit to her will. Men in Europe or the United States nearly always crumbled up before her. But in Mexico she had come to the wrong shop. The men were a law to themselves. While she was winning and rather lovely, with her blue eyes so full of light and her white skin glistening with energetic health, they expected her to become at once their mistress. And when they saw, very quickly, that she was having *none of that*, they turned on their heels and showed her their fat backs. Because she was clever, and remarkable, and had wonderful energy and a wonderful power for making people dance while she pulled the strings, they didn't care a bit. They, too, wanted *none of that*. They would, perhaps, have carried her off and shared her as a mistress, except for the fear of trouble with the American Government.

"So, soon, she began to be bored, and to think of returning to New York. She said that Mexico was a place without a soul and without a culture, and it had not even brain enough to be mechanically efficient. It was a city and a land of naughty little boys doing obscene little things, and one day it would learn its lesson. I told her that history is the account of a lesson which nobody ever learns, and she told me the world certainly *had* progressed. Only not in Mexico, she supposed. I asked her why she had come, then, to Mexico. And she said she had thought there was something doing, and she would like to be in it. But she found it was only naughty and mostly cowardly little boys letting off guns and doing mediocre obscenities, so she would leave them to it. I told her I supposed it was life. And she replied that since it was not good enough for her, it was not life to her.

"She said all she wanted was to live the life of the imagination and get it acted on. At the time, I thought this ridiculous. I thought she was just trying to find somebody to fall in love with. Later, I saw she was right. She had an imaginary picture of herself as an extraordinary and potent woman who would make a stupendous change in the history of man. Like Catherine of Russia, only cosmopolitan, not merely Russian. And it is true, she *was* an extraordinary woman, with tremendous power of will, and truly amazing energy, even for an American woman. She was like a locomotive-engine stoked up inside and bursting with steam, which it has to let off by rolling a lot of trucks about. But I did not see how this was to cause a change in the tide of mortal affairs. It was only a part of the hubbub of traffic. She sent the trucks bouncing against one another with a clash of buffers, and sometimes she derailed some unfortunate item of the rolling-stock. But I did not see how this was to change the history of mankind. She seemed to have arrived just a little late, as some heroes, and heroines also, today, always do.

"I wondered always, why she did not take a lover. She was a woman between thirty and forty, very healthy and full of this extraordinary energy. She saw many men, and was always drawing them out, always on the *qui vive* to start them rolling down some incline. She attracted men, in a certain way. Yet she had no lover.

"I wondered even with regard to myself. We were friends, and a great deal together. Certainly I was under her spell. I came running as soon as I thought she wanted me. I did the things she suggested I should do. Even among my own acquaintances, when I found everbody laughing at me and disliking me for being at the service of an American woman, and I tried to rebel against her, and put her in her place, as the Mexicans say—which means, to them, in bed with no clothes on—still, the moment I saw her, with a look and a word she won me round. She was very clever. She flattered me, of course. She made me feel intelligent. She drew me out. There was her cleverness. She made *me* clever. I told her all about Mexico: all my life: all my ideas of history, philosophy. I sounded awfully clever and original, to myself. And she listened with such attention, which I thought was deep interest in what I was saying. But she was waiting for something she could fasten on, so that she could 'start something.' That was her constant craving, to 'start something' But, of course, I thought she was interested in *me*.

"She would lie on a large couch that was covered with old sarapes—she began to buy them as soon as she came to Mexico—herself wrapped in a wonderful black shawl that glittered all over with brilliant birds and flowers in vivid colour, a very fine specimen of the embroidered shawls our Mexican ladies used to wear at a bullfight or in an open-air *fiesta*: and there, with her white arms glistening through the long fringe of the shawl, the old Italian jewellery rising on her white, dauntless breast, and her short, thick, blonde hair falling like yellow metal, she would draw me out, draw me out. I never talked so much in my life before or since. Always talk! And I believe I talked very well, really, really very clever. But nothing besides talk! Sometimes I stayed till after midnight. And sometimes she would snort with impatience or boredom, rather like a horse, flinging back her head and shaking that heavy blonde hair. And I think some part of her wanted me to make love to her.

"But I didn't. I couldn't. I was there, under her influence, in her power. She could draw me out in talk, marvellously. I'm sure I was very clever indeed. But any other part of me was stiff, petrified. I couldn't even touch her. I couldn't even take her hand in mine. It was a physical impossibility. When I was away from her, I could think of her and of her white, healthy body with a voluptuous shiver. I could even run to her apartment, intending to kiss her, and make her my mistress that very night. But the moment I was in her presence, it left me. I could not touch her. I was averse from touching her. Physically, for some reason, I hated her.

"And I felt within myself, it was because she was repelling me and because she was always hating men, hating all active maleness in a man. She only wanted passive maleness, and then this 'talk,' this life of the imagination, as she called it. Inside herself she seethed, and she thought it was because she wanted to be made love to, very much made love to. But it wasn't so. She seethed against all men, with repulsion. She was cruel to the body of a man. But she excited his mind, his spirit. She loved to do that. She loved to have a man hanging round like a servant. She loved to stimulate him, especially his mind. And she, too, when the man was not there, she thought she wanted him to be her lover. But when he was there, and he wanted to gather for himself that mysterious fruit of her body, she revolted against him with a fearful hate. A man must be *absolutely* her servant, and only that. That was what she meant by the life of the imagination.

"And I was her servant. Everybody jeered at me. But I said to myself, I would make her my mistress. I almost set my teeth to do it. That was when I was away from her. When I came to her, I could not even touch her. When I tried to make myself touch her, something inside me began to shudder. It was impossible . . . . And I knew it was because, with her inner body, she was repelling me, always really repelling me.

"Yet, she wanted me too. She was lonely: lonesome, she said. She was lonesome, and she would have liked to get me making love to her external self. She would even, I think, have become my mistress, and allowed me to take her sometimes for a little, miserable, humiliating moment, then quickly have got rid of me again. But I couldn't do it. Her inner body *never* wanted me. And I couldn't just be her prostitute. Because immediately she would have despised me, and insulted me if I had persisted in trying to get some satisfaction of her. I knew it. She had already had two husbands, and she was a woman who always ached to tell *all*, everything. She had told me too much. I had seen one of her American husbands. I did not choose to see myself in a similar light: or plight.

"No, she wanted to live the life of the imagination. She said, the imagination could master everything; so long, of course, as one was not shot in the head, or had an eye put out. Talking of the Mexican atrocities, and of the famous case of raped nuns, she said it was all nonsense that a woman was broken because she had been raped. She could rise above it. The imagination could rise above *anything*, that was not real organic damage. If one lived the life of the imagination, one could rise above any experience that ever happened to one. One could even commit murder, and rise above that . . . . By using the imagination, and by using cunning, a woman can justify herself in anything, even the meanest and most bad things. A woman uses her imagination on her own behalf, and she becomes more innocent to herself than an innocent child, no matter what bad things she has done."

"Men do that, too," I interrupted. "It's the modern dodge. That's why everybody today is innocent. To the imagination all things are pure, if you did them yourself."

Colmenares looked at me with quick, black eyes, to see if I were mocking him. He did not care about me and my interruptions. He was utterly absorbed in his recollections of that woman, who had made him so clever, and who made him her servant, and from whom he had never had any satisfaction.

"And then what?" I asked him. "Then did she try her hand on Cuesta?"

"Ah!" said Colmenares, rousing, and glancing at me suspiciously again. "Yes! That was what she did. And I was jealous. Though I couldn't bring myself to touch her, yet I was excruciated with jealousy, because she was interested in someone else. She was interested in someone besides myself, and my vanity suffered tortures of jealousy. Why was I such a fool? Why, even now, could I kill that fat, yellow pig Cuesta? A man is always a fool."

"How did she meet the bullfighter?" I asked. "Did you introduce him to her?"

"She went once to the bullfight, because everyone was talking about Cuesta. She did not care for such things as the bullring; she preferred the modern theatre, Duse and Reinhardt, and 'things of the imagination.' But now she was going back to New York, and she had never seen a bullfight, so she must see one. I got seats in the shade—high up, you know—and went with her.

"At first she was very disgusted, and very contemptuous, and a little bit frightened, you know, because a Mexican crowd in a bull-ring is not very charming. She was afraid of people. But she sat stubborn and sulky, like a sulky child, saying: Can't they do anything more subtle than this, to get a thrill? It's on such a low level!

"But when Cuesta at last began to play with a bull, she began to get excited. He was in pink and silver, very gorgeous, and looking very ridiculous, as usual. Till he began to play; and then there really was something marvellous in him, you know, so quick and so light and so playful—do you know? When he was playing with a bull and playing with death in the ring, he was the most playful thing I have ever seen: more playful than kittens or leopard cubs, and you know how they play; do you? Oh, marvellous! more gay and light than if they had lots of wings all over them, all wings of playing! Well, he was like that, playing with death in the ring, as if he had all kinds of gay little wings to spin him with the quickest, tiniest, most beautiful little movements, quite unexpected, like a soft leopard cub. And then at the end, when he killed the bull and the blood squirted past him, ugh! it was as if all his body laughed, and still the same soft, surprised laughter like a young thing, but more cruel than anything you can imagine. He fascinated me, but I always hated him. I would have liked to stick him as he stuck the bulls.

"I could see that Ethel was trying not to be caught by his spell. He had the most curious charm, quick and unexpected like play, you know, like leopard kittens, or slow sometimes, like tiny little bears. And yet the perfect cruelty. It was the joy in cruelty! She hated the blood and messiness and dead animals. Ethel hated all that. It was not the life of the imagination. She was very pale, and very silent. She leaned forward and hardly moved, looking white and obstinate and subdued. And Cuesta had killed three bulls before she made any sign of any sort. I did not speak to her. The fourth bull was a beauty, full of life, curling and prancing like a narcissus flower in January. He was a very special bull, brought from Spain, and not so stupid as the others. He pawed the ground and blew the breath on the ground, lowering his head. And Cuesta opened his arms to him with a little smile, but endearing, lovingly endearing, as a man might open his arms to a little maiden he really loves, but, really, for her to come to his body, his warm, open body, to come softly. So he held his arms out to the bull, with love. And that was what fascinated the women. They screamed and they fainted, longing to go into the arms of

Cuesta, against his soft, round body, that was more yearning than a fico. But the bull, of course, rushed past him, and only got two darts sticking in his shoulder. That was the love.

"Then Ethel shouted, Bravo! Bravo! and I saw that she, too, had gone mad. Even Cuesta heard her, and he stopped a moment and looked at her. He saw her leaning forward, with her short, thick hair hanging like yellow metal, and her face dead-white, and her eyes glaring to his, like a challenge. They looked at one another, for a second, and he gave a little bow, then turned away. But he was changed. He didn't play so unconsciously any more: he seemed to be thinking of something, and forgetting himself. I was afraid he would be killed; but so afraid! He seemed absent-minded, and taking risks too great. When the bull came after him over the gangway barrier, he even put his hand on its head as he vaulted back, and one horn caught his sleeve and tore it just a little. Then he seemed to be absent-mindedly looking at the tear, while the bull was almost touching him again. And the bull was mad. Cuesta was a dead man it seemed, for sure; yet he seemed to wake up and *waked* himself just out of reach. It was like an awful dream, and it seemed to last for hours. I think it must have been a long time, before the bull was killed. He killed him at last, as a man takes his mistress at last because he is almost tired of playing with her. But he liked to kill his own bull.

"Ethel was looking like death, with beads of perspiration on her face. And she called to him: 'That's enough! That's enough now! *Ya es bastante*! *Basta!*' He looked at her, and heard what she said. They were both alike there, they heard and saw in a flash. And he lifted his face, with the rather squashed nose and the yellow eyes, and he looked at her, and though he was far away, he seemed quite near. And he was smiling like a small boy. But I could see he was looking at the little place in her body, where she kept her courage. And she was trying to catch his look on her imagination, not on her naked inside body. And they both found it difficult. When he tried to look at her, she set her imagination in front of him, like a mirror they put in front of a wild dog. And when she tried to catch him in her imagination, he seemed to melt away, and was gone. So neither really had caught the other.

"But he played with two more bulls, and killed them, without even looking at her. And she went away when the people were applauding him, and did not look at him. Neither did she speak to me of him. Neither did she go to any more bullfights.

"It was Cuesta who spoke to me of her, when I met him at Clavel's house. He said to me, in his very coarse Spanish: And what about your American skirt? . . . I told him there was nothing to say about her. She was leaving for New York. So he told me to ask her if she would like to come and say goodbye to Cuesta, before she went. I said to him: But why should I mention your name to her? She has never mentioned yours to me. He made an obscene joke to me.

"And it must have been because I was thinking of him that she said that evening: Do you know Cuesta? . . . I told her I did, and she asked me what I thought of him. I told her I thought he was a marvellous beast, but he wasn't really a man. 'But he is a beast with imagination,' she said to me. 'Couldn't one get a response out of him?' I told her I didn't know, but I didn't want to try. I would leave Cuesta to the bullring. I would never dream of trying my imagination on him. She said, always ready with an answer: 'But wasn't there a marvellous *thing* in him, something quite exceptional?' I said, maybe! But so has a rattlesnake a marvellous thing in him: two things, one in his mouth, one in his tail. But I didn't want to try to get response out of a rattlesnake. She wasn't satisfied, though. She was tortured. I said to her: 'Anyhow, you are leaving on Thursday.' 'No, I've put it off,' she said. 'Till when?' 'Indefinite,' she said.

"I could tell she was tormented. She had been tormented ever since she had been to the bullfight, because she couldn't get past Cuesta. She couldn't get past him, as the Americans say. He seemed like a fat, squat, yellow-eyed demon just smiling at her, and dancing ahead of her. 'Why don't you bring him here?' she said at last, though she didn't want to say it. . . . 'But why? What

is the good of bringing him here? Would you bring a criminal
here, or a yellow scorpion?' 'I would if I wanted to find out about
it.' 'But what is there to find out about Cuesta? He is just a sort of
beast. He is less than a man.' 'Maybe he's a *schwarze Bestie*,' she
said, 'and I'm a *Blonde Bestie*. Anyway bring him.'

"I always did what she wanted me to, though I never wanted
to myself. So it was now. I went to a place where I knew Cuesta
would be, and he asked me: 'How is the blonde skirt? Has she
gone yet?' I said, 'No. Would you like to see her?' . . . He looked
at me with his yellow eyes, and that pleasant look which was really
hate undreaming. 'Did she tell you to ask me?' he said. 'No,' I
said. 'We were talking of you, and she said, bring the fabulous
animal along and let us see what he really is.' 'He is the animal
for her meat, this one,' he said, in his vulgar way. Then he pretended he wouldn't come. But I knew he would. So I said I would
call for him.

"We were going in the evening, after tea, and he was dressed to
kill, in a light French suit. We went in his car. But he didn't take
flowers or anything. Ethel was nervous and awkward, offering us
cocktails and cigarettes, and speaking French, though Cuesta
didn't understand any French at all. There was another old
American woman there, for chaperon.

"Cuesta just sat on a chair, with his knees apart and his hands
between his thighs, like an Indian. Only his hair, which was done
up in his little pigtail, and taken back from his forehead, made
him look like a woman, or a Chinaman; and his flat nose and little
eyes made him look like a Chinese idol, maybe a god or a demon,
as you please. He just sat and said nothing, and had that look on
his face which wasn't a smile, and wasn't a grimace, it was nothing.
But to me it meant rhapsodic hate.

"She asked him in French if he liked his profession, and how
long he had been doing it, and if he got a great kick out of it, and
was he a pure-blood Indian? . . . all that kind of thing. I translated
to him as short as possible, Ethel flushing with embarrassment.
He replied just as short, to me, in his coarse, flat sort of voice, as if

he knew it was mere pretence. But he looked at her, straight into her face, with that strange, far-off sort of stare, yet very vivid, taking no notice of her, yet staring right into her: as if all that she was putting forward to him was merely window-dressing, and he was just looking way in, to the marshes and the jungle in her, where she didn't even look herself. It made one feel as if there was a mountain behind her, Popocatepetl, that he was staring at, expecting a mountain-lion to spring down off a tree on the slopes of the mountain, or a snake to lean down from a bough. But the mountain was all she stood for, and the mountain-lion or the snake was her own animal self, that he was watching for, like a hunter.

"We didn't stay long, but when we left she asked him to come in whenever he liked. He wasn't really the person to have calling on one: and he knew it, as she did. But he thanked her, and hoped he would one day be able to receive her at her—meaning his— humble house in the Guadalupe Road, where everything was her own. She said: 'Why, sure, I'll come one day. I should love to.' Which he understood, and bowed himself out like some quick but lurking animal; quick as a scorpion, with silence of venom the same.

"After that he would call fairly often, at about five o'clock, but never alone, always with some other man. And he never said anything, always responded to her questions in the same short way, and always looked at her when he was speaking to the other man. He never once *spoke* to her—always spoke to his interpreter, in his flat, coarse Spanish. And he always looked at *her* when he was speaking to someone else.

"She tried every possible manner in which to touch his imagination: but never with any success. She tried the Indians, the Aztecs, the history of Mexico, politics, Don Porfirio, the bullring, love, women, Europe, America—and all in vain. All she got out of him was *Verdad!* He was utterly uninterested. He actually *had* no mental imagination. Talk was just a noise to him. The only spark she roused was when she talked of money. Then the queer half-

smile deepened on his face, and he asked his interpreter if the
Señora was very rich. To which Ethel replied she didn't really
know what he meant by rich: he must be rich himself. At which,
he asked the interpreter friend if she had more than a million
American dollars. To which she replied that perhaps she had—but
she wasn't sure. And he looked at her so strangely, even more like
a yellow scorpion about to sting.

"I asked him later, what made him put such a crude question?
Did you think of offering to marry her? 'Marry a — —?' he replied,
using an obscene expression. But I didn't know even then what he
really intended. Yet I saw he had her on his mind.

"Ethel was gradually getting into a state of tension. It was as
if something tortured her. She seemed like a woman who would
go insane. I asked her: 'Why, whatever's wrong with you?' 'I'll
tell you, Luis,' she said, 'but don't you say anything to anybody,
mind. It's Cuesta! I don't know whether I want him or not.' 'You
don't know whether he wants *you* or not,' said I. 'I can handle
that,' she said, 'if I know about myself: if I know my own mind.
But I don't. My mind says he's a nada-nada, a dumb-bell, no
brain, no imagination, no anything. But my body says he's marvellous, and he's got something I haven't got, and he's stronger than
I am, and he's more an angel or a devil than a man, and I'm too
merely human to get him—and all that, till I feel I shall just go
crazy, and take an overdose of drugs. What am I to *do* with my
body, I tell you? What am I to *do* with it? I've got to master it.
I've got to be *more* than that man. I've got to get all round him,
and past him. I've *got* to.' 'Then just take the train to New York
to-night, and forget him,' I said. 'I can't! That's side-tracking. I
won't side-track my body. I've got to get the best of it. I've got to.'
'Well,' I said, 'you're a point or two beyond me. If it's a question
of getting all round Cuesta, and getting past him, why, take the
train, and you'll forget him in a fortnight. Don't fool yourself
you're in love with the fellow.' 'I'm afraid he's stronger than I am,'
she cried out. 'And what then? He's stronger than I am, but that
doesn't prevent me sleeping. A jaguar even is stronger than I am,

and an anaconda could swallow me whole, I tell you, it's all in a day's march. There's a kind of animal called Cuesta. Well, what of it?'

"She looked at me, and I could tell I made no impression on her. She despised me. She sort of wanted to go off the deep end about something. I said to her: 'God's love, Ethel, cut out the Cuesta caprice! It's not even good acting.' But I might just as well have mewed, for all the notice she took of me.

"It was as if some dormant Popocatepetl inside her had begun to erupt. She didn't love the fellow. Yet she was in a blind kill-me-quick sort of state, neither here not there, nor hot nor cold, nor desirous nor undesirous, but just simply *insane*. In a certain kind of way, she seemed to want him. And in a very definite kind of way, she seemed *not* to want him. She was in a kind of hysterics, lost her feet altogether. I tried might and main to get her away to the United States. She'd have come sane enough, once she was there. But I thought she'd kill me, when she found I'd been trying to interfere. Oh, she was not quite in her mind, that's sure.

" 'If my body is stronger than my imagination, I shall kill myself,' she said. 'Ethel,' I said, 'people who talk of killing themselves always call a doctor if they cut their finger. What's the quarrel between your body and your imagination? Aren't they the same thing?' 'No!' she said. 'If the imagination has the body under control, you can do anything, it doesn't matter what you do, physically. If my body was under the control of my imagination, I could take Cuesta for my lover, and it would be an imaginative act. But if my body acted without my imagination, I—I'd kill myself.' 'But what do you mean by your body acting without your imagination?' I said. 'You are not a child. You've been married twice. You know what it means. You even have two children. You must have had at least several hours. If Cuesta is to be another of your lovers, I think it is deplorable, but I think it only shows you are very much like all the other women who fall in love with him. If you've fallen in love with him, your imagination has nothing to do but to accept the fact and put as many roses on the ass's head as you like.' She looked at me very solemnly, and seemed to think about it. Then she said: 'But my imagination has not fallen in love with him. He wouldn't meet me imaginatively. He's a brute. And once I start, where's it going to end? I'm afraid my body has fallen—not fallen in love with him, but fallen *for* him. It's abject! And if I can't get my body on its feet again, and either forget him or else get him to make it an imaginative act with me—I—I shall kill myself.' 'All right,' said I. 'I don't know what you are talking about, imaginative acts and unimaginative acts. The act is always the same.' 'It isn't!' she cried, furious with me. 'It is either imaginative or else it's *impossible*—to me.' Well, I just spread my hands. What could I say, or do? I simply hated her way of putting it. Imaginative act! Why, I would hate performing an imaginative act with a woman. Damn it, the act is either real, or let it alone. But now I knew why I had never even touched her, or kissed her, not once: because I couldn't stand that imaginative sort of bullying from her. It is death to a man.

"I said to Cuesta: 'Why do you go to Ethel? Why don't you stay away, and make her go back to the United States? Are you in love with her?' He was obscene, as usual. 'Am I in love with a cuttle-fish, that is all arms and eyes, and no legs or tail! That blonde is a cuttle-fish. She is an octopus, all arms and eyes and beak, and a lump of jelly.' 'Then why don't you leave her alone?' 'Even cuttle-fish is good when it's cooked in sauce,' he said 'You had much better leave her alone,' I said. 'Leave her alone yourself, my esteemed Señor,' he said to me. And I knew I had better go no further.

"She said to him one evening, when only I was there—and she said it in Spanish, direct to him: 'Why do you never come alone to see me? Why do you always come with another person? Are you afraid?' He looked at her, and his eyes never changed. But he said, in his usual flat, meaningless voice: 'It is because I cannot speak, except Spanish,' 'But we could understand one another,' she said, giving one of her little violent snorts of impatience and embarrassed rage. 'Who knows!' he replied imperturbably.

"Afterwards, he said to me: 'What does she want? She hates a man as she hates a red-hot iron. A white devil, as sacred as the communion wafer!' 'Then why don't you leave her alone?' I said. 'She is so rich,' he smiled. 'She has all the world in her thousand arms. She is as rich as God. The Archangels are poor beside her, she is so rich and so white-skinned and white-souled.' 'Then all the more, why don't you leave her alone?' But he did not answer me.

"He went alone, however, to see her. But always in the early evening. And he never stayed more than half an hour. His car, well known everywhere, waited outside: till he came out in his French-grey suit and glistening brown shoes, his hat rather on the back of his head.

"What they said to one another, I don't know. But she became always more distraught and absorbed, as if she were brooding over a single idea. I said to her: 'Why take it so seriously? Dozens of women have slept with Cuesta, and think no more of it. Why take him seriously?' 'I don't,' she said. 'I take myself seriously, that's the point.' 'Let it be the point. Go on taking yourself seriously, and leave him out of the question altogether.'

"But she was tired of my playing the wise uncle, and I was tired of her taking herself seriously. She took herself so seriously, it seemed to me she would deserve what she got, playing the fool with Cuesta. Of course she did not love him at all. She only wanted to see if she could make an impression on him, make him yield to her will. But all the impression she made on him was to make him call her a squid and an octopus and other nice things. And I could see their 'love' did not go forward at all.

" 'Have you made love to her?' I asked him. 'I have not touched the zopilote,' he said. 'I hate her bare white neck.'

"But still he went to see her: always, for a very brief call, before sundown. She asked him to come to dinner, with me. He said he could never come to dinner, nor after dinner, he was always engaged from eight o'clock in the evening onwards. She looked at him as much as to tell him she knew it was a lie and a subterfuge, but he never turned a hair. He was, she put it, utterly unimaginative: an impervious animal.

" 'You, however, come one day to your poor house in the Guadalupe Road,' he said—meaning his house. He had said it, suggestively, several times.

" 'But you are always engaged in the evening,' she said.

" 'Come, then, at night—come at eleven, when I am free,' he said, with supreme animal impudence, looking into her eyes.

" 'Do you receive calls so late?' she said, flushing with anger and embarrassment and obstinacy.

" 'At times,' he said. 'When it is very special.'

"A few days later, when I called to see her as usual, I was told she was ill, and could see no one. The next day, she was still not to be seen. She had had a dangerous nervous collapse. The third day, a friend rang me up to say, Ethel was dead.

"The thing was hushed up. But it was known she had poisoned herself. She left a note to me, in which she merely said: 'It is as I told you. Good-bye. But my testament holds good."

"In her will, she had left half her fortune to Cuesta. The will had been made some ten days before her death—and it was allowed to stand. He took the money—"

Colmenares' voice tailed off into silence.

"Her body had got the better of her imagination, after all," I said.

"It was worse than that," he said.

"How?"

He was a long time before he answered. Then he said:

"She actually went to Cuesta's house that night, way down there beyond the Volador market. She went by appointment. And there in his bedroom he handed her over to half a dozen of his bullring gang, with orders not to bruise her. . . . Yet at the inquest there were a few deep, strange bruises, and the doctors made reports. Then apparently the visit to Cuesta's house came to light, but no details were ever told. Then there was another revolution, and in the hubbub this affair was dropped. It was too shady, anyhow. Ethel had certainly encouraged Cuesta at her apartment."

"But how do you know he handed her over like that?"

"One of the men told me himself. He was shot afterwards."

The Test

Marguerite Steen

MARGUERITE STEEN (b. 1894) is the author of the bestselling The Sun Is My Undoing as well as two novels about bullfighting, Matador (1934) and Bulls of Parral (1954). This story illustrates how the young men of Spain seek to prove that they can be matadors by confronting a bull at a village capea—a kind of corrida where the animal may be plyed by anyone but is not usually killed.

At five o'clock every house had emptied itself as though by magic, save those around the square, where doors, windows, balconies, and roofs were crowded with a riotous, slightly tipsy audience that awaited the arrival of the bull. Down in the square itself a tatterdemalion mob collected, of bullfighters and would-be bullfighters, a thin, half-starved nondescript army, desperately bent on proving its valour, driven to doing so by a multitude of varying motives. For some it was the desire to show off in front of some woman; a few were serious aspirants, but of these there were not many; the bull was not to be killed, it was a mere matter of sticking a few darts, of flourishing a bit of red rag, of dodging about in a manner devoid of real skill, for the number of performers left little opportunity for studied work; some were there to test their valor with a bull that was known to be a formidable one; others for the mere love of danger itself, or from a more debased instinct still—the pleasure of seeing blood. A savage and diabolical spirit presides over the *capeas*, their tragedy is not the splendid tragedy of the corrida, but of something much lower, much more degraded, bestial and ruinous to those who take part, whether actively or as spectators.

The heat of the sun was still violent; it crimsoned the faces of those looking down into the square—mainly women and children, for a man, unless he wished to mark himself as a coward, remained at the lower windows, if not in the square itself. The walls of the square seemed to consist entirely of these faces, primitive and bestial for all their smiling. The faces down in the square were different; each one seemed thinned and sharpened by anticipation; on the faces of many was an unconscious listening look, as though they were on the alert for the footsteps of death. There was some high-pitched, unsmiling jesting, one or two drunken shouts. Don Cristobal, from his point of vantage over the church porch, roared a command to have one fellow taken out of the ring; he was so drunk that he would have made an instant victim for the bull.

There were some attempts of organisation among the various groups in the square. The aspirant bullfighters were to have their turn first; large amateur cuadrillas offered their services, and accepted their instructions as seriously as if a million pesetas hung on the result. Two of the bullfighters—one of whom had no shirt, and nothing save a pair of ragged trousers roped round his waist— were gipsies; the flat, Moorish faces were inscrutable, they stood like statues in the sun, their red cloths draped over their arms.

Tomas had the good fortune to get into one of the cuadrillas. Juan, watching from above, saw him hopping from foot to foot with excitement, flapping his old percale cape, although his usually merry face was as sober as a judge's. To Juan, who had never before witnessed a *capea*, the whole scene was utterly unreal.

He had come out of his sleep to find Tomas shaking his shoulder.

"Wake up, wake up! Don't you want to see me with old Satanas?"

As Juan grunted, turned over and sleepily rubbed his eyes, he found Tomas looking at him curiously.

"What have you done with Manuela to make her so angry with you?"

"I? I have done nothing. I've just—slept."

Tomas flung back his head and roared with laughter; then, as though in apology, smote Juan on the shoulder.

"*Hombre*, I'm afraid you're hopeless! If it is left to you, El Bailarin will never become a grandfather," he declared. His merry face grew sober. "You'll have to take care," he cautioned Juan seriously, "or people will begin to say you can't do it."

"Go to the devil," retorted Juan, who had wakened in a bad temper. But, as he followed Tomas, he was thinking: So that was what she wanted! He was guiltily aware of having missed an opportunity which might not occur again. After all that wine, it would have been easy—if he had been able to keep awake! But had she really expected him—a little girl like that?

A dull fury burned in him as he leaned over the balcony rail, looked at the scene below. The lovely dazzle and excitement of the morning had vanished; in its place was something sinister, something that took possession of Juan exactly as his former excitement had done. He scowled down at Tomas, who lifted an eager friendly face to receive his friend's encouragement.

The bull had been conveniently penned in a granary that opened on the square itself. The opening of the doors was a matter that presented much difficulty, for here were none of the pulley-and-rope arrangements you get behind the toril. Practically since daybreak the ardent citizens had been pounding on the doors, stirring up old Satanas to the anticipation of his duties. Muffled roars came once or twice from behind the doors, and in response to protracted hammering, a deadly crash and the trembling of the doors from top to bottom warned the performers of what they had to expect.

The difficulty of opening the doors lay in the fact that to get them open, two long iron staples had to be run back on either side; these had been carefully oiled, but even so they presented a problem: the slightest sound of the bars might cause an anticipatory rush of the bull, which would burst the doors open before the men in charge had time to get out of the way, and result in damage to somebody. So when Don Cristobal, who invariably presided over the ceremony, gave the signal and the bullfighters moved over to the farther side of the square, and when the trumpet blew, which was the signal to liberate old Satanas, a silence spread over the audience which was almost breathless.

All those who were not taking an active part in the bullfight were clambering out of the square, with varying degrees of haste as their age and dignity allowed them; the younger fry were scaling the trees that surrounded the square, those who were willing to pay a few centimos for the privilege were mounting the improvised tiers of the scaffolding erected behind the barricados.

Almost silently the bars slid back, the two men who manipulated them watching each other so as to time the run backward with the outward folding doors; on the face of each was terror, some of it real, much of it assumed, for your Andalusian peasant is before all things an actor, and each felt that he carried, as prologue, some of the responsibilities of the drama; each clowned his terror a little, as with a shout that echoed in the darkness of the granary, he rushed backward, dragging the door between himself and the bull.

From Tomas's description, Juan had visualised one of those bulls like houses Don Jose was fond of describing. The beast that trotted out into the sunlight was, relatively, a small one: rusty black, with a shimmer of muscle beneath the pelt; from either side of the broad forehead sprang the inimical arches of the horns, one of which, as Juan noticed, was splintered at the tip. The bull was a good fighting bull: all its weight was carried in its shoulders; its small feet were planted widely in the curling dust.

The instant the bull appeared, a burst of cheering broke out round the ring. "*Ole*, Satanas!" "*Buenos dias, toro!*" "*Huh, toro!*" "*Arre!*" Hats were waved, sticks flourished, in greeting to the bull, the upholder of the town's fame. Like many small towns, this one was too poor to allow its fighting bull to be killed. Satanas had made himself celebrated through many *capeas*; Tomas had spoken truly when he said, "He knows something, that one!"

He stood now, with reared head, thin tail quivering slightly, but otherwise still. Not for him any theatrical concessions to his audience; such cheap stuff as pawing the earth, snuffing into it, flinging up his head and sending his voice to echo round the square was for those bulls who had to make their effect and be quick about it, before the matador solved their problem once for all with the sword. It was an occasion of deadly seriousness for old Satanas; he knew exactly what was expected of him and what he meant to do; he had all his tricks pat and knew that the audience realized as much. He could take his time, and think out surprises in the brain behind that dark forehead.

The bullfighters shuffled with their feet, spread out their capes to incite; one of gipsies took a few paces forward, moving like a bunch of steel wires.

Suddenly, without giving the least warning, the bull charged. Down went his head sideways, as though with the right horn— the splintered one—he would cut the earth from corner to corner of the square. The suddenness of his opening took the bullfighters by surprise, scattered their group—several went flying towards the barricade, among the chaff of the safely bestowed audience, but the rest stood their ground, desperately inciting the bull from different points, relying on his rush to send him crashing into the stout fencing of logs around the square.

But, while they did this, Satanas executed the manoeuvre for which, among his own people, he was famous. With no apparent check in his stride, he swerved almost at right angles; down went the formidable head once more—and up—with the first victim impaled on the splintered horn.

Jesucristo! The *capea* had begun with a sensation. Old Satanas was out to-day to enhance his reputation. The hullabaloo was overwhelming. Not two minutes, hardly a minute in the ring, and he had got his first man. Juan, his own face yellow as tallow, his mouth open, the breath coming sharply, could see the face of the man who had received the *cornada*, blank with terror as he rocked up and down on the horn which had got him in the lower part of the back. *Huh, toro! Huh, toro!* The others were doing their best to make the beast fling him off, but the fearfulness and danger of the *capeas* lie in the fact that the fighters are handicapped, not only by their lack of skill and the restricted space in which they have to move, but by the freshness of the bull. There are no horses, no picadors, no banderilleros to prepare him for the act of the cape, which normally comes when his power is reduced. He is undamaged, in complete possession of all his wits and powers.

He charged down the square again, carrying his now fainting victim upon the horn. A woman screamed. Juan saw one of the gipsies rush in and seize the bull's tail, twisting it with both hands, as a washerwoman twists linen. Satanas lowered his head, the impaled man fell sprawling in the dust, which turned a bright crimson where he lay; the whole square became the scene of a monstrous scuffle as the bull pranced from one to another, now wrenching the red rag from the hands of one man and dragging it through the dust on a horn tip. There was no attempt at art in these manoeuvres; no man dared go nearer than five or six yards from the bull, and the cape work was wild, formless, and, so far as the bull was concerned, almost without effect. The wounded man was hoisted across the barricado, and died, almost at once, in the inexperienced hands of the doctor.

And suddenly the bull stood still again. The onlookers drew their breath through their teeth; they knew of old that his moments of stillness were his most ominous.

In the room at whose window Juan sat, he could hear the heavy breathing of the spectators. Manuela was among them; she did not now come near Juan, but contented herself with throwing at him looks of the most concentrated scorn and malice; it seemed to him amazing that a child's face could convey so much. He too was angry and occasionally glared back. On Manuela's farther side was a middle-aged, pregnant woman, who held her hands tightly over her distended body and stared down into the square with eyes like currants in a leaden face. A man spat across Juan's shoulder, and, by way of compensation, offered him a drink of water from an earthen crock—which, after one glance at the man's face, which was covered with a disease of the skin, he politely refused. He felt as though he had fallen into a very pit of savagery, yet something in himself responded to it. He had a fearful sense of having lost his own personality; as though being with these people, drinking their wine, sharing their food, had infected him with the same brutal spirit which seemed to be in all of them. The square and its occupants appeared to him hazed with a red mist; the forked shadows of the bullfighters took on an evil significance. The sun, beating straight into his face across the now empurpled tops of the sierras, held a savage magic. He was prepared for anything . . . anything. . . .

The gipsies were now displaying a hideous courage which would have brought scorn upon them in the formal corrida, so little relation had it to art or skill. Gradually they were working in closer to the bull; at last one had the temerity to allow the shoulder of old Satanas to jostle him, in the bull's mad rush after his companion. Juan watched Tomas darting from side to side with his ugly humped movement; working in now like the rest; anxious to prove his valour publicly. He had one or two narrow escapes, which, instead of making Juan's heart sink to the pit of his stomach, acted on him as some kind of stimulus. Two others had received unimportant wounds, and had retired covered with glory, as their garments were covered with gore. Some one executed a passable manoeuvre, and Juan, as behooved one of the aficion, applauded.

As the bull became more and more exhausted, more people poured into the ring; instigated by the shouts of the spectators, or by their own vanity, they started to take liberties with the animal, which, as the shreds of its dignity were torn from it, waxed more and more dangerous. Now it barely moved, save to make some deadly rush that ended in defeat, with the mob jeering on every side. The look in the eye of the bull was now the look of death; if he caught any one, he would finish him, but he was getting very tired.

Some tipsy dare-devil hooked the crook of his stick round the bull's horns, and a laugh went up as a toss of the powerful head splintered it. In the crowded space it was now almost impossible for the bull to avoid hitting some one; a youth of sixteen went flying through the air, and at the same moment a piercing shriek, followed by a groan, at Juan's elbow made him turn sharply. The woman on his left had been taken with her labour pains, and the rest of the women were crowding around her. Embarrassed to be present at such a scene, Juan, without thinking, threw his leg across the balcony rail.

As his feet hit the dust of the square, he realized, with a shock that drove through him, the fact that he was actually in the ring with the bull.

He could see nothing for the crowds that jostled him, that drove backwards and forwards with the movements of the bull. He felt himself shouldered aside by the supporters of a limp figure from whose fingers still hung a rag of red material. The rag dropped at Juan's feet, and his mind registered the fact that the bull had found another victim, as he bent mechanically to free his ankles of the stuff that dragged across them.

Suddenly a yell went up, and the crowd surged sideways in a mighty wave. Juan, left for a moment in an open space, saw the bull charging down on him, looking at him, and with the right horn lowered to scoop him up. His whole body seemed to go dead; his instinctive movement of flight was checked by the instantaneous remembrance that he was the son of El Bailarin. The movement that he made was purely mechanical and hereditary. Without the remotest notion of what to do, he shook out the cloak, which opened like a banner. Instead of Juan, the bull saw a great crimson cloud that fired his weary brain. He plunged for it. Icy with horror, Juan did he knew not what with the cape; he was positive afterwards that he had not achieved any of the classic manoeuvres his father had taught him. His feet were not together; he just stood and flapped his cape like a tyro. With a drugged sensation, he felt the bull's body rush past him like a gust of sultry air. He knew afterwards what he should have done, of course; he should have given the cape that flick in the opposite direction to the bull's rush, which would have checked the animal and doubled it on itself; he should have finished his *veronica*—it was a *veronica* of a sort—with the *recorte*. He had seen this done by the great matadors again and again; he could achieve it admirably himself—against the thin air. While he stood there shuddering, he felt himself flung out of the way.

It was Tomas who leapt in front of him, with cape outspread. With drained face, and a yell of anguish and despair, Tomas leapt at the bull, who was coming round again, and, using both hands, nailed the cape across his horns. The two horn tips came crackling through the rotten material, the swing of his head caught Tomas sidelong and ripped his trousers.

The dust came up towards Juan's face. The son of El Bailarin sank swooning in the arena.

"Don't tell me you fainted," said Tomas positively. "You were drunk. It would have been all right if you'd been sick, as I told you. That wine's nice, but it's bad. There's no getting away from it, it's bad. And your *veronica* was grand. It was the best of the afternoon. El Bailarin himself might have been proud of it."

The moon was up—a great flat silver disc in a sky of darkest emerald—when the boys again found themselves upon the hill track their faces set towards home.

Both were reeling with fatigue: Tomas's scratch, which he had proudly had iodized before the traditional poison had time to do its work, was deep enough to be painful and sufficiently awkwardly placed to make him limp. Their progress was slow; both were resigned to the fact that they were unlikely to make Granada before dawn of the following day.

Juan walked like one in a dream; slowly, very slowly, his own personality was returning to him, as though an evil spell were dissolving in the dews of night. All the events of the past day seemed now to him like a nightmare, from which he had awakened leaning on some one's arm, some one who had picked him, the son of El Bailarin, up from the dust of the square. No one seemed to realize that he had fainted; he realized gratefully that Tomas's heroism had drawn all attention from its object, himself. He had joined thankfully in feting Tomas, who was the hero of the day.

They had gone back to his mother's house, where the evening passed in carnival, while the mountains gulped the sun, and the sudden night brought out the lights of the town. Manuela would have nothing to do with them, but other girls would; both the boys were hustled, jostled, kissed—Tomas for his bravery; Juan because he was as handsome as an angel and the son of El Bailarin: he had also done something handsome with the cape— no one was clear what; no one particularly cared. His excitement and his rage both over, he was now stupefied, submitting himself blindly to whatever came his way. He was dragged to the hovel where the woman was, by now, delivered of her child, and made to stand godfather to a little wizened object more like a monkey than the offspring of human beings.

"Yes, that *veronica* of yours was perfect," Tomas was repeating. "Just as if you'd been inciting bulls all your life. *Hombre*, what I'd give to have a drop of matador's blood in me! Let me tell you not many bullfighters have come up against a bull like ours! You can tell that to your father, if you like."

Juan had not the least desire to mention the incident to his father, but he realized that it was his duty to do so, in order that Tomas might be suitably rewarded for his courage.

"What a pity you didn't fancy little Manuela!" said Tomas slyly. He stood still to rest his leg for a moment and laid his hand affectionately on Juan's shoulder. "*Hombre!* That would have been a day for you—if you'd fought a bull and kissed a girl! You'd have known about the two best things in the world."

A great and lonely regret penetrated Juan's whole being. Once again he had failed himself; in the crisis of such an emotion as the day had afforded him, he could surely have shown himself as much of a man as Tomas. His mean performance in the ring covered his soul with shame. He was even craven enough to accept Tomas's generous explanation of his swoon.

"Tomas," he said suddenly. "Do you know there is no such person as God?"

Tomas, a Catholic for practical purposes, looked startled.

"*Hombre!* You'll be getting yourself into trouble with Don Antonio if you talk like that."

"I mean there's no personal God," said Juan carefully. "God isn't *Him*; He's *It*."

"Have it your own way," said Tomas, wagging his head sagely. "I don't bother much about God. Now the Holy Virgin is quite another matter. When my uncle was down with bronchitis in the winter, my mother asked me to light a candle to Nuestra Senora de la Angustias for him."

"And did he get better?" asked Juan sceptically.

"Why, of course he did! She's the best Virgin that ever was for miracles. That's why they gave her her crown, isn't it? You don't get a crown like that for nothing, even if you're a Virgin."

"And do you believe in hell, and purgatory, and heaven?" asked Juan. Tomas shrugged his shoulders; he had no interest in this kind of conversation. Then his eyes twinkled.

"I heard a good tale about that the other day!" he began. "A man came into the shop the other day with a priest, and they got talking. The man said, 'I'm glad Mario Tonto is dead.' 'That's very wrong of you,' said the priest. 'Why are you glad he's dead?' 'I was owing him twenty pesetas. But I'll tell you what, Father,' he said. 'One doesn't want to quarrel with the people 'up there,' so when I die I'll tell my wife to put twenty pesetas in my coffin; then I can square it up with Mario when I meet him.' "

Behind his laughter Juan was envious of Tomas's light-hearted and practical acceptance of all matters on which he was not prepared to argue. His simple, good-natured features showed as little intellectual awareness as an animal's. It occurred to him that, all unconsciously, Tomas had managed to adapt himself to that Power of which Miguel spoke, which seemed now to be spinning him, Juan, as on a wheel. He felt so great and uncomfortable an inferiority to Tomas at that moment that it was necessary to assert his nobility by some fine gesture, such as his father might have made.

"You were a great hero to-day, Tomas," he said, a trifle grandly. "Anything might have happened but for your dressing the bull up like that. I shall not forget it."

"It was nothing—nothing at all," protested Tomas, crimson with pleasure. "A nice row I'd have got into if I'd allowed the son of El Bailarin to get hit by the bull! And any one could have done it after you'd got him all fuddled with that cape work of yours."

Deeply moved by this humility, Juan flung his arm round the shoulder of Tomas and kissed him.

"You'll be a great matador one day, Tomas," he said generously. Tomas shook a wise head.

"Not I. But you—when you make your first appearance in the ring at Madrid, perhaps you'll remember to-day, and allow me to pass you your sword."

"I'd die sooner than be a matador," said Juan violently.

The two boys stood staring at each other in the moonlight, under the black edges of the mountains.

"*Hombre*, I'd no idea you felt like that about it!" breathed Tomas. Juan laughed recklessly and bitterly now that he had given away his secret.

"Well, now you know. Now you see how it is with me," he muttered. Tomas seemed totally bereft of words; his mouth opened and closed grotesquely; he shrugged his shoulders, made a resigned gesture with his hands, and finally gripped Juan's in a clasp that hurt.

"That's bad, *hombre*. I'll say that's very bad."

The Undefeated

Ernest Hemingway

ERNEST HEMINGWAY (1898–1961) *was, and is, the single most important influence on the literature of toreo. His writings on the subject have introduced it to countless readers, and many an aficionado today owes his first appreciation to Hemingway's* Death in the Afternoon. *The short story included in this anthology is his fullest fictional portrait of a matador.*

Manuel Garcia climbed the stairs to Don Miguel Retana's office. He set down his suitcase and knocked on the door. There was no answer. Manuel, standing in the hallway, felt there was someone in the room. He felt it through the door.

"Retana," he said, listening.

There was no answer.

He's there, all right, Manuel thought.

"Retana," he said and banged the door.

"Who's there?" said someone in the office.

"Me, Manolo," Manuel said.

"What do you want?" asked the voice.

"I want to work," Manuel said.

Something in the door clicked several times and it swung open. Manuel went in, carrying his suitcase.

A little man sat behind a desk at the far side of the room. Over his head was a bull's head, stuffed by a Madrid taxidermist; on the walls were framed photographs and bullfight posters.

The little man sat looking at Manuel.

"I thought they'd killed you," he said.

Manuel knocked with his knuckles on the desk. The little man sat looking at him across the desk.

"How many corridas you had this year?" Retana asked.

"One," he answered.

"Just that one?" the little man asked.

"That's all."

"I read about it in the papers," Retana said. He leaned back in the chair and looked at Manuel.

Manuel looked up at the stuffed bull. He had seen it often before. He felt a certain family interest in it. It had killed his brother, the promising one, about nine years ago. Manuel remembered the day. There was a brass plate on the oak shield the bull's head was mounted on. Manuel could not read it, but he imagined it was in memory of his brother. Well, he had been a good kid.

The plate said: "The Bull 'Mariposa' of the Duke of Veragua, which accepted 9 varas for 7 cabballos, and caused the death of Antonio Garcia, Novillero, 27 April 1909."

Retana saw him looking at the stuffed bull's head.

"The lot the Duke sent me for Sunday will make a scandal," he said. "They're all bad in the legs. What do they say about them at the café?"

"I don't know," Manuel said. "I just got in."

"Yes," Retana said. "You still have your bag."

He looked at Manuel, leaning back behind the big desk.

"Sit down," he said. "Take off you cap."

Manuel sat down; his cap off, his face was changed. He looked pale, and his coleta pinned forward on his head, so that it would not show under the cap, gave him a strange look.

"You don't look well," Retana said.

"I just got out of the hospital," Manuel said.

"I heard they'd cut your leg off," Retana said.

"No," said Manuel. "It got all right."

Retana leaned forward across the desk and pushed a wooden box of cigarettes toward Manuel.

"Have a cigarette," he said.

"Thanks,"

Manuel lit it.

"Smoke?" he said, offering the match to Retana.

"No," Retana waved his hand. "I never smoke."

Retana watched him smoking.

"Why don't you get a job and go to work?" he said.

" I don't want to work," Manuel said. "I am a bullfighter."

"There aren't any bullfighters any more," Retana said.

"I'm a bullfighter," Manuel said.

"Yes, while you're in there," Retana said.

Manuel laughed.

Retana sat, saying nothing and looking at Manuel.

"I'll put you in a nocturnal if you want," Retana offered.

"When?" Manuel asked.

"To-morrow night."

"I don't like to substitute for anybody," Manuel said. That was the way they all got killed. That was the way Salvador got killed. He tapped with his knuckles on the table.

"It's all I've got," Retana said.

"Why don't you put me on the next week?" Manuel suggested.

"You wouldn't draw," Retana said. "All they want is Litri and Rubito and La Torre. Those kids are good."

"They'd come to see me get it," Manuel said, hopefully.

"No, they wouldn't. They don't know who you are any more."

"I've got a lot of stuff," Manuel said.

"I'm offering to put you on to-morrow night," Retana said. "You can work with young Hernandez and kill two *novillos* after the Charlots."

"Whose *novillos*?" Manuel asked.

"I don't know. Whatever stuff they've got in the corrals. What the veterinaries won't pass in the daytime."

"I don't like to substitute," Manuel said.

"You can take it or leave it," Retana said. He leaned forward

over the papers. He was no longer interested. The appeal that
Manuel had made to him for a moment when he thought of the
old days was gone. He would like to get him to substitute for
Larita because he could get him cheaply. He could get others
cheaply too. He would like to help though. Still, he had given him
the chance. It was up to him.

"How much do I get?" Manuel asked. He was still playing with
the idea of refusing. But he knew he could not refuse.

"Two hundred and fifty pesetas," Retana said. He had thought
of five hundred, but when he opened his mouth it said two hundred and fifty.

"You pay Villalta seven thousand," Manuel said.

"You're not Villalta," Retana said.

"I know it," Manuel said.

"He draws it, Manolo," Retana said in explanation.

"Sure," said Manuel. He stood up. "Give me three hundred,
Retana."

"All right," Retana agreed. He reached in the drawer for a
paper.

"Can I have fifty now?" Manuel asked.

"Sure," said Retana. He took a fifty peseta note out of his
pocketbook and laid it, spread out flat, on the table.

Manuel picked it up and put it in his pocket.

"What about a cuadrilla?" he asked.

"There's the boys that always work for me nights," Retana
said. "They're all right."

"How about picadors?" Manuel asked.

"They're not much," Retana admitted.

"I've got to have one good pic," Manuel said.

"Get him then," Retana said. "Go and get him."

"Not out of this," Manuel said. "I'm not paying for any cuadrilla out of sixty *duros*."

Retana said nothing but looked at Manuel across the big desk.

"You know I've got to have one good pic," Manuel said.

Retana said nothing but looked at Manuel from a long way off.

"It isn't right," Manuel said.

Retana was still considering him, leaning back in his chair, considering him from a long way away.

"There're the regular pics," he offered.

"I know," Manuel said. "I know your regular pics."

Retana did not smile. Manuel knew it was over.

"All I want is an even break," Manuel said reasoningly. "When I go out there I want to be able to call my shots on the bull. It only takes one good picador."

He was talking to a man who was no longer listening.

"If you want something extra," Retana said, "go and get it. There will be a regular cuadrilla out there. Bring as many of your own pics as you want. The charlotada is over by ten-thirty."

"All right," Manuel said. "If that's the way you feel about it."

"That's the way," Retana said.

"I'll see you to-morrow night," Manuel said.

"I'll be out there," Retana said.

Manuel picked up his suitcase and went out.

"Shut the door," Retana called.

Manuel looked back. Retana was sitting forward looking at some papers. Manuel pulled the door tight until it clicked.

He went down the stairs and out of the door into the hot brightness of the street. It was very hot in the street and the light on the white buildings was sudden and hard on his eyes. He walked down the shady side of the steep street toward the Puerta del Sol. The shade felt solid and cool as running water. The heat came suddenly as he crossed the intersecting streets. Manuel saw no one he knew in all the people he passed.

Just before the Puerta del Sol he turned into a café.

It was quiet in the café. There were a few men sitting at tables against the wall. At one table four men played cards. Most of the men sat against the wall smoking, empty coffee-cups and liqueur-glasses before them on the tables. Manuel went through the long room to a small room in the back. A man sat at a table in the corner asleep. Manuel sat down at one of the tables.

A waiter came in and stood beside Manuel's table.

"Have you seen Zurito?" Manuel asked him.

"He was in before lunch," the waiter answered. "He won't be back before five o'clock."

"Bring me some coffee and milk and a shot of the ordinary," Manuel said.

The waiter came back into the room carrying a tray with a big coffee-glass and a liqueur-glass on it. In his left hand he held a bottle of brandy. He swung these down to the table and a boy who had followed him poured coffee and milk into the glass from two shiny, spouted pots with long handles.

Manuel took off his cap and the waiter noticed his pig-tail pinned forward on his head. He winked at the coffee-boy as he poured out the brandy into the little glass beside Manuel's coffee. The coffee-boy looked at Manuel's pale face curiously.

"You fighting here?" asked the waiter, corking up the bottle.

"Yes," Manuel said. "To-morrow."

The waiter stood there, holding the bottle on one hip.

"You in the Charlie Chaplins?" he asked.

The coffee-boy looked away, embarrassed.

"No. In the ordinary."

"I thought they were going to have Chaves and Hernandez," the waiter said.

"No. Me and another."

"Who? Chaves or Hernandez?"

"Hernandez, I think."

"What's the matter with Chaves?"

"He got hurt."

"Where did you hear that?"

"Retana."

"Hey, Looie," the waiter called to the next room, "Chaves got cogida."

Manuel had taken the wrapper off the lumps of sugar and dropped them into his coffee. He stirred it and drank it down, sweet, hot, and warming in his empty stomach. He drank off the brandy.

"Give me another shot of that," he said to the waiter.

The waiter uncorked the bottle and poured the glass full, slopping another drink into the saucer. Another waiter had come up in front of the table. The coffee-boy was gone.

"Is Chaves hurt bad?" the second waiter asked Manuel.

"I don't know," Manuel said. "Retana didn't say."

"A hell of a lot he cares," the tall waiter said. Manuel had not seen him before. He must have just come up.

"If you stand in with Retana in this town, you're a made man," the tall waiter said. "If you aren't in with him, you might just as well go out and shoot yourself."

"You said it," the other waiter who had come in said. "You said it then."

"You're right I said it," said the tall waiter. "I know what I'm talking about when I talk about that bird."

"Look what he's done for Villalta," the first waiter said.

"And that ain't all," the tall waiter said. "Look what he's done for Marcial Lalanda. Look what he's done for Nacional."

"You said it, kid," agreed the short waiter.

Manuel looked at them, standing talking in front of his table. He had drunk his second brandy. They had forgotten about him. They were not interested in him.

"Look at that bunch of camels," the tall waiter went on.

"Did you ever see this Nacional II?"

"I seen him last Sunday, didn't I?" the original waiter said.

"He's a giraffe," the short waiter said.

"What did I tell you?" the tall waiter said. "Those are Retana's boys."

"Say, give me another shot of that," Manuel said. He had poured the brandy the waiter had slopped over in the saucer into his glass and drank it while they were talking.

The original waiter poured his glass full mechanically, and the three of them went out of the room talking.

In the far corner the man was still asleep, snoring slightly on the intaking breath, his head back against the wall.

Manuel drank his brandy. He felt sleepy himself. It was too hot to go out into the town. Besides there was nothing to do. He wanted to see Zurito. He would go to sleep while he waited. He kicked his suitcase under the table to be sure it was there. Perhaps it would be better to put it back under the seat, against the wall. He leaned down and shoved it under. Then he leaned forward on the table and went to sleep.

When he woke there was someone sitting across the table from him. It was a big man with a heavy brown face like an Indian. He had been sitting there some time. He had waved the waiter away and sat reading the paper and occasionally looking down at Manuel, asleep, his head on the table. He read the paper laboriously forming the words with his lips as he read. When it tired him he looked at Manuel. He sat heavily in the chair, his black Cordoba hat tipped forward.

Manuel sat up and looked at him.

"Hullo, Zurito," he said.

"Hello, kid," the big man said.

"I've been asleep." Manuel rubbed his forehead with the back of his fist.

"I thought maybe you were."

"How's everything?"

"Good. How is everything with you?"

"Not so good."

They were both silent. Zurito, the picador, looked at Manuel's white face. Manuel looked down at the picador's enormous hands folding the paper to put away in his pocket.

"I got a favor to ask you, Manos," Manuel said.

Manosduros was Zurito's nickname. He never heard it without thinking of his huge hands. He put them forward on the table self-consciously.

"Let's have a drink," he said.

"Sure," said Manuel.

The waiter came and went and came again. He went out of the room looking back at the two men at the table.

"What's the matter, Manolo?" Zurito set down his glass.

"Would you pic two bulls for me to-morrow night?" Manuel asked, looking at Zurito across the table.

"No," said Zurito. "I'm not pic-ing."

Manuel looked down at his glass. He had expected that answer; now he had it. Well, he had it.

"I'm sorry, Manolo, but I'm not pic-ing." Zurito looked at his hands.

"That's all right," Manuel said.

"I'm too old," Zurito said.

"I just asked you," Manuel said.

"Is it the nocturnal tomorrow?"

"That's it. I figured if I had just one good pic, I could get away with it."

"How much are you getting?"

"Three hundred pesetas."

"I get more than that for pic-ing."

"I know," said Manuel. "I didn't have any right to ask you."

"What do you keep on doing it for?" Zurito asked. "Why don't you cut off your coleta, Manolo?"

"I don't know," Manuel said.

"You're pretty near as old as I am," Zurito said.

"I don't know," Manuel said. "I got to do it. If I can fix it so that I get an even break, that's all I want. I got to stick with it, Manos."

"No you don't."

"Yes, I do. I've tried keeping away from it."

"I know how you feel. But it isn't right. You ought to get out and stay out."

"I can't do it. Besides, I've been doing good lately."

Zurito looked at his face.

"You've been in the hospital."

"But I was going great when I got hurt."

Zurito said nothing. He tipped the cognac out of his saucer into his glass.

"The papers said they never saw a better *faena*," Manuel said.
Zurito looked at him.

"You know when I get going I'm good," Manuel said.

"You're too old," the picador said.

"No," said Manuel. "You're ten years older than I am."

"With me it's different."

"I'm not too old," Manuel said.

They sat silent, Manuel watching the picador's face.

"I was going great till I got hurt," Manuel offered.

"You ought to have seen me, Manos," Manuel said, reproachfully.

"I don't want to see you," Zurito said. "It makes me nervous."

"You haven't seen me lately."

"I've seen you plenty."

Zurito looked at Manuel, avoiding his eyes.

"You ought to quit it, Manolo."

"I can't," Manuel said. "I'm going good now, I tell you."

Zurito leaned forward his hands on the table.

"Listen. I'll pic for you and if you don't go big to-morrow
night, you'll quit. See? Will you do that?"

"Sure."

Zurito leaned back, relieved.

"You got to quit," he said. "No monkey business. You got to
cut the coleta."

"I won't have to quit," Manuel said. "You watch me. I've got
the stuff."

Zurito stood up. He felt tired from arguing.

"You got to quit," he said. "I'll cut your coleta myself."

"No, you won't," Manuel said. "You won't have a chance."

Zurito called the waiter.

"Come on," said Zurito. "Come on up to the house."

Manuel reached under the seat for his suitcase. He was happy.
He knew Zurito would pic for him. He was the best picador living.
It was all simple now.

"Come on up to the house and we'll eat," Zurito said.

Manuel stood in the patio de caballos waiting for the Charlie Chaplins to be over. Zurito stood beside him. Where they stood it was dark. The high door that led into the bullring was shut. Above them they heard a shout, then another shout of laughter. Then there was silence. Manuel liked the smell of the stables above the patio de caballos. It smelt good in the dark. There was another roar from the arena and then applause, prolonged applause, going on and on.

"You ever seen these fellows?" Zurito asked, big and looming beside Manuel in the dark.

"No," Manuel said.

"They're pretty funny," Zurito said. He smiled to himself in the dark.

The high, double, tight-fitting door into the bullring swung open and Manuel saw the ring in the hard light of the arc-lights, the plaza, dark all the way around, rising high; around the edge of the ring were running and bowing two men dressed like tramps, followed by a third in the uniform of a hotel-boy who stopped and picked up the hats and canes thrown down on to the sand and tossed them back up into the darkness.

The electric light went on in the patio.

"I'll climb onto one of those ponies while you collect the kids," Zurito said.

Behind them came the jingle of the mules, coming out to go into the arena and be hitched onto the dead bull.

The members of the cuadrilla, who had been watching the burlesque from the runway between the barrera and the seats, came walking back and stood in a group talking, under the electric light in the patio. A good-looking lad in a silver-and-orange suit came up to Manuel and smiled.

"I'm Hernandez," he said and put out his hand.

Manuel took it.

"They're regular elephants we've got to-night," the boy said cheerfully.

"They're big ones with horns," Manuel agreed.

"You drew the worst lot," the boy said.

"That's all right," Manuel said. "The bigger they are, the more meat for the poor."

"Where did you get that one?" Hernandez grinned.

"That's an old one," Manuel said. "You line up your cuadrilla, so I can see what I've got."

"You've got some good kids," Hernandez said. He was very cheerful. He had been on twice before in nocturnals and was beginning to get a following in Madrid. He was happy the fight would start in a few minutes.

"Where are the pics?" Manuel asked.

"They're back in the corrals fighting about who gets the beautiful horses," Hernandez grinned.

The mules came through the gate in a rush, the whips snapping, bells jangling, and the young bull ploughing a furrow of sand.

They formed up for the paseo as soon as the bull had gone through.

Manuel and Hernandez stood in front. The youths of the cuadrillas were behind, their heavy capes furled over their arms. In black, the four picadors, mounted, holding their steel-tipped push-poles erect in the half-dark of the corral.

"It's a wonder Retana wouldn't give us enough light to see the horses by," one picador said.

"He knows we'll be happier if we don't get too good a look at these skins," another pic answered.

"This thing I'm on barely keeps me off the ground," the first picador said.

"Well, they're horses."

"Sure, they're horses."

They talked, sitting their gaunt horses in the dark.

Zurito said nothing. He had the only steady horse of the lot. He had tried him, wheeling him in the corrals, and he responded to the bit and the spurs. He had taken the bandages off his right eye and cut the strings where they had tied his ears tight shut at the base. He was a good, solid horse, solid on his legs. That was all he needed. He intended to ride him all through the corrida. He had already, since he had mounted, sitting in the half-dark in the big, quilted saddle, waiting for the paseo, pic-ed through the whole corrida in his mind. The other picadors went on talking on both sides of him. He did not hear them.

The two matadors stood together in front of their three peones, their capes furled over their left arms in the same fashion. Manuel was thinking about the three lads in back of him. They were all three Madrileños, like Hernandez, boys about nineteen. One of them, a gypsy, serious, aloof, and dark-faced, he liked the look of. He turned.

"What's your name, kid?" he asked the gypsy.

"Fuentes," the gypsy said.

"That's a good name," Manuel said.

The gypsy smiled, showing his teeth.

"You take the bull and give him a little run when he comes out," Manuel said.

"All right," the gypsy said. His face was serious. He began to think about just what he would do.

"Here she goes," Manuel said to Hernandez.

"All right. We'll go."

Heads up, swinging with the music, their right arms swinging free, they stepped out, crossing the sanded arena under the arc-lights, the cuadrillas opening out behind, the picadors riding after, behind came the bullring servants and the jingling mules. The crowd applauded Hernandez as they marched across the arena. Arrogant, swinging, they looked straight ahead as they marched.

They bowed before the president, and the procession broke up into its component parts. The bullfighters went over to the barrera and changed their heavy mantles for the light fighting capes. The mules went out. The picadors galloped jerkily around the ring, and two rode out of the gate they had come in by. The servants swept the sand smooth.

Manuel drank a glass of water poured for him by one of Retana's deputies, who was acting as his manager and sword-

handler. Hernandez came over from speaking with his own manager.

"You got a good hand, kid," Manuel complimented him.

"They like me," Hernandez said happily.

"How did the paseo go?" Manuel asked Retana's man.

"Like a wedding," said the handler. "Fine. You came out like
Joselito and Belmonte."

Zurito rode by, a bulky equestrian statue. He wheeled his horse
and faced him towards the toril on the far side of the ring where
the bull would come out. It was strange under the arc-light. He
pic-ed in the hot afternoon sun for big money. He didn't like this
arc-light business. He wished they would get started.

Manuel went up to him.

"Pic him, Manos," he said. "Cut him down to size for me."

"I'll pic him, kid," Zurito spat on the sand. "I'll make him
jump out of the ring."

"Lean on him, Manos," Manuel said.

"I'll lean on him," Zurito said. "What's holding it up?"

"He's coming now," Manuel said.

Zurito sat there, his feet in the box-stirrups, his great legs in the
buckskin-covered armor gripping the horse, the reins in his left
hand, the long pic in his right hand, his broad hat well down
over his eye to shade them from the lights, watching the distant
door of the toril. His horse's ears quivered. Zurito patted him with
his left hand.

The red door of the toril swung back and for a moment Zurito
looked into the empty passage-way far across the arena. Then the
bull came out in a rush, skidding on his four legs as he came out
under the lights, then charging in a gallop, moving softly in a fast
gallop, silent except as he woofed through wide nostrils as he
charged, glad to be free after the dark pen.

In the first row of seats, slightly bored, leaning forward to write
on the cement wall in front of his knees, the substitute bullfight
critic of *El Heraldo* scribbled: "Campagnero, Negro, 42, came
out at 90 miles an hour with plenty of gas—."

Manuel, leaning against the barrera, watching the bull, waved his hand and the gypsy ran out, trailing his cape. The bull, in full gallop, pivoted and charged the cape, his head down, his tail rising. The gypsy moved in a zig-zag and as he passed, the bull caught sight of him and abandoned the cape to charge the man. The gypsy sprinted and vaulted the red fence of the barrera as the bull struck it with his horns. He tossed into it twice with his horns, banging into the wood blindly.

The critic of *El Heraldo* lit a cigarette and tossed the match at the bull, then wrote in his notebook, "large and with enough horns to satisfy the cash customers, Campagnero showed a tendency to cut into the terrain of the bullfighters."

Manuel stepped out on the hard sand as the bull banged into the fence. Out of the corner of his eye he saw Zurito sitting the white horse close to the barrera, about a quarter of the way around the ring to the left. Manuel held the cape close in front of him, a fold in each hand, and shouted at the bull, "Huh! Huh!" The bull turned, seemed to brace against the fence as he charged in a scramble, driving into the cape as Manuel side-stepped, pivoted on his heels with the charge of the bull, and swung the cape just ahead of the horns. At the end of the cape he was facing the bull again and held the cape in the same position close in front of his body, and pivoted again as the bull recharged. Each time, as he swung, the crowd shouted.

Four times he swung with the bull, lifting the cape so it billowed full, and each time bringing the bull around to charge again. Then, at the end of the fifth swing, he held the cape against his hip and pivoted, so the cape swung out like a ballet dancer's skirt and wound the bull around himself like a belt, to step clear, leaving the bull facing Zurito on the white horse, come up and planted firm, the horse facing the bull, its ears forward, its lip nervous, Zurito, his hat over his eyes, leaning forward, the long pole sticking out before and behind in a sharp angle under his right arm, held halfway down, the triangular iron point facing the bull.

El Heraldo's second-string critic, drawing on his cigarette, his eyes on the bull, wrote: "the veteran Manolo designed a series of acceptable veronicas, ending in a very Belmontistic recorte that earned applause from the regulars, and we entered the tercio of the cavalry."

Zurito sat his horse, measuring the distance between the bull and the end of the pic. As he looked, the bull gathered himself together and charged, his eyes on the horse's chest. As he lowered his head to hook, Zurito sunk the point of the pic in the swelling hump of muscle above the bull's shoulder, leaned all his weight on the shaft, and with his left hand pulled the white horse into the air, front hoofs pawing, and swung him to the right as he pushed the bull under and through so that the horns passed safely under the horse's belly and the horse came down, quivering, the bull's tail brushing his chest as he charged the cape Hernandez offered.

Hernandez ran sideways, taking the bull out and away with the cape, toward the other picador. He fixed him with a swing of the cape, squarely facing the horse and rider, and stepped back. As the bull saw the horse he charged. The picador's lance slid along his back, and as the shock of the charge lifted the horse, the picador was already halfway out of the saddle, lifting his right leg clear as he missed with the lance and falling to the left side to keep the horse between him and the bull. The horse, lifted and gored, crashed over with the bull driving into him, the picador gave a shove with his boots against the horse and lay clear, waiting to be lifted and hauled away and put on his feet.

Manuel let the bull drive into the fallen horse, he was in no hurry, the picador was safe; besides, it did a picador like that good to worry. He'd stay on longer next time. Lousy pics! He looked across the sand at Zurito a little way out from the barrera, his horse rigid, waiting.

"Huh!" he called to the bull, "Tomar!" holding the cape in both hands so it would catch his eye. The bull detached himself from the horse and charged the cape, and Manuel, running sideways and holding the cape spread wide, stopped, swung on his heels, and brought the bull sharply around facing Zurito.

"Campagnero accepted a pair of varas for the death of one rosinante, with Hernandez and Manolo at the *quites,*" *El Heraldo's* critic wrote. "He pressed on the iron and clearly showed he was no horse-lover. The veteran Zurito resurrected some of his old stuff with the pike-pole, notably the *suerte*—."

"Olé! Olé!" the man sitting beside him shouted. The shout was lost in the roar of the crowd, and he slapped the critic on the back. The critic looked up to see Zurito, directly below him, leaning far out over his horse, the length of the pic rising in a sharp angle under his armpit, holding the pic almost by the point, bearing down with all his weight, holding the bull off, the bull pushing and driving to get at the horse, and Zurito, far out, on top of him, holding him, holding him, and slowly pivoting the horse against the pressures, so that at last he was clear. Zurito felt the moment when the horse was clear and the bull could come past, and relaxed the absolute steel lock of his resistance, and the triangular steel point of the pic ripped in the bull's hump of shoulder muscle as he tore loose to find Hernandez's cape before his muzzle. He charge blindly into the cape and the boy took him out into the open arena.

Zurito sat patting his horse and looking at the bull charging the cape that Hernandez swung for him out under the bright light while the crowd shouted.

"You see that one?" he said to Manuel.

"It was a wonder," Manuel said.

"I got him that time," Zurito said. "Look at him now."

At the conclusion of a closely turned pass of the cape the bull slid to his knees. He was up at once, but far out across the sand Manuel and Zurito saw the shine of the pumping flow of blood, smooth against the black of the bull's shoulder.

"I got him that time," Zurito said.

"He's a good bull," Manuel said.

"If they gave me another shot at him, I'd kill him," Zurito said.

"They'll change the thirds on us," Manuel said.

"Look at him now," Zurito said.

"I got to go over there," Manuel said, and started on a run for the other side of the ring, where the monos were leading a horse out by the bridle toward the bull, whacking him on the legs with rods and all, in a procession, trying to get him toward the bull, who stood, dropping his head, pawing, unable to make up his mind to charge.

Zurito, sitting his horse, walking him toward the scene, not missing any detail, scowled.

Finally the bull charged, the horse leaders ran for the barrera, the picador hit too far back, and the bull got under the horse, lifted him, threw him onto his back.

Zurito watched. The monos, in their red shirts, running out to drag the picador clear. The picador, now on his feet, swearing and flopping his arms. Manuel and Hernandez standing ready with their capes. And the bull, the great black bull, with a horse on his back, hooves dangling, the bridle caught in the horns. Black bull with a horse on his back, staggering short-legged, then arching his neck and lifting, thrusting, charging to slide the horse off, horse sliding down. Then the bull into a lunging charge at the cape Manuel spread for him.

The bull was slower now, Manuel felt. He was bleeding badly. There was a sheen of blood all down his flank.

Manuel offered him the cape again. There he came, eyes open, ugly, watching the cape. Manuel stepped to the side and raised his arms, tightening the cape ahead of the bull for the *veronica*.

Now he was facing the bull. Yes, his head was going down a little. He was carrying it lower. That was Zurito.

Manuel flopped the cape; there he comes; he side-stepped and swung in another *veronica*. He's shooting awfully accurately, he thought. He's had enough fight, so he's watching now. He's hunting now. Got his eye on me. But I always give him the cape.

He shook the cape at the bull; there he comes; he side-stepped. Awful close that time. I don't want to work that close to him.

The edge of the cape was wet with blood where it had swept along the bull's back as he went by.

All right, here's the last one.

Manuel, facing the bull, having turned with him each charge, offered the cape with his two hands. The bull looked at him. Eyes watching, horns straight forward, the bull looked at him, watching.

"Huh!" Manuel said, "Toro!" and leaning back, swung the cape forward. Here he comes. He side-stepped, swung the cape in back of him, and pivoted, so the bull followed a swirl of cape and was then left with nothing, fixed by the pass, dominated by the cape. Manuel swung the cape under his muzzle with one hand, to show the bull was fixed, and walked away.

There was no applause.

Manuel walked across the sand toward the barrera, while Zurito rode out of the ring. The trumpet had blown to change the act to the planting of the banderillos while Manuel had been working the bull. He had not consciously noticed it. The monos were spreading canvas over the two dead horses and sprinkling sawdust around them.

Manuel came up to the barrera for a drink of water. Retana's man handed him the heavy porous jug.

Fuentes, the tall gypsy, was standing holding a pair of banderillos, holding them together, slim, red sticks, fishhook points out. He looked at Manuel.

"Go on out there," Manuel said.

The gypsy trotted out. Manuel set down the jug and watched. He wiped his face with his handkerchief.

The critic of *El Heraldo* reached for the bottle of warm champagne that stood between his feet, took a drink, and finished his paragraph.

"— the aged Manolo rated no applause for a vulgar series of lances with the cape and we entered the third of the palings."

Alone in the center of the ring the bull stood, still fixed. Fuentes, tall, flat-backed, walking toward him arrogantly, his arms spread out, the two slim, red sticks, one in each hand, held by the fingers, points straight forward. Fuentes walked forward. Back of him and to one side was the peon with a cape. The bull looked at him and was no longer fixed.

His eyes watched Fuentes, now standing still. Now he leaned back, calling to him. Fuentes twitched the two banderillos and the light on the steel points caught the bull's eye.

His tail went up and he charged.

He came straight, his eyes on the man. Fuentes stood still, leaning back, the banderillos pointing forward. As the bull lowered his head to hook, Fuentes leaned backward, his arms came together and rose, his two hands touching, the banderillos two descending red lines, and leaning forward drove the points into the bull's shoulder, leaning far in over the bull's horns and pivoting on the two upright sticks, his legs tight together, his body curving to one side to let the bull pass.

"Olé!" from the crowd.

The bull was hooking wildly, jumping like a trout, all four feet off the ground. The red shafts of the banderillos tossed as he jumped.

Manuel, standing at the barrera, noticed that he hooked always to the right.

"Tell him to drop the next pair on the right," he said to the kid who started to run out to Fuentes with the new banderillos.

A heavy hand fell on his shoulder. It was Zurito.

"How do you feel, kid?" he asked.

Manuel was watching the bull.

Zurito leaned forward on the barrera, leaning the weight of his body on his arms. Manuel turned to him.

"You're going good," Zurito said.

Manuel shook his head. He had nothing to do now until the next third. The gypsy was very good with the banderillos. The bull would come to him in the next third in good shape. He was a good bull. It had all been easy up to now. The final stuff with the sword was all he worried over. He did not really worry. He did not even think about it. But standing there he had a heavy sense of apprehension. He looked out at the bull, planning his *faena*, his work with the red cloth that was to reduce the bull, to make him manageable.

The gypsy was walking out toward the bull again, walking heel-and-toe, insultingly, like a ballroom dancer, the red shafts of the banderillos twitching with his walk. The bull watched him, not fixed now, hunting him, but waiting to get close enough so he could be sure of getting him, getting the horns into him.

As Fuentes walked forward the bull charged. Fuentes ran across the quarter of a circle as the bull charged and, as he passed running backwards, stopped, swung forward, rose on his toes, arms straight out, and sunk the banderillos straight down into the tight of the big shoulder muscles as the bull missed him.

The crowd were wild about it.

"That kid won't stay in this night stuff long," Retana's man said to Zurito.

"He's good," Zurito said.

"Watch him now."

They watched.

Fuentes was standing with his back against the barrera. Two of the cuadrilla were back of him, with their capes ready to flop over the fence to distract the bull.

The bull, with his tongue out, his barrel heaving, was watching the gypsy. He thought he had him now. Back against the red planks. Only a short charge away. The bull watched him.

The gypsy bent back, drew back his arms, the banderillos pointing at the bull. He called the bull, stamped one foot. The bull was suspicious. He wanted the man. No more barbs in the shoulder.

Fuentes walked a little closer to the bull. Bent back. Called again. Somebody in the crowd shouted a warning.

"He's too damn close," Zurito said.

"Watch him," Retana's man said.

Leaning back, inciting the bull with the banderillos, Fuentes jumped, both feet off the ground. As he jumped the bull's tail rose and he charged. Fuentes came down on his toes, arms straight out, whole body arching forward, and drove the shafts straight down as he swung his body clear of the right horn.

The bull crashed into the barrera where the flopping capes had attracted his eye as he lost the man.

The gypsy came running along the barrera toward Manuel, taking the applause of the crowd. His vest was ripped where he had not quite cleared the point of the horn. He was happy about it, showing it to the spectators. He made a tour of the ring. Zurito saw him go by, smiling, pointing to his vest. He smiled.

Somebody else was planting the last pair of banderillos. Nobody was paying any attention.

Retana's man tucked a baton inside the red cloth of a *muleta*, folded the cloth over it, and handed it over to the barrera to Manuel. He reached in the leather sword-case, took out a sword and, holding it by its leather scabbard, reached it over the fence to Manuel. Manuel pulled the blade out by the red hilt and the scabbard fell limp.

He looked at Zurito. The big man saw he was sweating.

"Now you get him, kid," Zurito said.

Manuel nodded.

"He's in good shape," Zurito said.

"Just like you want him," Retana's man assured him.

Manuel nodded.

The trumpeter, up under the roof, blew for the final act, and Manuel walked across the arena toward where, up in the dark boxes, the president must be.

In the front row seats the substitute bullfight critic of *El Heraldo* took a long drink of warm champagne. He had decided it was not worth while to write a running story and would write up the corrida back in the office. What the hell was it anyway? Only a nocturnal. If he missed anything he would get it out of the morning papers. He took another drink of the champagne. He had a date at Maxim's at twelve. Who were these bullfighters anyway?

Kids and bums. A bunch of bums. He put his pad of paper in his pocket and looked over toward Manuel, standing very much alone in the ring, gesturing with his hat in a salute toward a box he could not see high up in the dark plaza. Out in the ring the bull stood quiet, looking at nothing.

"I dedicate this bull to you, Mr. President, and to the public of Madrid, the most intelligent and generous in the world," was what Manuel was saying. It was formula. He said it all. It was a little too long for nocturnal use.

He bowed at the dark, straightened, tossed his hat over his shoulder, and, carrying the *muleta* in his left hand and the sword in his right, walked out toward the bull.

Manuel walked toward the bull. The bull looked at him; his eyes were quick. Manuel noticed the way the banderillos hung down on his left shoulder and the steady sheen of blood from Zurito's pic-ing. He noticed the way the bull's feet were. As he walked forward, holding the *muleta* in his left hand and the sword in his right, he watched the bull's feet. The bull could not charge without gathering his feet together. Now he stood square on them, dully.

Manuel walked toward him, watching his feet. This was all right. He could do this. He must work to get the bull's head down, so he could go in past the horns and kill him. He did not think about the sword, not about killing the bull. He thought about one thing at a time. The coming things oppressed him, though. Walking forward, watching the bull's feet, he saw successively his eyes, his wet muzzle, and the wide, forward-pointing spread of his horns. The bull had light circles about his eyes. His eyes watched Manuel. He felt he was going to get this little one with the white face.

Standing still now and spreading the red cloth of the *muleta* with the sword, pricking the point into the cloth so that the sword, now held in his left hand, spread the red flannel like the jib of a boat, Manuel noticed the points of the bull's horns. One of them was splintered from banging against the barrera. The other was sharp as a porcupine quill. Manuel noticed while spreading the *muleta* that the white base of the horn was stained red. While he noticed these things he did not lose sight of the bull's feet. The bull watched Manuel steadily.

He's on the defensive now, Manuel thought. He's reserving himself. I've got to bring him out of that and get his head down. Always get his head down. Zurito had his head down once, but he's come back. He'll bleed when I start him going and that will bring it down.

Holding the *muleta*, with the sword in his left hand widening it in front of him, he called to the bull.

The bull looked at him.

He leaned back insultingly and shook the widespread flannel.

The bull saw the *muleta*. It was a bright scarlet under the arc-light. The bull's legs tightened.

Here he comes. Whoosh! Manuel turned as the bull came and raised the *muleta* so that it passed over the bull's horns and swept down his broad back from head to tail. The bull had gone clean up in the air with the charge. Manuel had not moved.

At the end of the pass the bull turned like a cat coming around a corner and faced Manuel.

He was on the offensive again. His heaviness was gone. Manuel noted the fresh blood shining down the back shoulder and dripping down the bull's leg. He drew the sword out of the *muleta* and held it in his right hand. The *muleta* held low down in his left hand, leaning toward the left, he called the bull. The bull's legs tightened, his eyes on the *muleta*. Here he comes, Manuel thought. Yuh!

He swung with the charge, sweeping the *muleta* ahead of the bull, his feet firm, the sword following the curve, a point of light under the arcs.

The bull recharged as the *pase natural* finished and Manuel raised the *muleta* for a *pase de pecho*. Firmly planted, the bull came by his chest under the raised *muleta*. Manuel leaned his head back to avoid the clattering banderillo shafts. The hot black body touched his chest as it passed.

Too damn close, Manuel thought. Zurito, leaning on the

barrera, spoke rapidly to the gypsy who trotted out toward Manuel
with a cape. Zurito pulled his hat down low and looked out across
the arena at Manuel.

Manuel was facing the bull again, the *muleta* held low and to
the left. The bull's head was down as he watched the *muleta*.

"If it was Belmonte doing that stuff, they'd go crazy," Retana's
man said.

Zurito said nothing. He was watching Manuel out in the center
of the arena.

"Where did the boss dig this fellow up?" Retana's man asked.

"Out of the hospital," Zurito said.

"That's where he's going damn quick," Retana's man said.

Zurito turned on him.

"Knock on that," he said, pointing to the barrera.

"I was just kidding, man," Retana's man said.

"Knock on that wood."

Retana's man leaned forward and knocked three times on the
barrera.

"Watch the *faena*," Zurito said.

Out in the center of the ring, under the lights, Manuel was
kneeling, facing the bull, and as he raised the *muleta* in both
hands the bull charged, tail up.

Manuel swung his body clear and, as the bull recharged, brought
around the *muleta* in a half-circle that pulled the bull to his knees.

"Why, that one's a great bullfighter," Retana's man said.

"No, he's not," said Zurito.

Manuel stood up and, the *muleta* in his left hand, the sword in
his right, acknowledged the applause from the dark plaza.

The bull had humped himself up from his knees and stood
waiting, his head hung low.

Zurito spoke to two of the other lads of the cuadrilla and they
ran out to stand back of Manuel with their capes. There were four
men back of him now. Hernandez had followed him since he first
came out with the *muleta*. Fuentes stood watching, his cape held
against his body, tall in repose, watching lazy-eyed. Now the two

came up. Hernandez motioned them to stand one at each side. Manuel stood alone, facing the bull.

Manuel waved back the men with the capes. Stepping back cautiously, they saw his face was white and sweating.

Didn't they know enough to keep back? Did they want to catch the bull's eye with the capes after he was fixed and ready? He had enough to worry about without that kind of thing.

The bull was standing, his four feet square, looking at the *muleta.* Manuel furled the *muleta* in his left hand. The bull's eyes watched it. His body was heavy on his feet. He carried his head low, but not too low.

Manuel lifted the *muleta* at him. The bull did not move. Only his eyes watched.

He's all lead, Manuel thought. He's all square. He's framed right. He'll take it.

He thought in bullfight terms. Sometimes he had a thought and the particular piece of slang would not come into his mind and he could not realize the thought. His instincts and knowledge worked automatically, and his brain worked slowly and in words. He knew all about bulls. He did not have to think about them. He just did the right thing. His eyes noted things and his body performed the necessary measures without thought. If he thought about it, he would be gone.

Now, facing the bull, he was conscious of many things at the same time. There were the horns, the one splintered, the other smoothly shrap, the need to profile himself toward the left horn, lance himself short and straight, lower the *muleta* so the bull would follow it, and, going in over the horns, put the sword all the way into a little spot about as big as a five-peseta piece straight in back of the neck, between the sharp pitch of the bull's shoulders. He must do all this, and must then come out from between the horns. He was conscious he must do all this, but his only thought was in words: "Corto y derecho."

"Corto y derecho," he thought, furling the *muleta.* Short and straight. Corto y derecho, he drew the sword out of the *muleta,* profiled on the splintered left horn, dropped the *muleta* across his body, so his right hand with the sword on the level with his eye made the sign of the cross, and, rising on his toes, sighted along the dipping blade of the sword at the spot high up between the bull's shoulders.

Corto y derecho, he lanced himself on the bull.

There was a shock, and he felt himself go up in the air. He pushed on the sword as he went up and over, and it flew out of his hand. He hit the ground and the bull was on him. Manuel, lying on the ground, kicked at the bull's muzzle with his slippered feet. Kicking, kicking, the bull after him, missing him in his excitement, bumping him with his head, driving the horns into the sand. Kicking like a man keeping a ball in the air, Manuel kept the bull from getting a clean thrust at him.

Manuel felt the wind on his back from the capes flopping at the bull, and then the bull was gone, gone over him in a rush. Dark, as his belly went over. Not even stepped on.

Manuel stood up and picked up the *muleta*. Fuentes handed him the sword. It was bent where it had struck the shoulder-blade. Manuel straightened it on his knee and ran toward the bull, standing now beside one of the dead horses. As he ran, his jacket flopped where it had been ripped under the armpit.

"Get him out of there," Manuel shouted to the gypsy. The bull had smelled the blood of the dead horse and ripped into the canvas cover with his horns. He charged Fuentes's cape, with the canvas hanging from his splintered horn, and the crowd laughed. Out in the ring, he tossed his head to rid himself of the canvas. Hernandez, running up from behind him, grabbed the end of the canvas and neatly lifted it off the horn.

The bull followed it in a half-charge and stopped still. He was on the defensive again. Manuel was walking toward him with the sword and *muleta*. Manuel swung the *muleta* before him. The bull would not charge.

Manuel profiled toward the bull, sighting along the dipping blade of the sword. The bull was motionless, seemingly dead on his feet, incapable of another charge.

Manuel rose to his toes, sighting along the steel, and charged.

Again there was the shock and he felt himself being borne back in a rush, to strike hard on the sand. There was no chance of kicking this time. The bull was on top of him. Manuel lay as though dead, his head on his arms, and the bull bumped him. Bumped his back, bumped his face in the sand. He felt the horn go into the sand between his folded arms. The bull hit him in the small of the back. His face drove into the sand. The horn drove through one of his sleeves and the bull ripped it off. Manuel was tossed clear and the bull followed the capes.

Manuel got up, found the sword and *muleta*, tried the point of the sword with his thumb, and then ran toward the barrera for a new sword.

Retana's man handed him the sword over the edge of the barrera.

"Wipe off your face," he said.

Manuel, running again toward the bull, wiped his bloody face with his handkerchief. He had not seen Zurito. Where was Zurito?

The cuadrilla had stepped away from the bull and waited with their capes. The bull stood, heavy and dull again after the action.

Manuel walked toward him with the *muleta*. He stopped and shook it. The bull did not respond. He passed it right and left, left and right before the bull's muzzle. The bull's eyes watched it and turned with the swing, but he would not charge. He was waiting for Manuel.

Manuel was worried. There was nothing to do but go in. Corto y derecho. He profiled close to the bull, crossed the *muleta* in front of his body and charged. As he pushed in the sword, he jerked his body to the left of the horn. The bull passed him and the sword shot up in the air, twinkling under the arc-lights, to fall red-hilted on the sand.

Manuel ran over and picked it up. It was bent and he straightened it over his knee.

As he came running toward the bull, fixed again now, he passed Hernandez standing with his cape.

"He's all bone," the boy said encouragingly.

Manuel nodded, wiping his face. He put the bloody handkerchief in his pocket.

There was the bull. He was close to the barrera now. Damn him.
Maybe he was all bone. Maybe there was not any place for the
sword to go in. The hell there wasn't! He'd show them.

He tried a pass with the *muleta* and the bull did not move.
Manuel chopped the *muleta* back and forth in front of the bull.
Nothing doing.

He furled the *muleta*, drew the sword out, profiled and drove
in on the bull. He felt the sword buckle as he shoved it in, leaning
his weight on it, and then it shot in the air, end-over-ending into
the crowd. Manuel had jerked clear as the sword jumped.

The first cushions thrown down out of the dark missed him.
Then one hit him in the face, his bloody face looking toward the
crowd. They were coming down fast. Spotting the sand. Somebody
threw an empty champagne bottle from close range. It hit Manuel
on the foot. He stood there watching the dark, where the things
were coming from. Then something whished through the air and
struck by him. Manuel leaned over and picked it up. It was his
sword. He straightened it over his knee and gestured with it to the
crowd.

"Thank you," he said. "Thank you."

Oh, the dirty bastards! Dirty bastards! Oh, the lousy, dirty
bastards! He kicked into a cushion as he ran.

There was the bull. The same as ever. All right you dirty, lousy
bastard!

Manuel passed the *muleta* in front of the bull's black muzzle.
Nothing doing.

You won't. All right. He stepped close and jammed the sharp
peak of the *muleta* into the bull's damp muzzle.

The bull was on him as he jumped back and as he tripped on a
cushion he felt the horn go into him, into his side. He grabbed
the horn with his two hands and rode backward, holding right on
to the place. The bull tossed him and he was clear. He lay still. It
was all right. The bull was gone.

He got up coughing and feeling broken and gone. The dirty bastards!

"Give me the sword," he shouted. "Give me the stuff."

Fuentes came up with the *muleta* and the sword.

Hernandez put his arm around him.

"Go on to the infirmary, man," he said. "Don't be a damn fool."

"Get away from me," Manuel said. "Get to hell away from me."

He twisted free. Hernandez shrugged his shoulders. Manuel ran toward the bull.

There was the bull standing, heavy, firmly planted.

All right, you bastard! Manuel drew the sword out of the *muleta*, sighted with the same movement, and flung himself onto the bull. He felt the sword go in all the way. Right up to the guard. Four fingers and his thumb into the bull. The blood was hot on his knuckles, and he was on top of the bull.

The bull lurched with him as he lay on, and seemed to sink; then he was standing clear. He looked at the bull going down slowly over on his side, then suddenly four feet in the air.

Then he gestured at the crowd, his hand warm from the bull blood.

All right, you bastards! He wanted to say something, but he started to cough. It was hot and choking. He looked down for the *muleta*. He must go over and salute the president. President hell! He was sitting down looking at something. It was the bull. His four feet up. Thick tongue out. Things crawling around on his belly and under his legs. Crawling where the hair was thin. Dead bull. To hell with the bull! To hell with them all! He started to get to his feet and commenced to cough. He sat down again, coughing. Somebody came and pushed him up.

They carried him across the ring to the infirmary, running with him across the sand, standing blocked at the gate as the mules came in, then around under the dark passageway, men grunting as they took him up the stairway, and then laid him down.

The doctor and two men in white were waiting for him. They laid him out on the table. They were cutting away his shirt.

Manuel felt tired. His whole chest felt scalding inside. He started to cough and they held something to his mouth. Everybody was very busy.

There was an electric light in his eyes. He shut his eyes.

He heard someone coming very heavily up the stairs. Then he did not hear it. Then he heard a noise far off. That of the crowd. Well, somebody would have to kill his other bull. They had cut away all his shirt. The doctor smiled at him. There was Retana.

"Hello, Retana!" Manuel said. He could not hear his voice.

Retana smiled at him and said something. Manuel could not hear it.

Zurito stood beside the table, bending over where the doctor was working. He was in his picador clothes, without his hat.

Zurito said something to him. Manuel could not hear it. Zurito was speaking to Retana. One of the men in white smiled and handed Retana a pair of scissors. Retana gave them to Zurito. Zurito said something to Manuel. He could not hear it.

To hell with this operating table! He'd been on plenty of operating tables before. He was not going to die. There would be a priest if he was going to die.

Zurito was saying something to him. Holding up the scissors.

That was it. They were going to cut off his coleta. They were going to cut off his pigtail.

Manuel sat up on the operating table. The doctor stepped back, angry. Someone grabbed him and held him.

"You couldn't do a thing like that, Manos," he said.

He heard suddenly, clearly, Zurito's voice.

"That's all right," Zurito said. "I won't do it. I was joking."

"I was going good," Manuel said. "I didn't have any luck. That was all."

Manuel lay back. They had put something over his face. It was all familiar. He inhaled deeply. He felt very tired. He was very, very tired. They took the thing away from his face.

"I was going good," Manuel said weakly. "I was going great."

Retana looked at Zurito and started for the door.

"I'll stay here with him," Zurito said.

Retana shrugged his shoulders.

Manuel opened his eyes and looked at Zurito.

"Wasn't I going good, Manos?" he asked, for confirmation.

"Sure," said Zurito. "You were going great."

The doctor's asistant put the cone over Manuel's face and he inhaled deeply. Zurito stood awkwardly, watching.

The Visitors

John Masters

JOHN MASTERS (b. 1915) is a keen student of tauromachia, and
he defends it strongly against attack, saying that he would
much rather view a corrida than a football match. "It is easy
to explain what happens in a corrida de toros—a bullfight—
but there is no way of explaining what a bullfight will mean
to you, for the experience is strictly personal. It only comes
directly, through the eyes, the ears, the nose, in the blood and
dust of the bullring. The message, whether of disgust or ex-
hilaration, of shame, or pride, goes direct to the bowels, and is
not subject to the rules of philosophy."

For the last two hundred yards they had been moving in
jerks, and stops, a few feet at a time. The people surged across the
road in front of them, and small boys darted under the wheels,
shouting and waving. Bill glanced at the temperature gauge and
stopped the car. It was hot, under a lowering grey sky.

The crowd surged past, so close packed now that the men
and women and ragged boys forming it had lost their separate
entities. Bill slid out from behind the wheel and struggled around
to open the door for Kit. The sound broke over him in waves, and
for a moment he felt like getting back into the big American car,
where he'd be protected by the tinted safety glass and shiny metal
and polished chrome. The Ford looked enormous, jammed in
there against the dusty kerb between two little European bugs.

Catherine Fremantle and Master Sergeant Olmbacher got
out after him, and the three of them joined the crowd surging
slowly down towards the bullring. Olmbacher gave Bill the tickets.

Bill looked at them and shouted, "Sergeant, what does
sombra mean?"

"Shade," Kit answered impatiently, before Olmbacher could speak.

The dust floated about them in a yellowish haze. The bullring loomed ahead over the heads of the shuffling crowd. It seemed to be like a football stadium, but there were two tiers or arches running all the way round, and it was a dusty, ochre colour, like the landscape beyond, and it was made of small bricks. Two flags hung limp on staffs above the main gate, one the national red and yellow of Spain, the other white with the shield of this city of Medina Lejo emblazoned on it.

The shape of the arches was Moorish, Oriental. Bill smelled blood in the dust. The bulls would die under his eyes, blood pouring from their mouths, their backs a bloody pulp of broken skin and torn flesh. He shouldn't have given her a carnation to wear at her shoulder. This was not a football game.

But she said she wanted to find out, that she *had* to find out. She said you had to find out about everything.

On the left now there was barren earth, and then the Milagro River, and low cliffs on the far bank. On the right—more bare earth, rising to stark, sun-baked hills, the same colour as the bullring. Behind, the street ran back between the dusty maples and the tenement buildings towards the sudden brown cliffs of the cathedral, and the hanging golden dome, all shimmering in the moving haze of the July afternoon. On top of the golden dome the glittering cross of steel was shaped like a sword.

In front of the cathedral was the big Plaza San Marco, and in the middle of the Plaza there was a huge bronze statue group on a high stone platform. The statue showed the saint, San Marco, dressed as a Roman soldier, kneeling, holding up his short sword like a crucifix. Standing beside him with head raised and body tensed was a huge bull. The bull had an enormous pair of testicles, almost twice life-size.

All that was outside the cathedral, and the people were coming from there to here to see the bullfight, and all this was something else that Kit kept saying she had to find out about, for the Spanish were truly devout and the statue was truly indecent; and the

Spanish were truly kind, and they were going to the bullfight.

Close to the bullring the crowd had become denser than ever as it funnelled slowly towards the high entrance. Sergeant Olmbacher took out his handkerchief and mopped his forehead. He grinned down at Kit—"Butterflies in the stomach?" She shook her head, and he said seriously, "It can be pretty unpleasant."

Bill yelled, "What got you so interested in bullfighting?"

The sergeant said, "I don't know, really. Unless it was to find out what makes the Spanish tick . . . since I was going to spend two years here."

Bill looked curiously at him. He was pale-skinned, blue-eyed, his thick, fair hair crew cut; a master sergeant and a master mechanic. Everyone on the base knew that Pete Olmbacher understood the working of machines. It was vaguely surprising, as Colonel Lindquist had hinted yesterday, to find him also delving into the working of people, especially of foreigners as strange to his character as Spaniards.

"Cold water! Lemonade! Eye-shades!" the vendors screamed.

They were at the entrance, the curved brick wall towering up directly over them. The shouting and the calling became hollow as they went in under the great arch. They passed out of the wide tunnel and into the arena. The reverberating sound fell back and Bill stopped involuntarily, wondering, where has it gone, everything, the noise, the crowd, the people? The stone tiers ran round in pale ochre rings, sweeping down in gradual steps to the circle of grey sand. The crowd was shuffling outwards along the stone banks, thinning again into individuals as they went to their places. The cries of the vendors drifted up, thin and dispersed, to the low, glaring overcast.

The circle of sand was surrounded by a barrier of thick wood, five feet high. Several narrow openings had been cut in the barrier, each guarded by a small outer barrier, so that a man, but nothing larger, could slip in and out. The front row of seats, in which the three of them sat, was some feet back from the barrier, and also higher, so that they were looking down into a narrow passage that ran the whole way around the ring. Two great arched entrances, guarded by gates, tunnelled under the stands into the arena, and close by to Kit's right there were two lower gates, heavily barred. Today there was no direct sunlight, and so no shade. The heat and the glare fell evenly everywhere.

Sergeant Olmbacher leaned across. ". . . That box up there, with the flags, is allotted to the president of the corrida. The wooden fence round the ring is called the *barrera*, and the passage down there is the *callejón*. . . ."

"*Perdóneme.*"

Bill looked around. Olmbacher was already on his feet, his knees pressed back against the stone platform on which they were sitting. Two women were edging past, heading for the vacant seats on Bill's right. The one in front was plump and middle-aged, dressed in black, wearing very high heels and dark glasses, her smoothed black hair streaked with grey. Behind her was a girl of Kit's age— slight but big-bosomed, dressed in a cool cotton print with white shoes. She carried the inevitable dark glasses in her hand and her eyes were dark, full, and deep. The two women passed, and the proud, fine curve of their noses and the straight dark lines of their eyebrows showed unmistakably that they were mother and daughter. They sank on to the stone next to Bill, the younger nearest to him, and the obsequious old attendant passed cushions along to them, cap in hand.

The tempo of preparation increased everywhere. An old high-wheeled wooden cart, drawn by two horses and carrying two huge barrels, ambled around the arena in concentric circles, water dripping unevenly from a steel cross-pipe under the tail-gate. The crowd came in faster, moving steadily down from the arches of the upper tier, streaming in through the entrance tunnels. The band began to play brass, martial music. Bill lit a cigarette, leaned over the broad wooden rail in front of them and peered down into the narrow circular passage, the callejón. There were men in business suits down there, smoking cigars, and talking to each other with their heads close, like men one saw in the theatre intervals in New York, or outside the little jewellery stores off Fifth Avenue in the lunch break; a big, coarse, blue-jowled policeman in a cheap grey cotton uniform with a red band round his hat, his belt sagging under his paunch from the weight of the pistol in its holster; two men in faded blue, meat hooks hanging from their belts and a motley of black and red and pink stains and splashes all over blouse and trousers.

"My God, look at those guys," Bill said suddenly. "That's blood on them, caked on. They can't have washed those clothes for a year."

Kit shook her head impatiently. She was in sulky mood today, he thought, ready to bite his head off at the slightest provocation, or without any. He returned to his study of the callejón.

There were men in white with red sashes, black berets and white sneakers down there, long switches in their hands; and another Broadway character, a real sharp cat, in a loud suit and pointed blue suède shoes. Olmbacher told him the man was an apoderado, a matador's agent.

A sudden stir of movement ran around the arena. The murmuring of the crowd voice checked, and then started again all together, a little louder.

From high in the stands a trumpet blew a slow, high call. The water-cart had gone, the circle of sand was empty. Across the arena three men struggled to open the tall gates of an entrance. The procession of the bullfighters entered the ring, three abreast. Olmbacher said, "The matadors are in the front row—Manrique on the right, in blue, Muralla on the left, in gold, Aguirre in the centre in black. Their clothes are called suits of lights."

Bill heard Kit repeating the names under her breath—"Manrique, Muralla, Aguirre."

Behind the matadors marched more men in brocade, then mounted men wearing Sancho Panza felt hats with a black bobble on one side, and long spears held upright, and armour on one leg; then the men in the red and white; and the mule team, the empty trace dragging in the sand behind them, red plumes bobbing on their heads, the men with whips walking beside them.

Bill lit another cigarette. Kit held out her hand and he gave her one and lit it for her. The matadors walked in a strange and insolent manner, stiff-legged, with slow and deliberate paces. The band played and the brilliant colours crossed the sand slowly. Under the president's box, they stopped. The matadors bowed slightly, not looking up, and lifted their hands to their heads; but they did not take off their winged black hats, only pressed them down more firmly on their heads. Then they all turned, insolent as ever. The horsemen left the ring, and the mule team.

The matadors and their peons came towards where they sat, fanning out a little—Manrique in blue to the right, Muralla to the left and Aguirre straight towards them, in black.

Directly below them Aguirre began to unwind the gorgeous parade cape that had been bound over his shoulder and under his arm. He was a slender, narrow-hipped man, very Spanish-looking, with a long upper lip and a long, dark, sad face, like those Bill had seen in a hundred portraits in the Prado—rather big ears, deep gashes in the skin from the sides of his nose to the corners of his lips. With a hint of a smile and a small bow he threw the dress cape across the callejón towards the women on Bill's right. The young one caught it, smiling, and began to arrange it over the rail in front of her, spreading it out so that the brilliant colours showed to the fullest advantage. She might be his girl friend, Bill thought, or perhaps his wife—if bullfighters ever got married. Kit and Olmbacher were watching her with interest.

There were two horses in the arena now, galloping round in opposite directions. The riders' black capes flowed out behind them, the red plumes in their sweeping black hats shook in the wind, and the band played louder.

Aguirre was in the callejón directly below them, a pink-and-yellow fighting cape in his hands. Bill watched him walk slowly towards one of the narrow passages that led into the arena. The suits of lights were scattered all around the barrier now. The fat policeman was talking to one of the Broadway characters. The horsemen left the ring.

The trumpet blew.

The crowd noise fell slowly away, ebbing out from the arena through the Moorish arches. Bill found his mouth suddenly dry.

The stone circles of the tiered stands wavered and were gone. There was no stone or brick here, only the people, standing on each other rank by rank from the pale sand to the sky. He gripped the railing, his right hand on the edge of Aguirre's dress cloak.

Beyond, a door slammed. Just in his line of vision, a broad black back slid out of the darkness under the stands towards the bright circle of sand. The crowd gave a deep, murmuring gasp, and the black bull was in the ring. For a moment he checked, and turned back so that Bill saw his bright eyes, wide horns, and small hoofs. Then he turned again and galloped wide-legged, heavy as a truck, light as a tiger, towards a trailing cape the other side of the arena. A roar, the cape flashed once, the bull turned like a cat outside the little gap into which the man had disappeared, came at full gallop towards the next cape. The crowd sighed, and sat down.

The minutes passed, in the sweeping of the pink-and-yellow cloaks across the sand, in the sway and stop and fierce turn of the black bull. The hour struck when, finally, the bull stood with his head down, his back slippery and shining dark, ten feet in front of the barrier and directly in front of Kit.

Manrique attacked it messily, with many thrusts. His eyes glittered and the sweat shone on the side of his face, turned to them, as he raised the sword slowly, for the fifth time. Bill saw the bull's flesh open to receive it and the sword slide in to the hilt. Manrique's tight lips exploded outwards in a gasp as he leaned far over and stood away, but the bull did not die. Manrique took another sort of sword, and stabbed down with it at the base of the hanging head, twice.

Whistles and catcalls rose and a cushion sailed past Bill's head into the ring, over the dying, unkillable bull. Bill felt his gorge rising. He muttered to Kit, "This is worse than a butcher's shop." He saw that she was holding tight to the wooden rail, and put out his hand to comfort her, but she pushed it away.

Manrique struck down again, and suddenly the bull dropped, suddenly as a light switched off. The crowd was eight thousand separate roars, and eight thousand piercing, angry whistles. All round they were standing on their seats and whistling. A score of cushions hurtled into the ring. Manrique stood in the arena by the dead bull's nose, slowly turning his head to look at every single person in the crowd. His lips moved once, forcibly spitting out a single word. Then he picked up his black hat, bowed very slowly towards the president, and walked out of the arena.

Bill spoke across Kit to Olmbacher—"You like *this*?"

The master sergeant said carefully, "Captain, you like baseball, and I guess you have to take the bad games with the good. Manrique's luck was out."

Bill said, "I guess I'd say the bull's was, being tapped for a fight in the first place, and meeting such a clumsy butcher when they got him here." He turned to Kit. "Are you sure you want to stay for the rest of this?"

"Oh yes," she said. "It's no good running away."

The mule team dragged the carcass out of the ring with shouts and cries and cracking of the whips. Again the trumpet blew, and again the heavy door thudded, and again the black back slid from the pen into the circle of sand. . . . Muralla, gold. The bull stopped, and would not charge the tantalizing, dragging capes, but stood with lowered head and brooding eye, watching.

Bill found that the ugly slaughter of the first bull had aroused a strong emotion of anger in him. He was no longer a disinterested spectator. Now he muttered under his breath, "Go on, charge. Don't take any notice of the cape."

For the rest of the playing of that bull he could feel his own hostility flowing out towards the bullfighters, and his sympathy towards the brave, tortured bull. When it died, fairly cleanly and at the far side of the ring, he sat back and mopped his face with his handkerchief. He said, "There must be things about us that the Spaniards understand as little as we understand this. The only thing to do is leave it that way."

Olmbacher said, "If you can."

Kit was looking at him coldly. After a while, their looks meeting and holding, Bill grinned and said, "Whatever it is you're feeling, it suits you." He stretched out the fingers of his hand and slowly she touched them with hers. It was a private sign which she sometimes answered, sometimes didn't. He saw that her anger of a moment before was drifting away from her grasp, and saw that she resented his power to make it go.

He hesitated, but he had to speak. He said, "Are you sure you don't want to go now, honey? Because, really, I do. I can't enjoy this . . . it's so unfair. And I know you're trying to understand what it's all about, and I'm afraid you'll get mad at me."

Sergeant Olmbacher said, "It isn't supposed to be fair, captain. It isn't a contest at all. As far as I can make out it's more like a performance of *Hamlet*. It would be all wrong if the actor playing Hamlet was able to alter the result. We know how it's going to end, and what matters is how it's done."

Bill said, "Well, I say it *is* a contest, and an unfair one." The trumpet blew for the third bull, and Bill raised his voice rebelliously. The trumpet ended in a sudden hush and in the hush Bill heard his own voice loud and clear—"And I say I'm on the side of the bull."

The matador Aguirre was standing behind one of the small outer barriers directly below him. He turned slowly and looked at Bill, the hint of an inverted smile pulling down the corners of his long, wide mouth. From somewhere behind an American voice called, "I'm with you. Bill."

Bill turned and saw Captain Fisher and his wife, five rows back, Paul's finger and thumb together in the gesture of approval. Other American faces sprang out at him from the Spanish sea. There seemed to be hundreds of them, all turned in his direction, some nodding, some frowning in disapproval.

"Bill!" Kit said sharply. "You're making us conspicuous."

"I'm sorry," he said doggedly. "I didn't mean anyone else to hear. But it's true."

The pink-and-yellow capes began once more to make their swirling patterns in the sand, and the crowd roar rose in a jerky crescendo. Pete Olmbacher muttered, "*Verónica* . . . and another . . . and another . . . *media-verónica*, and *recorte*." The figure in black turned and strutted away from the bull, coming towards them. He walks like a fairy, Bill thought sourly. All the matadors walked like fairies.

Aguirre was there beneath him now, leaning over the barrier to take a pair of long, paper-ribboned, barbed darts from an assistant. His eyes moved up and he stared briefly at Bill before turning, the darts in his hand, and walking out towards the bull. The swing of his hips seemed more exaggerated now, as he placed one pink-stockinged foot directly in front of the other in his steps, the darts held high with delicately arched hands, arms raised.

The bull charged, Aguirre leaped gracefully in the air, his arms swung down, the darts stuck into the bull's shoulder. Aguirre ran off and the bull turned sharply, the darts hanging down his withers, held in the flesh by the barbs. Aguirre slowed to a walk. "Christ," Bill muttered. "How would *he* like a pair of those in his back." The matador was at the barrier, his hands outstretched for another pair of darts. Bill thought that this one was the worst of the lot. He seemed to be enjoying the cruelty.

Kit whispered, "Bill, if you're not quiet, I'm going to sit somewhere else."

Bill said nothing. The bull ran back and forth across the sand in slower, heavier charges. The time came when Aguirre walked to the barrier and the man in blue suède shoes rested a sword on the barrier in its scabbard, its hilt towards the matador, and Aguirre pulled out the sword and walked towards the president's box. He stood a moment there, looking upward, the winged hat extended in his right hand, his head and pigtail bare, then he dropped the hat to the sand and, turning, walked slowly towards the bull.

"*Natural*. Another. Another. Another, to the left. . . . *Pase de pecho*. And again. *Manoletina*. And again. And again. *Recorte*. . . . This is a lot better, captain. He's building a good *faena*."

The red cloth moved, the bull charged. The man was on his knees and the bull charging. Bill was quiet. The lonely black figure in the sand, and the black bull joined to him by the red cloth, made a single shape and suddenly, breathlessly, laid hold of all his attention. The skin of his scalp prickled, his hands were wet and the roar of the crowd lifted up in huge steps of sound, rhythmic as slow breakers on the shore—"Olé!" one, two, three, four, "Olé!" a single crashing shout, "Olé!"

The bull stood still, head down, feet together. Aguirre sighted along the raised blade. His left leg bent at the knee, toe pointed as in the step of a minuet. He flowed into action, forward. The bull tossed its head, the sword-hilt sticking out of its shoulders. Aguirre watched it for a moment. The bull charged him, and the helpers ran forward, capes swirling.

All the magic was gone, as quickly as it had come. "Not again," Bill muttered. But it was, again, and again.

Kit said, "What bad luck."

Olmbacher agreed. "He would have got an ear, at least. Now, he'll be lucky if he gets anything."

Bill muttered, "Do it right, for God's sake."

And again, when the sword failed to kill that time, he whispered savagely, "I bet it would make a better job on you if it had the chance." The attempts to kill went on and on, and Bill grew more angry.

The failing, gallant bull, its back in shreds, tottered half a pace forward after another downward stroke with the long cross-pieced sword. Aguirre's face was clenched in a furious horror.

Bill cried in agony, "This goddamned fairy couldn't pop a paper bag."

Kit's elbow jerked savagely into his ribs and she was saying furiously, "What do you think he feels like?" Olmbacher leaned across and muttered in a low voice, "The ladies on your right are Aguirre's sister and mother. The sister speaks very good English."

Bill looked at the Spanish ladies quickly from the corner of his eye. What had he said, while those wretched women sat and suffered?

The crowd sighed and he knew that the bull had died at last. The shouting became confused and contradictory, but slowly the applause overcame the whistling. The matador began to make a circuit of the ring, followed by his brocaded peons. Bill watched him glumly, feeling that Fate had once more trapped him into doing the wrong thing. The man was a public performer, and getting paid for it, and it was sheer bad luck that he had to be sitting next to his sister.

Kit was on her feet, clapping hard. Bill thought, I should do that too, if I want to make up to her; but I can't. The matador and his peons were coming closer, running a few paces, then walking. A leather wine bottle sailed down. Aguirre caught it dexterously, drank, and swung it back into the sands. Flowers flew out in single blossoms and small bouquets. . . . Now he was here, directly below them on the sand, his hand raised.

Kit tore the big red carnation from her shoulder, wrenched it free of the pin and threw it towards him.

Aguirre caught it neatly, and held it up Looking towards her, and slowly, with exaggerated motion he had used when raising the darts, he bowed, the red flower held out at arm's length to her. Slowly he brought it to his lips, and kissed it. Cheers and laughter from all around. A man's voice shouted, *"Que guapa es, y rubia!"* Something about pretty. Aguirre left the arena, carrying the flower in his hand, and Kit sat down. She stared at Bill and said, "Well?"

Bill said, "It was your flower."

How did Olmbacher know who the women in the next seats were, and if he knew why didn't he say so earlier? The women were looking into the ring, where the fourth bull had just entered. The girl half-turned and, as she did, Kit leaned across Bill and spoke to her. "He had bad luck at the end, didn't he?"

The girl smiled shyly, and answered, "Yes. The bull was made of rubber. It is so painful then . . . the poor bull, the poor matador. Everyone is unhappy." She made a small unhappy gesture with her hands, but still smiling shyly. She spoke a pure, accurate English of England, a little halting, some of the accents dragged out so that she said *thee bull* instead of *th' bull.* Beyond the older woman turned, and smiled, and made a small nodding motion of acknowledgment. Bill, pressed back into his seat between the smiling women, tried to smile in a neutral manner.

The girl said, "He is my brother, César. That matador."

Kit said, "Oh," and then, "I didn't know. . . ."

Looking at the Spanish girl Bill thought he could now see the family resemblance. She had the same mouth and eyes as the matador, only there was nothing cruel about them in her.

Manrique, in blue. Bill supposed it must be good, because the crowd was again in that rhythm of shouting, and the band played and the red cloth swirled. At the end Manrique too walked round the arena in triumph, holding an ear of the dead bull in his hand. The crowd had forgiven him for the earlier butchery, but he had not forgiven them. He held the bull's ear and shook it at them as though he wished it were theirs, singly and collectively. The leather bottles arched through the air and Manrique took no notice, but only shook the ear and stalked on round the arena, never once breaking into a run.

Trumpets again; gold, Muralla. He began to see the pattern of the spectacle, and once or twice, as the cape swirled long and low and arabesque across the sand, he almost found himself on his feet shouting, as the people roared and the band played.

The sixth and last bull entered the arena, and he didn't need Olmbacher's confirmation to know that this was a "good" one. The sigh of the crowd said it, and the way the bull ran hard and straight, lifting its forelegs off the ground when it struck, letting out a short grunt of fury and effort each time, turning fast, striking again. One, two, three; the swirl to a count of two; and three —"Olé" like a thunderclap; and begin the silent count again. Now the sad horse and the bull, locked into a single heaving shape right below him. Now the horse down, the rider down, his leg pinned under the horse and the white horns plunging down at him. Bill was on his feet . . . but a pink cape swirled the bull away. The horse struggled up, the bull trotted back, paused, rammed in against the lance point.

The horses left, other men ran out with darts.

Aguirre strode out alone with the sword and the red cloth, took off his black hat and held it out to his mother. The crowd cheered thunderously, and Aguirre threw the hat towards her. It went wide, so that it was Olmbacher who leapt up and caught it. Bill held out his hand for it, but Olmbacher leaned across and, smiling, gave it to the Spanish girl.

Aguirre passed the bull six times, closer and slower each time, and the band began to play. His sister turned shyly across Bill to Kit. "They're playing 'El Rondeno de Aragon.' It is his own *paso doble*."

Kit said, "His own? Composed in his honour?"

The girl said, "He composed it himself, and it is his own. El Rondeno de Aragon is one of his nicknames."

Aguirre passed the bull behind his back, three times, then turned it short so that it stopped, head down. The crowd sound died and the music stopped. Aguirre moved the red cloth slowly down, a little sideways, the sword extending it. Olmbacher was muttering, "Watch this. He has to get the bull's fore-feet level with each other, or the shoulder-blades close the gap he has to put the sword through. . . . And the head down. Ah, he's moved again."

A low thunderous roar filled the arena . . . louder, louder. Who was shouting, where was that sound coming from? Was it the bulls in the pens? No, they were dead. Or the crowd booming so? Was this what they did at the moment of the killing of the last bull? Senorita de Aguirre was staring at him, and her mother too, their faces full of fear. *They* didn't know. The crowd was silent, everyone staring at his neighbour and the roar growing louder. On the sand the motion was frozen, the splashes of gold and scarlet and yellow and green, frozen all in their places, the trodden sand violet in the lateness of the afternoon. Aguirre himself frozen, the red cloth down and the bull's nose glued to it, the long sword out from shelter now, ready in his hand.

Bill jumped to his feet. Of course he knew! Anywhere but in the bullring, in a medieval century, he would have recognised it long since. The sound burst directly overhead and all round, simultaneously the whining scream in the sky, and the moan of the crowd. An enormous silver bulk blacked out the sky, flashed light into his eyes.

"The 52s!" Bill shouted.

The bull jerked up its head, bellowed, and ran twenty paces towards the centre of the arena. The crowd was on its feet, everyone staring up.

Slowly the near-panic subsided. The crowd sank back with a

long sigh—all except the American airmen among them, who
continued to stare upwards. The huge swept-back wings sliced
across the sky and vanished. The first was gone and another behind it, wheels down, flaps down, nose up, engine intakes and
turbines screaming, and high overhead the thunder of a fourth
and fifth, dragging vapour trails from their engines as they circled
for the landing.

The Americans sat down. Aguirre walked to the bull, lowered
his cape, and plunged in over the horn in a single savage thrust.
The bull's head jerked up and Aguirre spun round, red sword and
red cloth flying away. He fell on his knees in the sand. The weary
bull watched as he struggled to his feet almost beneath its nose.

Backing away from the bull, Aguirre looked at his left hand,
and shook his arm. The hand flopped loose at the end of it. Turning his back on the bull he walked to the barrier, and everyone in
the arena heard him call curtly, "José! Bandage!" His face was
tightly pulled together in rage. The man in blue suède shoes
expostulated in whispers. Aguirre pushed his arm over the barrier,
and a doctor from the pen below hurried forward. More argument,
but in the end the man called José slit the red cloth a little,
pushed it into Aguirre's left hand, closed his fingers tight round
it, and held them there while the doctor bandaged the fingers into
that position, so that the cloth and the stick to which it was
fastened could not fall out of his hand. The bull watched, standing alone in the ring.

The dulled sword in his right hand, Aguirre walked towards the
bull. Reaching it, he paused, lowered his left arm with the cloth
dangling inertly from it, and ran in with the sword. The sword
went in, and sprang out. Again; and all the time the crowd was
silent. Again; this time the sword stayed in; but the bull did not
die. Aguirre jerked his head, and a peon ran out to him with the
other sword, with the crosspiece. Once, twice, three times Aguirre
struck down. A trumpet sounded, and at the fourth attempt the
bull fell.

His sister threw him his hat. He caught it, bowed curtly towards his mother, and strode quickly out of the ring and out of sight. The frozen silence of the crowd began to dissolve. Shouts rose, and handkerchiefs waved. A voice cried in Spanish and Bill turned to Kit. "What was that?"

She said, " 'The Rich One has no luck but by God he's got guts.' That must be another nickname. . . . Now they're saying, 'Give him an ear'. . . . 'He's gone'. . . . 'Give the ear to the Americans, then.' "

"Are they saying that?"

"One man did. Because of the 52s. We certainly know how to make ourselves popular."

Olmbacher said, "That was just bad luck. They only have three corridas a year here."

Olé la Señorita Americana!

Robert Ruark

ROBERT RUARK (1915–1965) *wrote "Olé la Señorita Ameri-cana!" to satirize those people who take part in the fake cor-ridas that are especially staged—"Try bullfighting for yourself: guaranteed no danger!"—at certain tourist centers. Ruark came to Spain in the last years of his life to study bullfighting. He is perhaps best known for his two novels set in Africa,* Something of Value *and* Uhuru.

Alec Barr sat lonely in the *dueño's* seats of the private bullring. Nearly everyone had a crack at the *becerros.* The two professional bullfighters—one fair, one nothing—had performed some flashy capework in taking the two-year-old heifers away from the man on the horse. The host, Don Juan, had strapped on his leather chaps, and had produced some more flashy capework in the *quites,* performing acceptable *reboleras* and *chiquelinas,* wrap-ping the cape around him in a flash of magenta and yellow. The brother, Tomas, was playing the part of picador, maneuvering the horses well, leaning stoutly on the *vara,* laying the iron into the shoulders of the calves without unduly brutalizing them.

There are some damned good embryo bulls down there on that yellow sand, Alec thought, blinking against the slanting sun of the late afternoon, sitting off to himself in the white plaster of the little private ring. That last one took sixteen before she quit. She will be put to the seed bulls and yield some mighty calves for the brave festival.

I wonder, he thought, what makes me so bloody ornery? I led that poor bastard, Juan, into a cul-de-sac at the lunch table. I was unforgivably rude. I guess it's merely insecurity in strange places, but I would love to see one of those big mouths with the amateur capes and the country clothes go up against a really nasty elephant in thick bush, or a leopard suddenly in the lap. He massaged his welted wrist as he remembered the screeching fury he had peeled off himself, so many years ago, choking it finally to death with the barrels of a shotgun.

I got books to write, he thought. *I got bills to pay. I don't need no horn up my ass.* Not, he thought, unless I can sell the product via Marc Mantell. This business of the drunk socialites playing with half-grown bulls is like playing chicken with cars, where the first one to swerve is a coward. You remember that actress that got kicked in the face with a horse, in this same Spain, when she was learning how to bullfight from horseback? It took a lot of plastic surgery to get that dimple straightened out again, and she still does her close-ups from the left side of her face on account of the lip don't turn up on the right side of her face when she smiles.

The hell with it, he said, and took a sip of the brandy. Now we got the star turn. Little Miss Twitchett, the Barbará Bah-een from Hollywood, is going to fight a bull. *Que tengas la suerte,* he whispered. That you should have luck.

Barbará looked marvellous out there on the golden sands of the arena. (Golden sands of the arena? What kind of writing is that? *Arena* means "sand" in Spanish, unless you are in Cataluna, where it's spelled *arenys.* Smart-ass.)

She had her Cordobés sombrero tipped at exactly the right angle, a little forward. Her backside was right and trim in the striped pants. Her shoulders were braced well back, and those fantastic breasts pushed the frilled shirt forward, with the vest-cut jacket swinging free as she raised the cape to cite the little cow. (Little cow? Enough horns there to unzip her from navel to neck.)

"Olé Barbará! Olé la Señorita Americana! Olé la actriz brava!"

The voices swelled, all twenty of them, as Barbará planted her feet, one-two, as brave as Manolete, who is dead, and cited the *becerra*. (Barbará had the actor's gift of magnificent mimicry. At the moment she was playing *Blood and Sand*—second version, Tyrone Power—with himself, Alec Barr, playing critic by courtesy of the late Laird Cregar.)

"*Huh! Huh! Huh! O hey, toro!*" He heard that trained actress voice saying the words just like something out of Hemingway. "*Eh hah! Hohohoho Hah! Toro!*"

Perfect take. *Cut.*

Now here came the brave cow. (Horns a good fourteen inches long, and sharp as needles. Weight four hundred pounds, and full of *plomo*.)

Barbará (Belmonte) Bayne swung the cape with nice slow gypsy wrists, taking the cape low, sculpturing, head bowed, looking at the feet, as the calf came roaring, blood from its pic-ing streaming thickly from its shoulder. *Ay, que torera!*

The calf passed her and took the cape with her as she went. Then the calf shook the cape irritably from the horn and looked again for an enemy. She found the enemy. It was wearing beautifully cut *trajes cortos*—tight pants, fine bolero jacket, correct Cordobés hat, bosoms swelling under frilled shirt. Standing alone and uncertain.

"*Huh!*" This time it was the calf who cited, and charged. The host and his brother ran into the ring with capes, but not soon enough. Barbará ran for the *burladero*—the jokemaker, the little pantry in which bullfighters sometime find it necessary to hide—with the calf goosing her all the way.

Barbará tripped and fell, just as she achieved the entrance to the *burladero*. The cow lowered her head (she's left-handed, bad left-hook, Alec noted) and unzipped Barbará's tight pants as she crawled to safety behind the *burladero*.

The host and his brother caped the calf away, and Barbará emerged from the *burladero*.

Her backside shone white in the Sevillan sun. She had lost her hat. Her pants were down around her ankles. She had badly torn the front of her blouse, and her nose was scraped by sand. Her face was ashen, and she had begun to cry.

The host, Juan, ran up and wrapped her in a fighting cape.

Alec shuddered. He decided, if somebody could find her a pair of pants or something fairly decent to wear until she got back to the hotel, that this was going to be no night to spend on a late dinner with *flamenco* until dawn.

It is not, he muttered, the hasty ascent up the thorn tree when you are being chased by a rhino that hurts so much. It is that long trip down. It was going to be a long trip back to the Alfonso Trece, and a smart man would be well advised to keep his mouth shut.